MODERN LIGHTWEIGHT
CAMPING

Also by Hazel Constance

Gear for Outdoors

MODERN LIGHTWEIGHT CAMPING

A handbook

Pat and Hazel Constance

ROBERT HALE · LONDON

First published in Great Britain 1985

ISBN 0 7090 1751 0 (*cased*)

ISBN 0 7090 1868 1 (*paperback*)

Robert Hale Limited
Clerkenwell House
Clerkenwell Green
London EC1R 0HT

Photoset in North Wales by
Derek Doyle & Associates, Mold, Clwyd
Printed in Great Britain by
St. Edmundsbury Press, Bury St. Edmunds, Suffolk
Bound by Woolnough Bookbinding Ltd

Contents

Photographs

Credits

27, Karrimor International Ltd; 31 and 32, F. Hutt; 34, Field & Trek (Equipment) Ltd; all other photographs by Pat Constance

Diagrams

Credits

Diagrams 10 and 16 reproduced by permission of Mountain Equipment Ltd; Diagram 23 reproduced by permission of Karrimor International Ltd

Foreword

Over the years a number of books have appeared dealing with different aspects of camping, be it 'lightweight' or otherwise. Some of these have been of limited scope, whilst others describing specific equipment have quickly become dated. Details of new designs and materials, or the latest ideas, continually appear in the outdoor Press, and the prospective or practising lightweight camper must find it a daunting task to know where to find the information he needs, let alone to digest it all.

For this reason we have attempted to gather together knowledge from many sources and to present it in a form which will, we hope, guide beginners and old hands alike towards a choice of suitable equipment and suggest ways of using it whilst camping in small tents.

We remember a group of us once trying to define a Lightweight Camper. Simple enough, one would think – but it wasn't. The problem was, of course, that we were not all backpackers, neither were we all cycle campers. Some of us were both, and among the party were canoe campers and others. We could not define our theoretical person in terms of the total weight he or she would or could carry; neither could we talk about how the necessary equipment would be carried. It was eventually agreed that what we were really concerned with was camping in small tents – not frame tents, not large ridge tents, certainly not trailer tents or vans, but just small tents. We even put a limit of six feet on the height of the 'small tent', and everyone went away satisfied.

Our definition, as you will see, conveniently ignores the question of transport. We have written this book for anyone who camps in small tents, whether they be backpackers, cycle campers, canoe campers, travellers by car or motorcycle or any other means, the common denominator being their use of a small tent and simple, lightweight equipment. Much of the equipment we shall be considering can be used by anyone, regardless of their means of transport.

There is no one single 'right way' of doing things when camping lightweight. Neither is there any such thing as the ideal set of equipment to suit all conditions and circumstances. The newcomer to the game is faced with a bewildering choice when it comes to collecting together the necessary kit, and he will find out very quickly that, although he may be planning to camp in a small tent, the amount of money which can be spent is anything but small.

Our hope in writing this book is that by pointing the newcomer in the right direction we may help him with his choice. Perhaps we can also offer some fresh ideas to those who are already enjoying the freedom of camping lightweight, of enjoying making the maximum use of the minimum of equipment to ensure their safety and comfort, and who can get up and go, at a moment's notice, to enjoy the odd unexpected break or fine weekend.

Situations and circumstances seem to remain the same, our weather is its usual unpredictable self, and the basic requirements for dealing with all this do not change. What does change is the introduction and adaptation of new materials and equipment to enable campers to cope with these conditions. During the past few years there has been a great increase in interest, accompanied by a rush of new ideas and designs. For this reason, any book which describes and catalogues specific models of, for example, tents will be out of date before it reaches the shelves of the booksellers. To attempt to avoid this fate, we will try to describe the basic requirements and ways of satisfying them, with suggestions as to what the buyer should look for. We can, in this way, offer advice and reasons for it – after that, the choice is yours.

We also hope we can help with ideas on how to use the equipment to the best advantage, how to look after it and how to get the maximum enjoyment from the pastime with the minimum of effort.

Although we have tried many different ways of lightweight camping and have used a variety of equipment, we are by no means tough 'super-people', neither do we enjoy a spartan way of life. When camping with lightweight gear there is no need to 'rough it'. The looks of amazement on the faces of some campers when they see sleeping-bags, mattresses, chairs and other things being produced out of a rucksack or cycle pannier have to be seen to be believed!

If, like us, you are still enjoying camping in small tents and still learning new wrinkles after forty years, we shall be more than satisfied.

Our thanks must go to many camping friends and individuals in the trade who have helped, perhaps unknowingly, over the years with ideas and suggestions, and to all those who have encouraged us to go ahead with this book.

Special thanks must be given to our daughter Heather for producing the majority of the drawings for us, and to Peter Moore and Tony Pearson of Field and Trek (Equipment) Ltd, for the generous loan of equipment. Special thanks too, to Ron Etherington of Mountain Equipment Ltd, for his help. Our thanks also to the following companies: DuPont (UK) Ltd, Epigas, Fjallraven Sports Equipment (UK) Ltd, Karrimor International Ltd, AB Optimus Ltd, Primus-Sievert UK Ltd, Silva (UK) Ltd, Ultimate Equipment Ltd.

1 Getting Started

Very few of us are in a position to walk into our nearest camp shop and buy everything we need in one go, even if we knew what we needed. In the following chapters we shall be describing in some detail the various pieces of equipment which are required to meet different situations, and making suggestions as to what to look for when buying or otherwise obtaining what you need. For a start, however, you should ask yourself some questions.

How? You may be thinking of walking or cycling, travelling by car or motor cycle, by canoe or by some other form of transport. You may be planning to try more than one of these ways, but the basic kit will be similar in most respects, apart from how you pack and carry it. You should also have some idea as to whether you will be travelling alone or with a companion.

When? The time of year, with the weather to be expected, must have an important bearing on what you need and how you will use it. Late spring to early autumn in this country may be warmer, but rain and wind can still cause you problems.

Where? Lowland routes or trips into the hills and mountains are all possibilities. Do you plan to move or to stop at one site for a while? Do you plan to go abroad?

Why? For many people, the actual camping is a means to an end, and this is especially so with lightweight campers. For them, the camping should be second nature compared with the pursuit of the interest which is the prime object of the exercise. Simple but adequate gear is a must in these circumstances.

When you have answers to these basic questions, you can

tackle the remaining question, which is 'What?' What do you need to get started?

Collecting the gear together

If you are already a camper, you will have some equipment which may be used, but your first requirement will be a tent. It will probably be the most expensive single item, so care is needed in choosing one to suit your particular needs. Obtain a selection of catalogues from different manufacturers or retailers, and study them in conjunction with the information given in Chapter 2. Before making a final decision, try to see some of the tents in use.

Try to borrow or hire a tent, or at least go to a campsite or club meet where you can talk to the owners of tents of the type you have in mind. It is sometimes very surprising how the user will have opinions about a product quite different from those of the salesman. The temptation to buy, especially when there are end-of-season bargains on offer, is very great, but do remember that once you have bought your tent it may be a long time before you can change it.

At this stage, if you have a car or other means of transport, and some basic kit such as a sleeping-bag, stove and cooking utensils, it is a good idea to go off for a night and try out the tent. Go somewhere not too far away and not too difficult for pitching. If you really cannot put up with the restrictions of living in a small tent, now is the time to find out. We say 'living' because there may well be occasions when that is what you have to do if the weather is so bad that you have to 'stay put' for a while.

While you are trying your tent, you will probably find that there is quite an art in disposing of all your gear in the restricted space available. Your sleeping-bag may be rather bulky. Perhaps the ground felt rather cold and hard. Comfort at night is a vital requirement, as without a good night's sleep you will not enjoy your camping. So your next move is to have a look at our ideas on sleeping in comfort in Chapter 3, and again study the catalogues. Car camping will let you take advantage of the rather bulkier but cheaper synthetic fillings, but before buying, think if you are likely to try some other way of travelling. Not many of us can afford the luxury of several pieces of basic equipment for use in different circumstances at the beginning of our lightweight career.

It is of course possible to depend on cafés or pubs for the main meal of the day, so making do with the means of brewing up in the morning and evening, with just a minimum amount of cooking. Pans can probably be found around the home, as can a number of other things. It is surprising what good use can be made of empty containers which are normally thrown away at home.

So far we have been talking mainly in terms of using a car for transport. If you do not have one, you will have to decide how you will carry the equipment. If your intention is to walk after using public transport for the main part of your journey to your destination, you will need to consider the purchase of a rucksack.

Having everything conveniently on your back, out of the way, is by far the best method. If you are thinking of more serious walking, the choice of pack will require more care. Maybe you can defer your final decision until after you have been able to borrow or hire one to try. Make sure it is of a suitable size to fit you if you do so. Be warned against spending money on a cheap rucksack which lets you down by breaking at a most inconvenient time and place. Not only will it be weak; it most likely will not be comfortable to carry, and *that* can put you off lightweight camping. We consider the choice and use of rucksacks in some detail in Chapter 8.

One situation in which you should never use a rucksack is if you plan to ride a bicycle. The means of carrying all your equipment on a cycle is covered in Chapter 9.

One of the secrets of success in every type of lightweight camping is to try out your gear – tent, rucksack, cycle with load on board, and so on – preferably in your own garden. If this is not possible, go a very short distance to a campsite where you can quietly set up your shelter, cook and eat, sleep and then go home to think over what you have done. You will learn a lot, and if you make mistakes, you will probably learn even more.

As you continue to go out, you can gradually collect all

the little things which help to make your life easy, but any individual will have different ideas as to what he or she needs. Look at what others do; talk to other campers. Some of their ideas may not suit you, but do not just reject them out of hand. As you gain confidence in yourself and your gear, you can go further afield and attempt more ambitious trips, but as a beginner do not let yourself be put off by those individuals you will always find who think they know it all and try to give you the impression you are completely incompetent.

It is possible to feel dissatisfied with various items of equipment after having used them for a while, but to replace everything because of that is not really a practical or economic possibility. Perhaps some modifications, on a 'Do-it-Yourself' basis, can be done. Replacing a single tent pole by an A-pole to improve the access, adding extra hooks or rings, maybe replacing a rubber tension loop with a guyline and runner; all these are little jobs which you learn the need for as you go. Make small bags to hold pegs, cutlery, pans and so on: all the little things which, in the long run, help to make your life as a lightweight camper that much simpler and more comfortable. Of course you can spend a fortune buying many such things, but it just is not worth it. The thing you make or improvise to suit your own need is much better, and cheaper, in the end.

Saving money on the small things is all very well, but what about those major items such as the tent, the sleeping-bag, the stove, the rucksack or panniers? It seems that one of the perverse facts of the lightweight camper's life is that to save pounds weight he has to spend more pounds of his hard-earned money. To obtain the performance from your gear that you require whilst keeping down the weight does mean that the materials and design must be good, and so must the workmanship. Good products cost money. On the other side of the picture, low prices do not always mean cheap products. Early repair or replacement may be the least of your worries in the event of failure, whereas good equipment should be capable of giving many years of satisfaction, especially if used properly and looked after.

Without sound advice and a certain amount of financial

help, it is all too easy for young people to set out with completely unsuitable equipment and high hopes, only to become disillusioned when they encounter the problems of gear failure and discomfort. Many will have their first taste of lightweight camping through schools or youth organizations, possibly as part of a school outdoor-activity programme or participation in the Duke of Edinburgh's Award training. In these circumstances it is likely that major equipment such as tents, sleeping-bags, stoves and so on will be provided by the organizers. It is a fact that such equipment is not always ideal. Often education authorities and similar bodies tend to go for rugged, "youth-proof" gear which will inevitably be heavy and not necessarily of the best design for its intended use.

Costs, clubs and insurance

We return once more to the question of cost. It has been suggested that suitability for the purpose, weight, size and durability should determine *what* you buy. The matter of price should determine *where* you buy. Perhaps this is rather an over-simplification, but, as always, there is a certain amount of truth in it.

A quick glance through the advertisements in some of the specialist magazines will show quite wide variations in the price different firms ask for the same product, and this can be affected even further by sales and special offers which seem to occur at almost any time of the year.

In general, the well-known and reputable manufacturers can usually be relied on to introduce new developments only after considerable research and field testing. Although many new ideas are really innovative, the basic design of reliable equipment does not change very rapidly, it is the details and materials that change. Good gear is simple. It has to be. One must always try to imagine what to do with it in the dark with a gale of wind and heavy rain!

We have already mentioned that a good starting point is to get catalogues from firms. Apart from retailers, it is useful to obtain the brochures from the leading manufacturers of equipment. Sometimes these have to be paid for, but they are normally very informative guides, with much useful and interesting information on the design and use of their products. We are often asked for advice from people who say they have no good retailer of lightweight equipment near where they live. In such a case, one alternative is to deal with a specialist mail-order business, but provided a reputable firm with expert knowledge of the subject is used, no trouble should result.

It is possible to take advantage of discount prices by joining some clubs or organizations who have bulk-buying or similar arrangements with retailers. In the Appendices we give details of a number of manufacturers and importers and some firms we know operate mail-order business. A number of clubs and other organizations are described in Chapter 14 and addresses are given in Appendix I.

When you have obtained your equipment, or at least several of the major items, you should consider the question of insurance. Any camping equipment can represent a fairly heavy financial outlay. Lightweight gear is by no means an exception. Your household contents insurance may cover the gear whilst at home, but you need cover against all normal hazards of damage, fire and theft while you are travelling to and from your campsite and while actually in camp. Do not forget third party cover – just in case you knock into someone on the bus with your heavy rucksack! Many clubs have some insurance cover included in the membership or can arrange insurance for members at additional cost, but do make sure you understand exactly what you are covered for and, more important, what you are not. Many insurance policies for campers seem to be designed for "heavyweight" campers staying on one site. The needs of the more mobile lightweighter are not always fully met, so be warned.

2 Lightweight Shelter

The lightweight camper needs shelter. This usually means a tent, and his tent will be his home from home. Although the intention may be to use the tent only for a night stop, weather or other circumstances may dictate that the overnight shelter must become a daytime refuge. All this from a piece of equipment which must be easy to pack and carry when you move on. It is asking a lot, but by choosing wisely, a good, modern, lightweight tent can be all this and more besides.

The right choice

The right choice for you must be determined by going back to our starting point and asking those basic questions again – how, when where and why? How you travel will give you some idea as to the weight and size of your portable house, both in use and when packed. When and where should start you thinking about the weather conditions your shelter must withstand and the sort of ground on which you will build your refuge. Why you want to camp lightweight can possibly suggest other needs, such as storage for equipment additional to your camping kit, or maybe extra space for working at your particular hobby or interest.

All the differing individual requirements should add up to a tent which will be safe, simple and comfortable, and at the same time light in weight. An excellent piece of advice we read some while ago is still valid now: "Do not buy a tent that is intended for use in warm, sunny summer weather, but choose one as though there was always a storm outside." The tent-maker will try to satisfy requirements by making good use of suitable materials and good design based on knowledge of what happens in practical use. Add to that quality of workmanship and good after-sales service and you will realize that by paying perhaps a little more you are really making an investment which it will be worth looking after.

Materials

We will look for a start at the various materials in use for lightweight tents, and their advantages and disadvantages.

Cotton

Formerly, all lightweight tents were made from finely woven cotton, and today some of the most expensive lightweight tents are made from this material. Damp and condensation will pass through or be absorbed by the fabric, and a well-designed and pitched tent will resist a lot of rain and wind. The disadvantages of cotton are that when wet it weighs heavier, will take more time to dry out and must be very thoroughly dried before being packed away, to prevent rot and mildew damage. In general cotton tends to be heavier than other comparable fabrics. Modern methods have improved the waterproofing properties of cotton tent materials, but there is still the problem that if the roof of the tent is touched, rain can come through. This problem can be minimized by using a double roof.

Polyester/Cotton

This fabric, lighter in weight than pure cotton of equivalent thickness, is also cheaper. It 'breathes' in the same way as cotton, which is an important factor in avoiding condensation problems. It is normally used for the inner of a double-skin tent and has a similar feel to cotton.

Nylon

Fabric woven from nylon thread is probably the most commonly used material for lightweight tents today. Light and strong, it does not absorb water with corresponding increase in weight – an important consideration, when you have to pack up a wet tent. Although not so affected by rot, a nylon tent should be dried and aired as soon as possible before packing away. In order to give the woven material the required waterproofing properties, the fabric is coated with thin layers of polyurethane (PU) or acrylic resin, the latter being cheaper and less durable. The better-quality PU-coated fabrics have two or three layers. Nylon fabric can also be given a silicone treatment, and this is normally, used for inner tents, as it 'breathes'. Coated fabrics are used for the outer flysheet. One important point to note is that the coating, whether PU or acrylic, produces a completely waterproof material through which moist air and rain cannot pass. A variant of plain woven nylon is the so-called 'rip-stop' nylon, in which a coarse mesh of stronger threads is incorporated into the material to increase its tear strength.

Nylon has some disadvantages compared with cotton. It is difficult to achieve a good set to a nylon tent, although good design and manufacture will go a long way to overcoming this. Seams will normally require sealing to prevent leakage through the stitching holes. Strong sunlight will, in time, have a deteriorating effect on the material. However, development and research have gone a long way in the past few years to reduce many of the problems. Heavier nylons, coated with PU or maybe PVC or other plastics, can be used for the groundsheet or floor of the tent.

Other woven materials

We have already said that today nylon is probably the material most commonly used for lightweight tents. Polyester fabric treated with silicone and coated with PU has increased resistance to sunlight and can have increased tear strength and resistance to stretching. A variant of this is coated with a reflecting layer of aluminium to reflect the sun's rays, so maintaining a cooler inner-tent temperature.

Before leaving the subject of materials we should consider the problems of condensation and how they may be minimized. It is not possible to produce a tent which is a hundred per cent free from condensation on the inner surface. We have experienced it even with a tent using cotton for the inner and outer tents, in conditions of cold when the condensed moisture had frozen inside the inner-tent roof. That was in Surrey, not in the high hills. So let us consider the cause of the problem.

During the night, when asleep, each person loses about one third to one half pint of moisture. This output is in the form of warm, moisture-laden air, which will rise towards the roof of the tent. Here it encounters the inner surface of the tent fabric, which will be cooler because of the surrounding night air. If our tent roof is made of cotton material, in any but extreme conditions the moist air will either be absorbed by the material or pass through to the outside.

However, when we consider the coated nylon or other synthetic materials used on many modern lightweight tents, we are faced with a completely waterproof material through which neither air nor water will pass. The nylon fabric will be colder than natural cotton, so the moisture-laden air will condense its water content on the surface. From here, it will simply drip off and back onto you, your bedding and anything else inside the tent. If you are having to do any cooking under cover, or even if you are just enjoying a hot drink with the tent closed, the additional steam will aggravate the problem.

With the introduction of coated nylons for use in tent manufacture, this problem was tackled in two ways. The first was to try to ensure adequate ventilation to carry away the warm, moist air. The other way was to use a double-tent construction, with an inner tent, and an outer tent or flysheet spaced a few inches away. The air space between the two provides an insulating layer which helps to keep the surface of the inner tent warmer. The outer flysheet is made of the completely waterproof, coated material, the inner tent of breathable material which allows the moist air to pass through, and any condensation which does occur will be on the inner surface of the flysheet. Any water which drips off will fall onto the inner tent, but if this is made of showerproof fabric (e.g. silicone-treated), the drips will not come through. The amount of condensation on the flysheet will be controlled by the flow of air between the inner and outer tents, depending on the efficiency of the design.

There have been many criticisms of nylon lightweight tents by people who say that condensation is inevitable and unacceptable. We are trying to point out that, with good

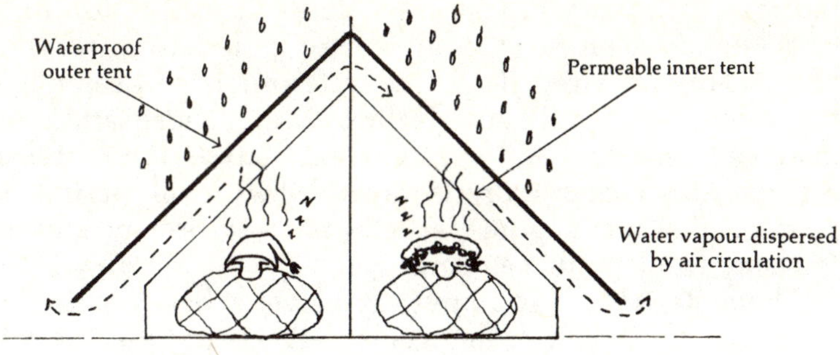

Diagram 1 Control of condensation
Double-tent construction keeps condensation away from the occupants

design and good materials, plus an understanding of the basic causes of the effect, it can be reduced to acceptable levels. It is perhaps worth explaining that the reason for using the double-tent construction in cotton has little to do with avoidance of condensation. It is partly to provide an insulating layer of air to help keep the inner tent warm in cold weather, and cool in summer. The main reason is to maintain a space between the outer and inner tents to prevent the occupants from touching the cotton outer roof when it is raining outside, as this will allow wet to penetrate the fabric.

Using an inner tent with an outer flysheet does, of course, add to the total weight and the packed size of the tent, and for those who want to keep both of these to the barest minimum the solution would seem to be to use a single-skin tent. In cotton, this is feasible in fine weather, and if it rains, the main problems are the avoidance of touching the roof, and the fact that heavy rain will produce a fine spray. The single-skin construction using nylon brings with it the certainty of heavy condensation or, if this is not too serious, it simply means that the nylon material is permeable, which is the same as saying it will let in the rain.

In Chapter 5, dealing with waterproof clothing, we mention the fairly recent introduction of what are termed moisture-permeable waterproof fabrics. On the face of it, these seem to be just what we are looking for. In fact, a number of single-skin tents have been made using such fabrics, with varying success. The difficulty lies in an understanding of exactly how these materials work. They are highly water-repellent and waterproof, so keeping out the rain is no problem; dealing with condensation is a different matter. As we explain later, these fabrics incorporate a microporous layer which will permit the passage of water-vapour particles but will present a barrier to water droplets such as rain.

The material acts as a one-way valve. When it is used for clothing, the body heat generated inside the garment produces a pressure differential which drives the saturated air out through the layer. The same effect can occur when the material is used for an outer shell on a sleeping-bag. With a small tent, whose door is closed, sufficient heat can be generated by an active occupant to produce the same effect. However, with the door open, pressures inside and outside will become equal, and if the tent roof is cooler than the air inside, condensation will form. Similarly, when the camper settles down in his sleeping-bag, the heat radiation from his body is minimized, and again the pressure difference is reduced. It follows that single-skin tents using these materials must be small, and to be effective the door must remain closed – not a happy thought when trying to reduce condensation while cooking. Normal conditions of use in the hills of Britain involve freezing temperatures and driving rain, and both of these can have the effect of blocking the exit of vapour through the pores of the fabric, so apart from the question of expense, there is a long way to go yet in this matter.

So much for the materials used for the tent itself. There will, of course, be other materials incorporated for rubber rings, guyline cord, tape and poles. Guyline cord is best made of braided nylon – avoid the polypropylene used on some cheap tents. The latter also often use steel poles, which are hardly lightweight, liable to rust and often badly finished, but we shall be coming back to the subject of poles later.

Design – shape, size and weight

Earlier in this chapter, we suggested that a good lightweight

Diagram 2 Walls increase sleeping space

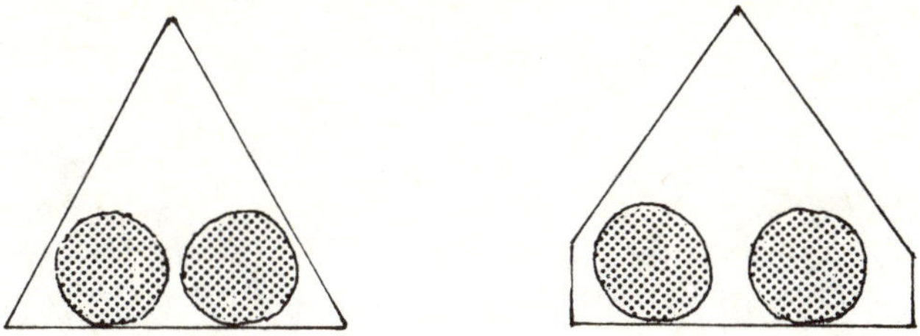

tent needs to be safe, simple, comfortable and light. Safety implies that shelter can be obtained quickly in adverse conditions of rain and wind and in the dark, and that the resulting refuge will continue to protect you whatever the conditions. To achieve this aim, the design should be essentially simple. Comfort requires that there is sufficient space for the number of people using the tent, together with all their equipment. Finally it needs to be easily carried.

Leaving aside for a moment the question of pitching, we start with the fairly obvious fact that, if the roof of the tent is flat or at a shallow angle, it will collect rain or snow, hence a sloping or curved top is necessary. If we have a roof sloping down to the ground, there will be some of the floor area which cannot be used fully, so vertical walls come into the design. That deals with the situation when the occupants are lying down, but what happens when they are sitting up? There needs to be adequate head-room and shoulder-room to allow the one or more campers in the tent to sit up in comfort, in or near the entrance, without pressing against the sides or roof. If the overall height of tent is not to be excessive, so adding to the weight and packed bulk, some other solution is necessary, such as 'squaring off' the entrance and supporting it on extra poles. Sheltering porches which can be closed against the elements but which are large enough to meet the requirements of space outside the sleeping area are necessary. Balanced against this we must not forget the wind and need for stability.

We can now begin to visualize certain shapes and forms which may satisfy the requirements, and in fact most lightweight tents fall into relatively few basic types. Each has its advantages and disadvantages, and we will try to

Diagram 3 Increasing sitting space

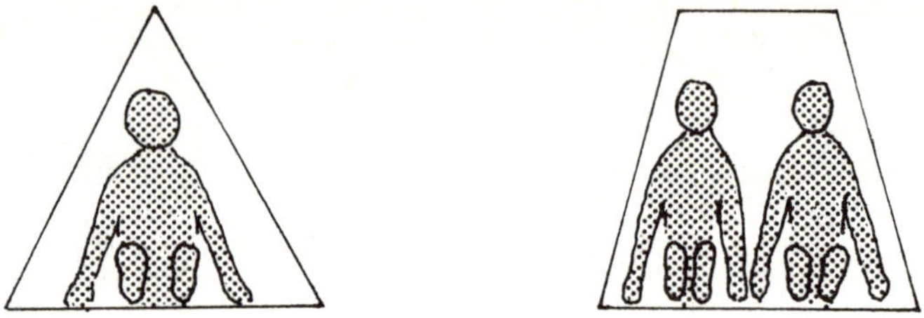

'Squared-off' design gives more head-and-shoulder room when sitting

summarize these, helped by the accompanying diagrams.

Ridge
This is a basic design in the form of an inverted V. Steeply sloping roof panels assist rain shedding, and the floor is usually rectangular with an entrance at one end. Two upright or A-poles support the tent and may be linked by a horizontal ridge pole. The design in its simplest form is cost effective as regards material and provides excellent stability. Interior space is restricted by the sloping roof, but the addition of vertical walls gives a marked improvement. Ideally some protective porch is required over the entrance to provide shelter against driving rain and to provide sheltered cooking space. Some protection is also advisable at the rear.

Sloping ridge
This is a development of the basic ridge shape in which the roof and sides taper towards the rear. In this way, space is

Diagram 4a

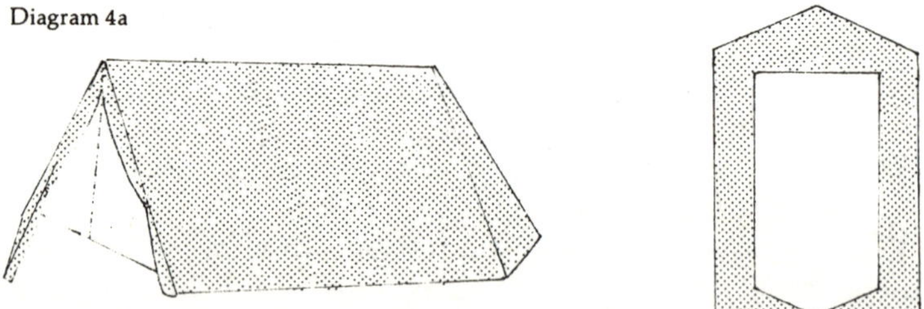

Standard ridge tent

Diagram 4b

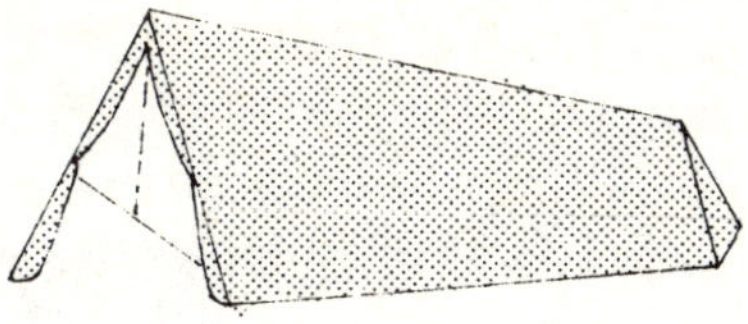

Sloping ridge tent

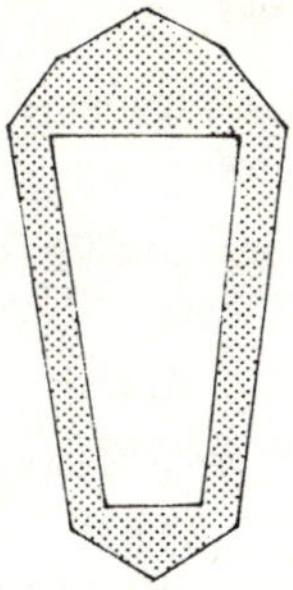

reduced at the end where the user's feet will be, but sufficient room is left at the entrance for sitting and storage. By so doing, weight and bulk can be reduced, and the more streamlined shape will withstand wind better. The omission of a ridge pole gives additional saving in weight, but in order to achieve a satisfactory 'set' without wrinkles, the ridge must be cut in a curve. This may lead to some reduction in head-room around the centre of the tent but should not be unacceptable. There should be a sheltered porch or bell end over the door.

Transverse ridge

In this design the ridge is short and is at right-angles to the direction in which the occupants lie. This allows wider entrance doors to be provided for the inner tent, and usually two bell ends are fitted to shelter two doors. The design provides a very roomy arrangement with plenty of sheltered storage and cooking space. It is not so stable in exposed positions unless pitched carefully, but this can be improved by use of a ridge pole.

Diagram 4c

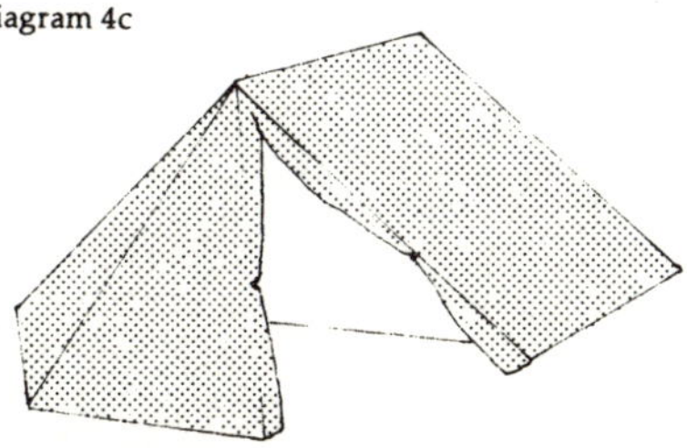

Transverse ridge tent

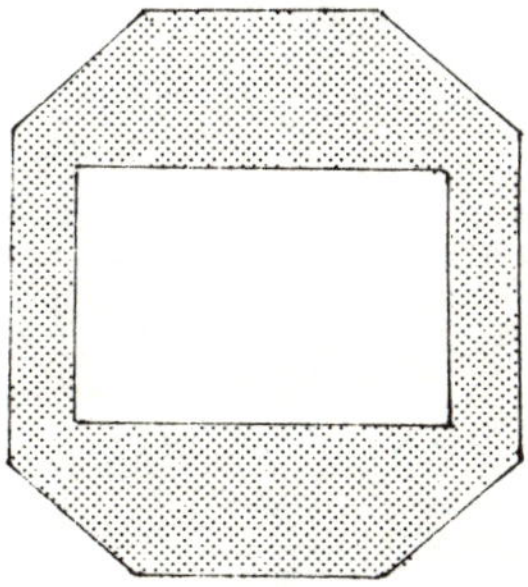

Diagram 5

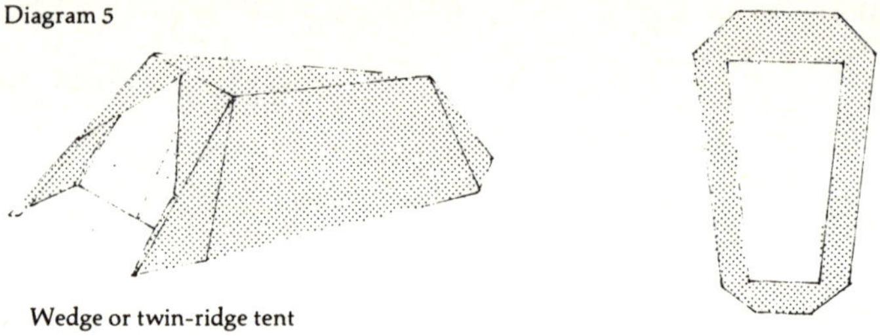

Wedge or twin-ridge tent

Wedge or twin ridge

By introducing twin front poles tapering down to a single short pole at the rear, head- and shoulder-room when sitting is improved, at the expense of poorer rain-shedding by the roof.

Single pole

This basically simple, stable and reliable shape requires more space for pitching. Without walls, the usable floor area is restricted, but there is increased head-room in the centre. A symmetrical pyramid shape is good for snow shedding but usually has reduced shelter over the entrance. Single-pole tents with extended closed-in flysheet entrances give good protection and storage space and are fairly easy to pitch but do require very long head guylines to ensure a good set.

Tunnel or hoop

Flexible poles or wands form hoops which extend the fabric, leaving unobstructed floor space. The tent can be either parallel-sided or tapered towards the rear. With almost vertical sides they provide the maximum usable space and

Diagram 6

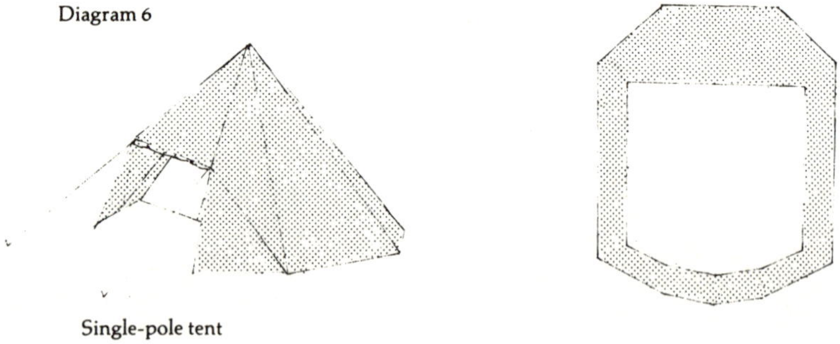

Single-pole tent

storage and are stable. A variation is the transverse hoop tent which gives generous storage space under cover.

Dome

Dome-shaped tents are held in position by long, flexible hoops crossing in the centre of the roof. They are stable and provide very generous space inside but storage and sheltered cooking areas are sometimes restricted, giving little protection against rain when the outer entrance is open. The packed size may be bulky, and ventilation is not always generous.

Diagram 7

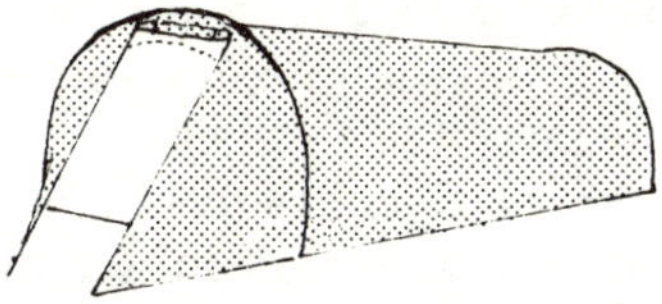

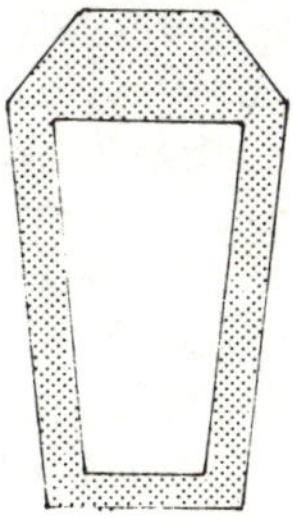

Tunnel or Hoop tent

Diagram 8

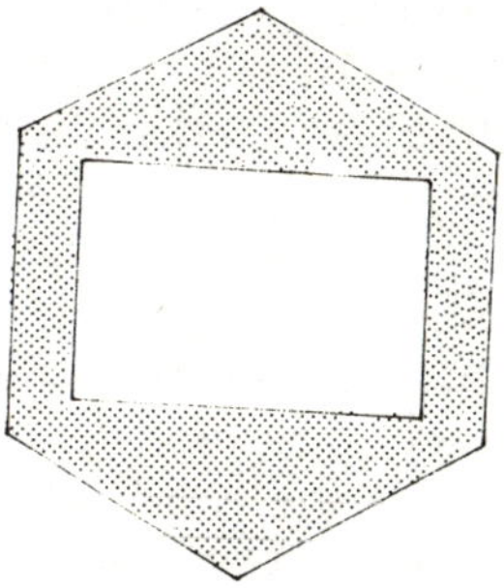

Dome tent

In addition to the above basic shapes and variations on them, there is a group of tent designs specifically for mountain use which are generally stronger and heavier than those intended for less rigorous conditions. Stability is attained by the use of A-poles or hoops in sleeves at each end. Sleeved entrance doors may be provided at one end, and snow flaps along the walls assist in holding the tent against strong winds.

Diagram 9

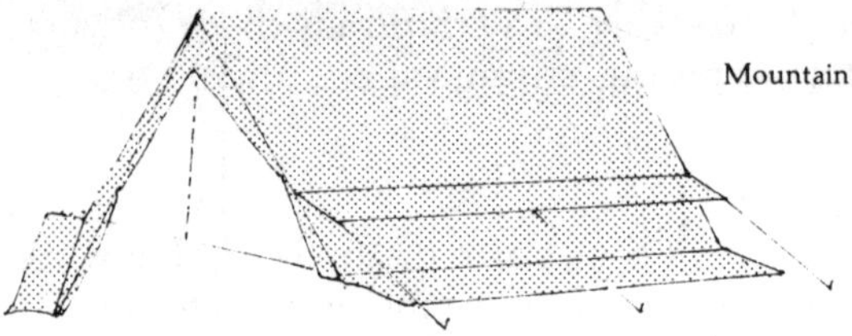

Mountain tent

In general in the British Isles we experience what has been described as a wet mountain climate. Tents for use here require the stability of the mountain tent combined with adequate shelter against rain and wind, and, knowing that in some conditions a considerable time will have to be spent under cover, sheltered space for cooking in safety.

One way to assess the useful size of a tent is to sit cross-legged and see if you have sufficient clearance to avoid touching the roof or side without having to bend your neck. Next you need to compare your height with the length of the inner tent. You should allow at least 6 inches over your own height (or length) when lying down, as you need to consider the thickness of the sleeping-bag over your head and feet. For general use each person occupying the tent will need about 18 inches to 24 inches minimum width, and space is needed for dressing and undressing and stowage of small items of kit, remembering that things should not be allowed to press against the walls. Space is needed under the flysheet at the entrance to enable you to take off waterproofs, boots etc under cover, and space for storing spare gear and food. Sheltered space for safe cooking is a must. Some designs such as the transverse-ridge tents have two bell ends, one each side, with corresponding entrances to the inner tent. Since the wind is always liable to change direction at night, this is a useful idea.

After size, the next factor in your choice will probably be weight. Lightness does, however, bring with it the possibility of restricted space, weaker materials, instability in high wind and reduced waterproofness. To maintain these properties will usually result in higher cost. However, as a general rule one should aim at four pounds per person as an average weight. Two or more people can share the load, but the target of four pounds each should be kept.

Coupled with the matter of weight is the equally important one of bulk, or packed size. First there is the bulk of the tent and flysheet when folded or rolled. It should be possible to separate the two articles for packing in case the flysheet is dripping wet. Second is the pole assembly. Whatever system is used, when taken apart for packing the result always seems to be several lengthy bundles of loose items. Two methods of dealing with poles are common. First, the sections of pole may be linked together with elastic shock cord. This is intended to prevent sections of pole becoming lost and to make pitching easier, but the result as regards packing is a rather bulky bundle of tube sections which cannot be reduced in size any further. The alternative way is to have separate sections of tube which slide or nest one inside the other. You finish up with one single tube with everything else inside. We prefer this type for vertical poles and linked metal sections for tunnel or dome tents, where we are dealing with very long flexible poles. The alternative fibreglass wands with brass ferrules can cause problems by coming apart at the joints.

There are a number of other design features which should be taken into account when trying to make your choice. We are talking in general terms of tents suitable for backpacking or cycle camping as these will be useful for many other types of lightweight camping as a matter of course. We consider that it is essential for such tents to be capable of erection flysheet first, with a minimum of time spent on getting basic shelter. When packing up, the reverse should hold good. We also feel that any tent designed for use by two or even three people should be capable of being pitched without difficulty by one person, even in bad weather or in the dark. Obviously this needs practice, but it is not unreasonable. If the tent has the flysheet and inner tent attached to each other, they must be capable of being separated, so that the two parts can be carried separately and can be dried and aired more easily before packing away.

Desirable details would include a completely enclosed bell end (or bells) to the flysheet providing a sheltered area outside the inner door. When zipped entries are opened, there should still be adequate shelter to prevent rain or condensation from dripping into the open door of the inner tent. To avoid undue strain on the zip-fasteners, they should have hooks or tabs to fix across the end so that the pull of the adjoining fabric is taken away from the track. Provision is needed to hold back the open doors when cooking. Such fastenings can be tie tapes, toggles and loops, or Velcro tabs. The tapes should be sewn in such a way that water cannot 'wick' through from the outside, and they should preferably be waterproof.

The inner tent should, in the case of a double-skin design, be spaced at least ten centimetres (four inches) away from the flysheet, and means must be incorporated to ensure that this separation is maintained even when conditions are windy. One way is to provide linking bands between inner and outer about the centre of each side, in line with guylines from the outer flysheet. The inner tent should have a tray groundsheet without seams at the corners or across the floor. This may not be possible to achieve, in which case any seams must be well made and sealed to prevent ingress of water from below. Added comfort is obtained if the front edge of the groundsheet is turned up to form a low wall across the door. The inner tent door is best closed by means of zips coming up each side and meeting at the top in the centre. This will allow the door to be opened slightly, so giving ventilation without draught.

Ventilation panels covered with mosquito net are useful in the door tops, with a corresponding panel in the rear wall of the tent. If intending to camp in places where midges and other flying pests abound, a separate inner door made of mosquito net which can be completely closed whilst the normal doors are open is very desirable. Other useful features to look out for are pockets on the walls for such things as spectacles, watches and so on at night, and tape loops attached to the ridge for hanging lamps, although not gas or oil lamps.

Good-quality workmanship is important and it might be as well to consider some of the things you should look for after deciding what type of tent you want. Whenever possible, you should examine the tent or another like it in the fully erected condition. Look at the seams to see if they are neatly made, with evenly spaced stitching, straight, without missing any edges of fabric. Coated nylon flysheet seams should ideally be sealed. If not, then it is something you should consider doing yourself.

Points of stress such as guyline attachment points, fastenings for peg loops or grommets should be reinforced. The ridge seam should be reinforced along its length with tape or webbing, and the points where the tops of the poles enter the ridge require something more than just a thin brass eyelet. They should have a good reinforcement, preferably a leather patch, with a ring or grommet sewn in. Major guylines should have taped seams running from their attachment points to distribute the strain. Examine the groundsheet for any seams, and if present check that they are well made and sealed. Ensure that all zips run freely.

Poles should be made of aluminium or light alloy. Look carefully at the finish. Any roughness on the ends can cause damage to the tent fabric as well as causing difficulties in assembly. If flexible fibreglass poles are supplied, examine them carefully for any signs of splitting or rough ends. If the tent is intended to have the poles standing inside on the groundsheet, there should be reinforcing patches for the pole foot, and plastic cups should be supplied. One thing which is almost certain is that if the guylines are attached with good knots, which do not immediately work loose, you will have a well-made tent. It seems that few manufacturers take the trouble to tie effective knots!

Flammability

Before leaving the subject of choice of tent and looking at how to use it, we feel we should mention a subject which has caused much discussion among consumer protection organizations. This is the matter of protection from fire.

Several years ago work was commenced on the drafting of a British Standard to cover the question of safety of tents. The final version was published as BS 5576 in May 1978, under the title *Safety Features of Camping Tents*. It deals solely with recommendations on the provision of means of escape from and advice to users of camping tents in the event of fire. The recommendations are applicable mainly to large tents, not to those we would consider lightweight, although the Standard does not specifically exclude lightweight tents. One recommendation we would question is that all zip-fasteners used for openings of tents, both inner and outer, should be fitted so that the puller is at the bottom when closed. In the case of a backpacking tent, this would mean lying on the ground and trying to pull the fastener upwards to open, which we find most difficult. It is also in conflict with our suggested arrangement for ventilation at the top. A definite recommendation is also made to attach a label to all tents warning the user to remember that his tent can burn. We have seen such labels on American tents imported into this country, and we understand that regulations on such matters as safety from fire are very much stricter in the USA than here.

Following the publication of BS 5576, another Standard has been published (BS 6341:1983) entitled *Fabrics for Camping Tents*. This Standard contains requirements in terms of flammability for the materials used in manufacturing tents, together with other requirements such as tear strength, shrinkage, colour fastness and water resistance. Fabrics may be graded according to their properties. One thing which we feel can be misleading is that a claim that a given fabric meets a flammability classification according to this Standard does not necessarily mean that a tent made from the fabric is non-flammable. In fact, we would say that in the case of a lightweight tent it is far safer not to try to state a degree of non-flammability but to assume always that danger from fire exists. Heavy fabrics such as those used for frame tents or marquees may be treated to retard the spread of flame, but such treatment is of doubtful use on the sort of lightweight fabrics with which we are concerned.

So, having purchased a tent, the next thing to do is to take it home and check everything. It is too late if you are out in the hills and find something missing. Having checked that everything is there, preferably against the instruction sheet which should be supplied by the manufacturer, you should pitch it in either your own garden or a nearby park.

Pitching

The sequence to be followed will, of course, vary depending on the style of tent. For most ridge tents the procedure will be very similar. We will take as an example a small sloping-ridge model without ridge pole, and of course, one in which the flysheet can be erected first.

Before unpacking the tent select the spot on which you intend pitching, pointing the low rear end towards the wind but ensuring that your head will not be downhill when you are lying in your sleeping-bag. Clear the ground of loose twigs, stones, pine cones and other such objects – keep an eye open for ants' nests!

Before unfolding tent or flysheet, it is a good idea to assemble both poles and lay them ready. They are unlikely to blow away, but put their empty bag in a safe place. Open the peg bag and lay it handy. Never scatter loose pegs on the ground, as you will certainly lose some in the grass. This is particularly important if you are working in the dark or rain.

Having decided exactly where you are going to position the tent, unfold the flysheet and peg the back point and corners to the ground, judging the peg positions by holding the rear pole grommet up at about the correct height. It should then be possible to slip this pole into position and move it upright, and by holding the front end of the flysheet ridge against the pull of the back pegs, the whole shape of the flysheet will appear. Slip the front pole into position and quickly peg down the front point or points of the flysheet. You will then have the basic shelter standing. Front and back guylines should next be set out, either from their attachment points or by hooking them over the pole tops, depending on the design. These main guylines should then be tensioned and pegged securely, to obtain a very tight ridge line. Some adjustment to the pegs around the flysheet will probably be needed and the remainder of the pegs inserted. You then have a basic shelter in a matter of a very few minutes.

We suggest that it is worth the very slight extra weight to carry a sheet of fairly thin plastic to lay on the ground underneath the inner groundsheet. This will protect it from mud and possible damage from small stones, twigs etc.

The next task is to lay it down inside the flysheet, and lay out the inner tent on top. A good technique to adopt is to crawl on your knees with your booted feet up in the air. Position the groundsheet of the tent in relation to the rear pole, and peg the two back corners to the ground, making sure there are no creases across the width. Then hook the back peak of the tent up to the attachment inside the flysheet, before backing carefully out towards the front entrance, pulling the tent and groundsheet smooth as you go. Peg the front corners to the ground, pulling the sides straight as you do so, then hook up the front peak to the attachment point.

While you are pegging out both flysheet and tent, the doors should be closed. Next, you need to check and if necessary re-adjust pegs, peg out any guys on the inner tent, and generally 'square things up'. Of course details will vary with different models, and you may have linking elastic loops with hooks to maintain the spacing between inner and outer tent along the sides. The method of attaching the inner tent may also vary, although the simplest idea is a hook and ring arrangement.

When you have completed pitching, your tent should look neat and tidy, with a tight ridge and smooth sides without creases or wrinkles. The sides should be tight enough to prevent flapping in the wind. Many people who are unfamiliar with nylon tents do not achieve this tight, smooth pitch, mainly because they do not realize that, unlike natural materials like cotton, nylon tends to stretch and slacken when wet. For this reason, after you have pitched your tent, if it is raining or just becoming damp with dew in the evening, everything needs re-tightening. Otherwise you will have a very untidy-looking tent with sagging ridge, which in turn will reduce the separation between inner and outer, and the flapping of the material in the wind will not do the proofing coating any good. So for appearance and efficiency, maintain a tight pitch at all times. The first thing to tension is the ridge itself, then the main corner points to ensure the sides are straight, and finally set up the mid-guys along the sides. These latter must not be so tight that the ridge is pulled down in the centre. The 'set' of your tent should be checked at intervals including last thing at night and first thing in the morning.

The same basic ideas apply to transverse-ridge tents, with perhaps the addition of the ridge pole. This slips over the tops of the poles, under the flysheet. There is usually some form of loop midway along to suspend the inner tent below the ridge pole. If this loop is fixed so that the pole must be slipped through first before erection, it is usually easy and worthwhile to carry out a small DIY modification to allow the flysheet to be pitched first, otherwise you have the problem of a wet inner tent when pitching in the rain.

With tunnel and dome tents, again the procedure should be to clear the area, assemble the flexible poles, get things ready, then start assembly. The main difference between these and tents with rigid poles is that the long wands must be threaded through sleeves before erection, and this can prove a problem if working single-handed in windy conditions. Four hands are better than two here, as one person can push the rod through while the other holds the sleeve out straight and eases the end through. The other tricky operation can be flexing the poles and inserting their ends into the pockets provided. This requires a certain amount of strength and skill, especially with a new tent, and at this point in the game a gust of wind can have interesting if not actually disastrous results. For this reason it is advisable to peg down the windward edge of the tent first. Most tunnel and dome tents have fairly simple arrangements for attaching and erecting their inner tents once the outer shell is up and secured to the ground. Do not forget the latter task, as the guys at corners and intermediate points are necessary to prevent the whole structure being blown over, as also are the ground pegs.

Some general ideas on guylines and pegs may apply to all types of tent. The guylines themselves should pass through rings, either metal or plastic, which in turn are secured to the tent or flysheet by strong tape loops. The guylines should have a slider or adjuster to vary the length and tension, and the line should be almost double the length required between the tent and the required peg position. We favour fitting guylines in such a way that, when pulling the adjuster, you are pulling against the tent seam; in other words the slider should move down the line to tighten it. A loop or ring should be provided at the peg end, remembering that small rings may not fit over all types of peg. The line passes freely through the ring on the tent and back to the adjuster. A secure 'stopper knot' should ensure that the line cannot slip out of it, and ends of line should be heat-sealed.

Pegs are available in a number of different designs, most of which are intended for different types of ground conditions. For inner-tent ground pegging, straight pins of light alloy with hooked or ringed tops are probably most useful. Similar but larger pegs are usually adequate for inner-tent guylines. Most conditions are suited to the use of alloy angle pegs for the outer and main guylines. These are available in different sizes, and it is a good idea to carry some slightly larger ones for the main guys. For special conditions such as snow, sand or rock, other designs are available, but we have found very few situations in which a combination of straight pins and angle pegs does not prove effective.

The way in which you position your guylines and pegs plays an important part in the setting and security of your tent, and to ensure peace of mind and comfort it is worth paying some attention to this matter. The guylines should be pulled out in line with tent seams or out at an angle from corners. In general, side guys should come out in line with the sloping roof surface, or even slightly further out, so as to hold the vertical side walls up. This may mean that the guyline adjusters must be set to give a long line, especially when the ground is uneven and sloping down away from the tent. The pegs must be inserted into the ground at an angle sloping away from the tent, in such a way that the pull of the guyline naturally tends to make it slip down the peg to ground level. This is the most secure way. We have very rarely found the need for using a mallet or hammer, even on hard or stony ground. If your guylines are sufficiently long, when you hit a stone in the ground it is usually possible to reposition the peg slightly or lean it at a different angle, when all will be well. When you encounter strong, gusty wind, you may well find that double pegging is advisable on main guys and perhaps corners. This is achieved either by inserting a second peg across the guyline peg or by putting another peg through the ring or hole in the top of the first peg.

Finally, when all is set up, lock the runners or adjusters to prevent them from slipping. This is done by setting the cord into a slot on the side of the small alloy slider, depending on the design.

Having completed the operation of pitching, place any spare pegs and the empty bags all together in a safe place under the flysheet where they are to hand but cannot get blown away.

Packing up

When the time comes to pack and move on, the general procedure will be reversed.

Take out all the inner-tent guyline pegs, and put them together in a neat pile where you will not lose them. Then, in the case of our sloping-ridge tent, unhook the peak from the pole top, and work your way back and repeat the process at the rear. Lay the tent down onto the groundsheet and fold it as flat as possible. Then, and not before, take out the corner pegs on one side, fold the groundsheet with tent over to the centre line, then repeat with the other side. In this way you will have the groundsheet folded so that any wet or mud on the bottom will not lie on the tent material. Finish by folding again lengthways, pressing the trapped air out as you do so, then fold up into a size to fit the tent bag.

Now turn your attention to the flysheet. Go round taking out all intermediate pegs, making sure there are sufficient pegs left in on the windward side or end to prevent the whole thing from blowing away. Every time you remove a guyline, pull out the peg at the same time, otherwise you will never find them hidden in the grass later. Finally collapse the flysheet, laying the poles on the ground, and fold the material up as quickly and neatly as possible, pressing out the air as you go. If the fabric is wet but it is not raining, try to shake off as much as possible before folding and then complete the task by dismantling the poles, and finally scrape off as much mud as possible from the pegs before putting them in their bag.

One problem which seems to be with us every time we have to pitch in bad conditions is that the guylines have a habit of getting tangled. We have tried various ways of coiling them, but eventually we have concluded that, with the exception of the long main guys, it is just as easy to lay the lines loosely onto the material of the tent or flysheet and fold them in with it. Another very practical idea is to place your hand over the spike on the top of the pole when pulling the flysheet over before fitting the grommets onto the spike, to avoid damage to the material. Finally get into the habit of never leaving small items such as plastic pole cups or loose guylines lying on the ground but place them immediately together on the peg bag so they do not get lost or overlooked. The same principles apply to tunnel and dome tents. With their thin, flexible poles, as with the thicker poles of other tents, it is very important to avoid getting mud or grit and sand on the joints, so when laying them on the ground, watch out for this. Wipe the joints when you pack up, to avoid jammed sections on your next pitch.

Care and maintenance

With your tent being one of the most expensive single items of your equipment, it follows that some time and thought given to care and maintenance will pay dividends. The golden rule for all your gear should be to unpack, check, clean and repack everything when you return at the end of a trip, and your tent certainly requires this treatment.

Three main areas require care. First the flysheet and inner tent. Any loose twigs or particles of dried mud or grit should be brushed or shaken out from the inside. Mud or dirt sticking to the underside of the groundsheet should be brushed off or wiped with a damp cloth – no detergent or other substance to be used. Then the whole article – cotton or nylon – should be hung up where it can dry and air thoroughly. Check the guylines and retie any which have become loose. From time to time give a check to any points of strain, particularly the grommets where the tops of the poles fit, to see if the stitching requires attention. Check the groundsheet for signs of abrasion or punctures.

Next, look over all the pegs, if necessary wash them free of all mud, dry them thoroughly and repack in their bag. Straighten any bent pegs. Remember never to pack loose pegs in with the tent. They will easily damage the thin fabric, no matter how strong it may be.

Finally, remember the pole sections. Unpack them, check them carefully for any damage, scratches or burred ends, and correct these with fine emery cloth or other means. Such flaws can cause jammed poles next time, or even prevent correct assembly. Most important, and often overlooked, is to dry all the pole sections before packing away. Aluminium does not rust, but it *does* become affected with white oxidation, and this can cause the joints to jam. Wipe off the tubes and give them a very light rub with a dry cloth on which is a little silicone polish. This will give the surface of the tubing a slightly slippery and smooth feel, and is better than using oil.

If you have any doubts about the zips on your tent, check them over carefully. If they are not damaged but just fail to slide easily, you can obtain products in aerosol cans to ease the situation.

Normally a good-quality coated nylon tent will not require re-proofing for some considerable time. If, however, you feel this is necessary, there are a number of proprietory treatments available, for brushing, spraying or use from aerosol cans. Similarly, seam sealants can be obtained for treating the seams. Cotton and polyester/cotton fabric can also be re-proofed using the appropriate products. It is worth remembering that detergents will destroy proofing on tents and flysheets. For this reason, never use such products to clean dirty marks on your shelter. Sponge with plain water, and avoid at all costs children on campsites who are playing at blowing bubbles.

Repack everything after airing, cleaning and checking, and you will then know that all will be ready when needed. If you are packing things away for the winter, it is preferable to pack tents loosely, rather than tightly rolled in their stuff sacks. Do not leave them always folded tightly in the same folds, as this may weaken the material and coating. The best way of keeping a tent in good condition is to use it, provided you use it carefully.

Most of what we have written so far on shelter applies equally to single-skin bivouacs made of moisture-permeable proofed materials. In other words, the general methods of pitching, packing and so on will apply, modified according to the design. Follow the instructions supplied by the manufacturers. These specialized fabrics do depend for their action on the fact that the micro-pores are kept clean, so they may require washing from time to time. Take care, and follow the manufacturers' recommendations on this matter.

3 Sleeping in Comfort

Whatever type of lightweight camper you are you will not enjoy yourself if you do not get a good night's rest between your daily travels. You will find that you become irritable from lack of sleep, and you will be unable to travel as far as you had planned.

Heat Balance

At night, man is at his most defenceless. He needs rest and sleep. A warm body can rest during sleep, but if it gets cold, it has to work to keep warm. The happy medium has to be found between shivering and overheating.

To be comfortable, man needs to lose heat at the same rate as he produces it. When he is awake he can react to the prevailing conditions by adding or removing clothing, but when sleeping he needs a protective layer to give his body the extra help it needs in the form of insulation, to retain the body heat and prevent it from being lost at a faster rate than it is produced. The natural processes of breathing and perspiration cause heat loss by evaporation, and to remain comfortable, this must be allowed to escape freely. The body also loses heat by radiation (although at low temperatures this only amounts to under ten per cent of the total heat loss), by conduction and convection.

Loss by conduction is caused by contact between the skin and its surroundings, such as air, clothes etc; loss by convection occurs when moving currents of air surrounding the body carry its heat away.

There are a number of factors which affect the rate of heat loss, such as shelter, wind velocity and humidity. Winds will decrease the efficiency of the insulation by circulating cold air across the surface, so drawing heat away by convection. High humidity will have some control over the rate of evaporation, and can also reduce the efficiency of certain insulation materials.

For a comfortable night, the balancing of heat loss and heat gain should result in an average skin temperature within a few degrees of 91°F (33°C), but the 'deep core' temperature is more important. By this we mean the temperature of the vital organs of the body – heart, lungs and brain – and to survive, this must be maintained at around 98.6°F (37°C). In temperate and cold climates, where the air temperature around us is much colder than 91°F, we need clothing by day and bedding by night in order to maintain heat balance.

Insulation

The most convenient form of bedding for the lightweight camper is a sleeping-bag. A good bag will be far less bulky than its equivalent warmth value in blankets, and of course will be much lighter in weight. It is immediately ready for use when required, can be packed quickly and easily into a small space, and will be so designed as to give sufficient insulation to reduce the heat loss by conduction and convection to a minimum. Conduction loss is best reduced by means of a barrier layer of air surrounding the body. However, if that layer is too thick, convection currents can circulate within the open space and continually carry the heat away. To overcome this problem, the space needs to be divided up to trap the air and keep it as still as possible. This can be achieved by means of an inner and outer 'shell' whose purpose is to retain a suitable filling which traps the insulating layer of air. This is the basic idea behind a

Diagram 10 Insulation

A layer of air – the best barrier to loss of heat by conduction

Too thick a layer means that convection currents circulate and carry heat away

The space needs to be divided and filled with a suitable filling to trap the air sleeping-bag.

Loft

The term 'loft' is used to describe the ability of the filling to expand within the confines of the shell construction, so producing the required layer of still air. The maximum loft is obtained when the bag is fluffed up, and a good filling will retain its resilience and ability to loft over a long period of use. The construction of a sleeping-bag is specially designed to make the best use of the filling. The shell materials must retain this in position, should be durable and lightweight and must allow the body moisture to escape. The outer shell must be fairly draughtproof and the inner shell comfortable in feel.

When considering the loss of body heat, it should be remembered that as much as thirty per cent of this can come from the head. For this reason, a sleeping-bag will have some form of hood. In general it should be possible to pull this up without the feet being pressed hard into the foot of the bag, and there should be room inside to allow the wearing of extra clothes if necessary.

Other features to consider are whether or not zips are fitted for easy entry, and for cooling in warm weather. Sometimes it is possible to join two bags together to make a double. Adequate means must be provided to prevent draughts penetrating the zips.

Fillings for sleeping-bags

We can now consider the various fillings which are used for sleeping-bags, together with the construction methods used for each type of filling.

Down

In dry conditions, down is by far the best insulator there is. It is light, breathable, compressible and very resilient. There is nothing man-made to equal its softness and lofting capabilities. It has a much longer life – if treated correctly – than synthetic fillings. It will keep you warm for less weight and bulk than any other material. A synthetic bag with equal performance is likely to be $1\frac{1}{2}$ times as heavy and bulky as its down equivalent and is liable to lose its loft much earlier. There are, however, some drawbacks to down. It is a natural substance, for which the demand is high. It takes seven mature geese to supply two pounds of down – just about sufficient for a four-season sleeping-bag. Hence it is more expensive than man-made fibres. It is also useless as an insulator when wet, and takes a very long time to dry. Despite these drawbacks, it is still the most popular filling for specialist sleeping-bags, particularly when problems of weight and bulk have to be considered.

Down is the undercoating beneath the feathers of waterfowl – that is to say, geese and ducks. It consists of thousands of particles, each with a number of light, fluffy filaments growing from a single quill point, but with no quill shaft. When used as an insulator, these down filaments cling to one another, forming thousands of tiny pockets which trap the air. It is these air pockets which inhibit the passage of both cold and heat through the down. When positioned uniformly around the body, down insulates efficiently against loss of body heat, whilst at the same time allowing body moisture to wick through the cellular structure, just as it does for the ducks or geese from which it came. It can be compressed into a space a fraction of its normal size and will spring back to full size again and again.

Quality of natural fillings The best guide to quality is the name of a good manufacturer on the label of the sleeping-bag. The filling should be new; recycled down is very soft but tends to lose its loft rather quickly. There are British Standards for down used for bedding. BS 1425 details the specifications for cleanliness of fillings and stuffings to be used. BS 2005 describes the various fillings used.

Because of the problems involved in the separation of down from feathers, the inclusion of separate fibres, and of up to fifteen per cent by weight of fine, small, light, fluffy feathers is usually acceptable. There must be at least eighty-five per cent down.

Down and feathers is a mixture containing not less than fifty-one per cent by weight of down as defined above.

Feathers and down must contain not less than fifteen per

cent weight of down as defined above.

There is no British Standard for sleeping-bags as such, but BS 5335 refers to Continental quilts. The filling for these must comply to the standards of cleanliness laid down by BS 1425, and any down and feathers used *must* be new and from waterfowl.

Most reliable manufacturers will adhere to these standards, but it is important to make sure that you know what the filling is. Here again, the reliable manufacturer will label his product. 'All new down' will be exactly that. Nevertheless, there are differing qualities within each type of filling. Be sure too, that you are not confused by the terms 'down/feather' and 'feather/down'. Ask to see the manufacturer's brochure which refers to the bag you are buying. If there is any doubt about the quality of the filling, take care. There are some lesser-known manufacturers who make use of recycled down. Although it is unlikely that any label will state this, the price should give you a guide, and the bag itself will have less 'loft' than those of higher quality. Such fillings should, therefore, be avoided.

Prior to 1939, the very best down bags were filled with eiderdown. Unfortunately, much confusion has arisen because the term 'eiderdown' began to be used as a general term referring to bed quilts, which often as not were filled with *anything but* eiderdown! The eider duck nests in the Arctic, in very hostile conditions. Its nest is simply a hollowed area of stony ground, filled with down from its breast, and, although it might seem quite incredible, this does not blow away but stays in place, each tiny particle of down clinging to its next-door neighbour. It is very fine and springy, and a dull, mousey-brown in colour. The eider duck is now very rare and is a protected species, and the down is extremely difficult to obtain, so it is no longer used for commercially produced bags. Down bags today are filled with either duck down or goose down, or a mixture of the two.

Construction of down bags There are numerous different methods of making sleeping-bags to ensure the best use of the filling. These days, most down-filled bags will be

Diagram 11 Internal walls of sleeping-bags

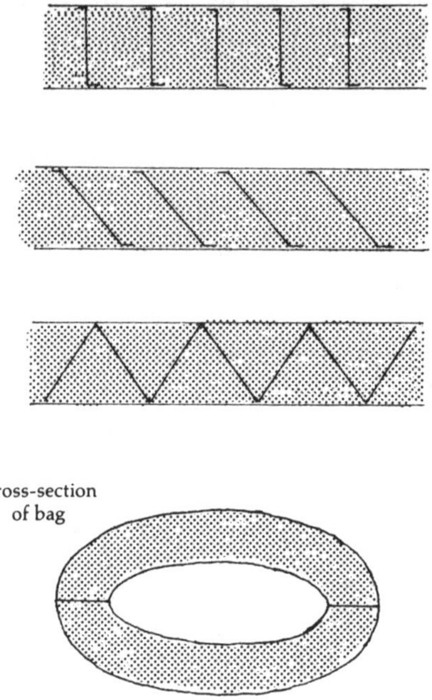

constructed with internal walls to prevent the down from shifting around, and to prevent cold spots from occurring. These walls, or baffles, may be constructed in different ways.

The simplest form of wall-quilting is straight-wall quilting, where the walls are sewn at right angles to the fabric of the outer and inner shell. Although they do a reasonable job in keeping the down evenly distributed, it is possible for cold spots to occur when the filling migrates away from the walls. Slant walls, which, as their name suggests, are sewn at an angle to both inner and outer shells, help to prevent this migration and are more generally used in better-quality bags.

Continuous V-baffle construction (sometimes called overlapping tube construction) makes for excellent distribution of the filling but tends to make the bag heavier, because more material is used.

Side baffles prevent down from shifting from the top of the bag to the underneath, and vice versa, and will always be present in top-quality bags.

In addition to baffled construction, there are two other methods of quilting which are occasionally still used. Simple quilting, where the two shells are sewn straight through, is used on some bags of the lower price range, often with feather/down fillings. Such bags are only really suited to use in very warm conditions, and there will be cold spots at all points of stitching, as there will be no filling at these points. Double-quilt construction is where two separate bags are made of simple quilting, and one is sewn inside the other. The stitching is 'offset' to prevent cold spots. At one time this was the standard method of making expedition bags, but it is seldom used today for down-filled bags.

Diagram 12 Stitched-through quilting

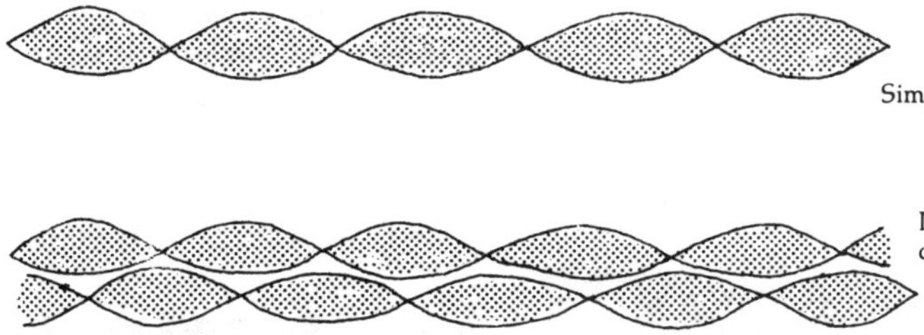

There are other important features which should be incorporated if the bag is to be really efficient. A good foot piece, which should be baffled around the edge and not stitched through, and large enough to accommodate the feet comfortably, is needed. In the better-quality bags, the inner will be cut smaller than the outer, to allow the down to loft fully. This is known as differential cut. A hood is required, which can be pulled up around the head when needed, with a toggle on the cord to keep it drawn up to the required amount.

Synthetics

Most synthetic bags will be filled with some kind of

polyester batt. This is formed by assembling polyester fibres into a controlled width and thickness, and then spraying with a resin to maintain the shape. There are various brand names referring to different types and makes.

The general term 'polyester filled' is used for cheaper bags with unspecified fillings which are often by-products of fibres made for other uses, cut or shredded and sold as fillings to manufacturers at about half the cost of branded polyesters. However, they lack the loft and durability of these.

Branded fillings include Terylene from ICI and Dacron* Fiberfill 2H from DuPont. The latter is the filling material used by manufacturers of sleeping-bags and clothing who are licensed by DuPont to use the name Dacron 'Hollofil'.

Polyester fibres are normally about $2\frac{1}{2}$ inches long. Hollofil consists of polyester fibres of the same length, but each fibre is hollow, allowing the air to collect inside it. This provides the Hollofil with a good heat-insulating capacity. It is also soft, resilient and fluffy, and almost as comfortable as down, and, although cheaper, it is considerably heavier and bulkier. The branded fillings are far superior to the unspecified polyesters as they give a much better loft.

Diagram 13

Dacron* Hollofil **Conventional Polyester Fibre**

*DuPont's registered trade mark

In addition to polyester batts, there is now a polyester filling which can be blown into sleeping-bag shells in a similar manner to down. This is ICI's 'Terylene Superloft', consisting of gossamer-fine continuous-filament Terylene fibres, which are blown into sleeping-bags with walled channel construction. This has led to significant improvements in the warmth-to-weight ratio of polyester bags, with consequent advantages of lighter bags, and bags which pack into smaller spaces.

Perhaps the biggest advantage of synthetic fibre is its performance in wet conditions. It is insensitive to moisture, mould and salt water and retains its insulating properties even when wet. Because they are not as compressible as down bags, those filled with polyester will be more efficient in providing insulation under the body. Unfortunately, this factor of less compressibility means that they take up much more room when packed.

Construction of polyester-filled bags Most polyester-filled bags will be made using the double-quilt method of construction, with offset stitching. (See Diagram 12.) The batt is covered on both sides with a suitable fabric, which is then stitched through to form a quilted sandwich. The filling does not then shift around, but the disadvantage is that, however resilient the filling, it cannot loft beyond the limits set out by the proximity of the nearest stitch line. The addition of a 'radiant barrier' to synthetic bags can increase the performance, weight for weight, by about twenty per cent. In practice, this will reduce the weight and bulk by twenty per cent for the same level of performance. This places the radiant barrier bag midway between down and normal synthetics for weight/bulk/warmth ratio but carries with it the wet-performance advantage of synthetics. This radiant barrier (a specially formulated reflective film) achieves these savings by retaining the heat normally lost by radiation – around ten per cent of the body's total heat loss. To make the combination of radiant barrier and synthetic filling work successfully, the barrier itself must be light *and* breathable. The best performance is achieved when it is sandwiched between two layers of insulation. This slows

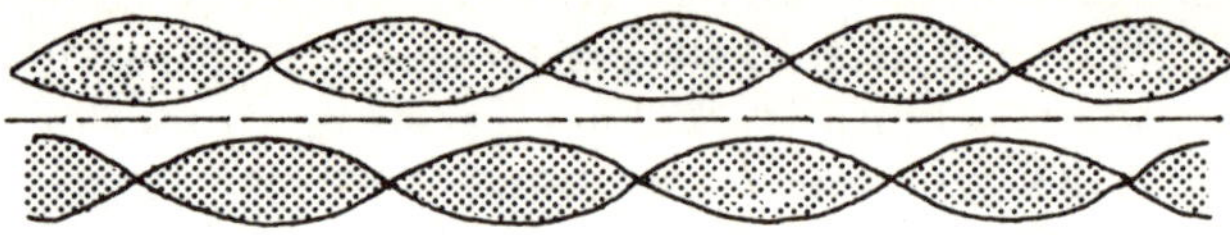

Diagram 14 Radiant barrier construction

Double quilt construction with permeable radiant barrier to let water vapour through

down the convection currents between the two layers of filling, thereby increasing efficiency.

Blown filled bags can use the straight or slant-baffle systems to give the excellent distribution and loft associated with down-filled bags. Cold spots are eliminated and the construction is lighter than the double-quilt method. Care has to be taken to eliminate any tendency to shift away from the baffles; there must be sufficient filling to prevent this. For this reason, this method of construction is best suited to bags intended for use in colder conditions. Other features, such as a good foot piece, differential cut and a hood with draw-cord should also be incorporated in bags made of synthetic fibres.

Shell materials

Most bags these days are made of an all-nylon shell construction, with perhaps a different type of nylon for the inner, of a more comfortable texture. Some manufacturers make bags with cotton or polyester/cotton inner shells for those who prefer them, but few bags are now made with all-cotton coverings. The most common fabric in use is a two-ounce plain woven nylon. This is very strong and reasonably cheap and has most of the qualities required for both shells. A two-ounce ripstop nylon, similar to but tougher than the above, is often used for outers, and a very lightweight $1\frac{1}{2}$-ounce nylon taffeta may be used for inners as it has a comfortable feel. The lightness is particularly important when weight is of prime consideration.

Cotton is rather heavier than nylon. It also has a shorter life and needs more care in use. Polyester/cotton, although tougher than pure cotton, is still quite heavy in comparison with nylon. Undoubtedly, however, there are those who prefer a cotton lining in a sleeping-bag.

Gore-Tex fabric is now used as a covering on some specialist bags. It makes the outer shell virtually waterproof, yet allows body moisture to evaporate. It is therefore useful when bivouacking.

Fibre-pile bags

In addition to conventional sleeping-bags with down or polyester fillings, it is possible to obtain ones which are made from fibre-pile fabric. They are available in various weights to suit different temperatures. Fibre-pile fabric is very warm and comfortable and performs exceptionally well in wet conditions. It is an excellent under-body insulator and has a long effective life. Its biggest drawbacks are weight and bulk, bags being rather heavier and bulkier than those filled with polyester. Perhaps their greatest advantage is in their use as supplementary bags to extend the range of lightweight down- or polyester-filled bags, enabling them to be used in colder conditions.

Sheet linings

A number of manufacturers make a sheet lining to fit inside their sleeping-bags. These help to keep them clean and will also add a certain amount of insulation due to the air space between the two. A shaped lining is not essential; many prefer to use a hostel-type liner with a built-in pillow cover. This may be pulled over the head or can be stuffed with clothes to make a pillow. Sheet-liners give additional comfort, especially when using a nylon-lined bag. They can be tied in with tapes which helps to avoid any 'twisting up'.

Choosing a sleeping-bag

There is no point in buying a bag which is intended for the very coldest conditions if you are going to be out camping only in the summer. If you are likely to be camping throughout the year, you will need to consider the range of temperatures you could encounter. It may be worthwhile getting a lighter bag and wearing extra clothing when it is very cold. On the other hand, if you know that you are going to do a lot of camping high up in the hills, the warmest bag

Diagram 15 Sleeping-bag shapes

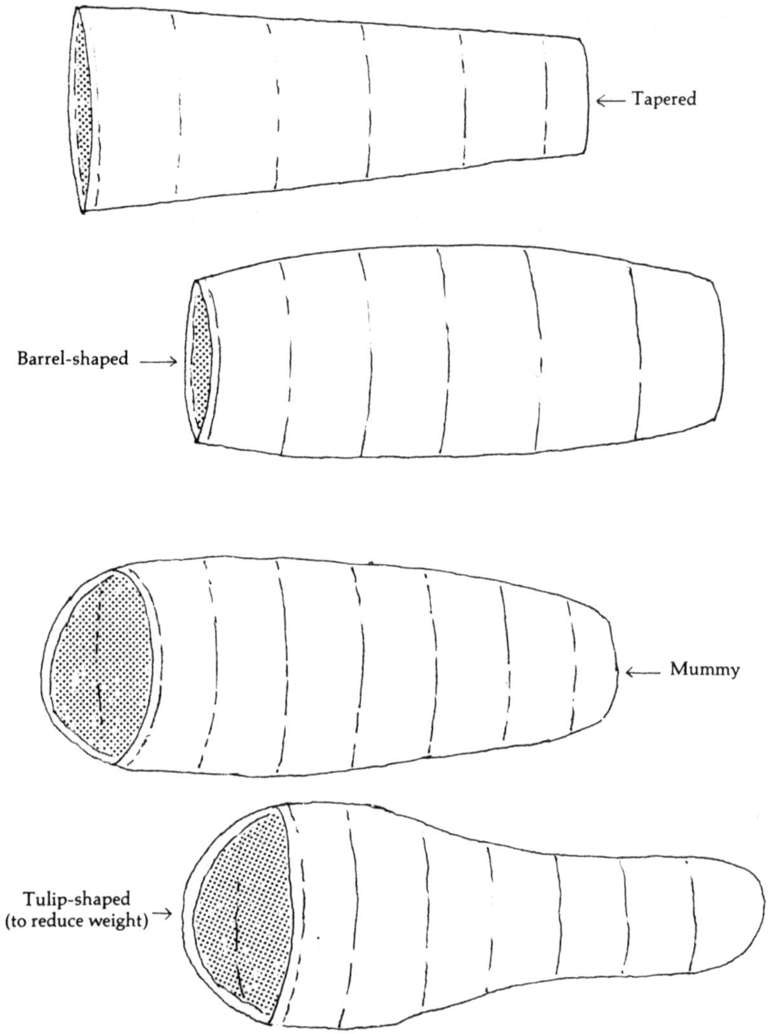

might be worth considering. You also have to take into account your method of camping. If you are backpacking or cycling, weight and space are important factors. A down bag which will pack very small will be useful here. If, however, you are likely to come into contact with water, choose a bag filled with polyester. Obviously you will need to use this type of bag if you are allergic to feathers and down.

Another point to consider is your own personal size. It is useless to buy a bag that is too small, but if you are not very tall, you certainly do not need one which is extra-long. Some backpacking bags are very narrow at the foot end, mainly to save weight, but if you like plenty of room for your legs, avoid this shape. If you are of a heavy build, it is possible to buy a 'barrel-shaped' bag, which is larger round the trunk than the shoulders, and you may prefer one of these.

You may wish to join two bags together to make a double bag, in which case you need to be sure to buy two which pair up properly – one must have a right-hand and the other a left-hand zip and there should be baffles behind them to prevent draughts.

You also have to decide how much money you are prepared to pay out, and how long you want your bag to last. Down will cost more but will outlast synthetics and will therefore be cheaper in the long run.

Many manufacturers group their sleeping-bags into 'classes' which relate to the approximate minimum temperatures for which they are suitable. Mountain Equipment Ltd, who are regarded as the world's top specialist sleeping-bag manufacturers, produce a range that fits into five different classes. A bag which contains twenty-six ounces of down will be in the same class as one filled with a double seven-ounce batt (that is seven ounces per square yard), or a blown-filled bag containing forty ounces of Terylene Superloft. These would all be suitable for 'three-season' use – spring, summer and autumn – in the hills, and all-year round at valley level. The lowest temperature for which they are recommended is given as 20°F (−6°C). Most other manufacturers class their bags in a similar manner.

Ground insulation

No sleeping-bag will give its best performance without good insulation beneath the body. Fibre-pile bags will provide this, but other bags will need an additional thermal

Diagram 16 Choosing your sleeping-bag

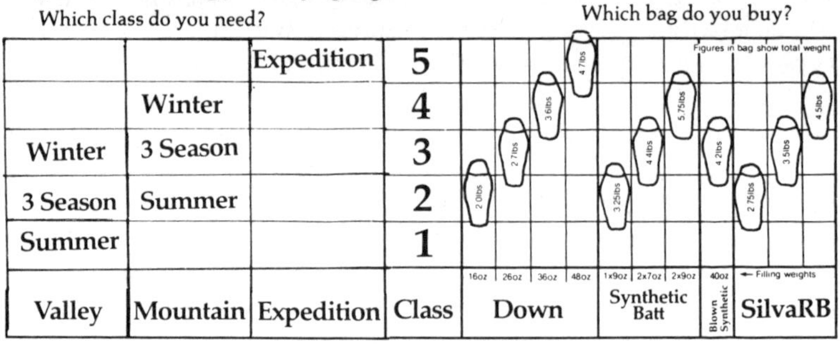

Approx minimum temperatures Class 1 50°F Class 2 35°F Class 3 20°F
Class 4 −5°F Class 5 −35°F

insulation layer of some kind. Air-beds are comfortable but rather heavy and tend to be cold as the air inside transfers heat from the body to the ground by conduction and convection. A partial remedy is to cover the air-bed with a thin piece of closed-cell foam, which will form an insulating barrier between it and the body. There are some air-beds available which are made from PVC and have been specially designed for lightweight campers. These are small units which can be buttoned together to create larger beds. They have small air channels with double walls separating them, so that the air inside is kept reasonably still, offering good insulation.

It is also possible to obtain self-inflating mattresses. These, filled with open-cell foam, which is soft and comfortable, are covered with nylon and are reasonably compact when packed. Their disadvantage is that they are expensive to buy, although they offer excellent insulation.

Probably the most favoured type of insulating mat is the closed-cell foam pad, obtainable in various thicknesses to suit the intended conditions of use, and different makes are available, probably the best known being 'Karrimat'. The main disadvantage is that, although it is an excellent insulator, it is somewhat hard to lie on. Open-cell foam on its own does not offer good insulation, as it soaks up moisture like a sponge, both from the body and from the surrounding atmosphere.

Getting the best from your sleeping-bag

You will need to remember some general points if your bag is to give good service. First of all, never store it in its compressed state but in a large pillow case or the manufacturer's storage bag, where provided. The latter is often made from nylon net and can also be utilized for washing the sleeping-bag. Always air your bag thoroughly to dry out any moisture; this is particularly important with down-filled bags. If the weather is too wet to lay it out in the fresh air, turn it inside out for as long as you can before packing up. When you reach your next night's camp, take the bag out as soon as possible and open it to finish airing off. In any case, it is a good idea to take it out of its stuff sack so that there is an opportunity for it to reach its maximum loft before nightfall. Only store your bag when perfectly dry.

You can extend the range of your sleeping-bag by adding a pile liner or overbag and by wearing extra clothing at night. However, it is important to remember that clothing must not be too tight, or it will restrict the circulation. If you wear socks, they should be loose fitting and should not be the ones you wore during the day. Keep a special set of clothes for wearing at night – clothing which has been worn during the day will undoubtedly be damp.

Both down and polyester fibres can be damaged by excessive heat; therefore your bag should be stored in a dry, warm but not hot place.

Cleaning your sleeping-bag

It is most important to keep your sleeping-bag clean. Down bags need treating with great care. They *can* be dry-cleaned, but this should only be done by a reputable company who know about cleaning down products. The majority of quality manufacturers now recommend laundering down bags, using one of the special products specifically designed for the purpose, as certain dry-cleaning agents and detergents will have a very harmful effect on the down fibres. We think there is a better chance of giving your bag a longer life if it is hand-washed, but of course great care has to be taken not to strain the walls and fabric by the weight of wet down. The main thing to remember is that you will need a lot of patience, as it will take a long time to do the job properly, and, once started, it must be finished as speedily as possible. A down bag must not be allowed to remain wet for any length of time.

You should buy one of the specialist down cleaners available from good camping shops – there are six or seven brands currently available. Check your bag to ensure that there are no tears in the fabric, and that no stitching is coming undone, as repairs must be undertaken before washing. Do not use a washing-machine, as the constant turning and tumbling of a wet bag could cause the walls to collapse. Use the bath, rather than the kitchen sink, so that your bag has room to be moved around in the water.

Put about ten gallons of hand-hot water into the bath. Dissolve the cleaning agent in the water according to the instructions on the container, and stir around with your hand until plenty of suds appear. Put the sleeping-bag into the water, still rolled up, and unroll it under the water, keeping it there until it is really wet. Alternatively, put the bag in the water in its storage bag. Leave to soak for about twelve hours, agitating occasionally during this time, still keeping it under water. On no account lift the bag while it is soaking wet. Push it down gently with open hands to work the suds into the bag, kneading it under the water. Do not twist or wring. Holding the bag to one side, drain the dirty water from the bath, then rinse in clean water several times until the water is clear, making certain that all traces of soap are removed. Now press out as much water as you can, again with open hands, pushing out the maximum possible without wringing or twisting the bag. This can be quite hard work, as you have to get rid of a lot of water in this manner.

The next step is to remove the bag *very carefully* from the bath. To do this, pick it up like a baby, supporting all its weight in your arms and hands. You may wish to give your bag a light spin in a spin dryer, but be very careful only to give it a short spin when you have pressed out the maximum amount of water possible by hand. Never use a fast spin. On no account put a soaking wet bag in a spin dryer.

Drying should be achieved as quickly as possible. Hanging on the washing-line cannot be recommended, as the weight of the wet down could cause the internal walls to break away. If you do have to hang it up, make sure the walls hang *vertically* rather than horizontally. The best way to dry a down bag is to tumble it dry on a low-heat setting. Most domestic tumble dryers are too small for all but the lightest bags, so it is best to ask at your local launderette if you may use one of theirs, during a slack period.

Be careful that the heat setting remains on 'low', as vibration sometimes causes it to shift to the hotter positions. Too great a heat could cause damage to both the nylon covering fabric and the down filling. Put an old, clean tennis shoe in an old pillowcase or nylon bag, tie it up tightly and put it in with the sleeping-bag. This will create a certain amount of static electricity and will help to break up the down clumps and renew the loft. Take the bag out of the dryer at intervals, and break up the clumps of down by hand. It will take about two hours, or possibly even longer, to get the bag really dry. Remember that the cover will dry relatively quickly, but the down inside will take much longer. Turn the bag at intervals, and shake it as it gets drier. Finally, give it a good airing, preferably in the sun. Pat the down channels to distribute the filling evenly, and shake the bag again when completely dry. Only wash the bag occasionally – possibly once a year – and keep the bag as clean as possible.

Polyester bags can be washed by hand or machine. However, the best machine to use is the large front-loading type. Do up any zips before you wash the bag, and make sure you have a full load in the machine so that the bag cannot move around too much, thus reducing the strain on seams and stitching. Use a mild detergent and a warm, gentle wash. Do not use soap, as it can coat the fibre and reduce the lofting power. If washing by hand, soak the bag for about half an hour, then squeeze the water through the bag several times. If it is very dirty, you may need to give it a second washing. Rinse thoroughly until all traces of dirt and detergent have been removed. Press out all the water, as for a down bag, and dry in a large commercial dryer on a low-heat setting, or you can hang it on a line to dry.

If polyester fibres are heated to a temperature above

140°F, they begin to lose their crimp, and hence your bag will lose its loft if you use water in excess of that temperature, or dry it on too high a heat setting. Dry-cleaning is not recommended as some cleaning solvents remove the fibre coatings, again destroying the lofting properties. Also, cleaning solvents may not be completely removed during dry-cleaning, and you could find yourself breathing in lethal fumes if the bag is not properly aired.

In an emergency, if you cannot obtain the special cleaners for down bags, pure soap flakes may be used for cleaning, but do not use too much. Alternatively, baby shampoo is safe to use, as it will not remove the natural oil from the down.

Gore-Tex covered bags will need special care, and the manufacturer's instructions should be followed to the letter to prevent damage.

Fibre-pile sleeping-bags can be washed and dried in a washing-machine and spin dryer without any risk of damage.

4 Cooking and Eating

We are often highly amused at articles appearing in camping journals extolling the virtues of the latest gas-stoves produced for campers. The writers so often seem to think that the 'old-style' camper with a Primus stove, or worse, a wood fire never managed a hot drink, let alone a decently cooked meal. Yet with care and practice it is perfectly possible to produce an excellent meal in bad conditions on a single-burner backpacking stove, just as it is equally possible to have a disaster with a new shiny marvel.

There are very few opportunities in Great Britain these days for using a small fire for cooking when backpacking. The risk of damage to the environment is too great, and it must be admitted that the means of getting something hot to eat and drink, and getting it quickly at the end of the day, favours the use of one of the many highly efficient and reliable stoves which are now available. We are faced again with having to make a choice. How shall we carry the stove and its fuel? When and where shall we be using it?

Fuels

Fuels may be solid, liquid or gas, and we will take them in that order.

Solid fuel

Normally available in the form of solid tablets, this fuel has low heating power and is suitable for use only in an emergency or for an occasional 'brew-up'. It has its use also as a pre-heating fuel for some of the liquid-fuel stoves since the tablets are dry and easy to carry. There are a number of makes of solid-fuel tablet on the market, and we suggest you try several of them because some seem to produce fumes which are rather unpleasant both in the dry state and when burning. Solid fuel cannot be controlled when burning, and with its low heat output it cannot be considered for serious cooking.

Liquid Fuels

Methylated spirit Often called 'meths', when burned in its liquid state, it is not as hot as other liquid fuels, but if vaporized it can produce a very hot flame. Purer forms burn with a very clear, almost invisible blue flame, but additives can affect this characteristic. If spilled, it evaporates fairly quickly and does not leave any oily, unpleasant residue. Normally methylated spirit is easy to light in the liquid form, although some difficulty can be experienced at temperatures around 0°C. Once burning, however, it provides a satisfactory fuel.

Supplies are readily available in England and Wales, although Scotland, particularly in rural areas, can be difficult. In some cases it is necessary to sign the Poisons Register when purchasing. In England and Wales it is available in most ironmongers, builders' merchants and chemists in screw-topped plastic bottles or metal cans. Both are suitable for carrying the fuel. It is reasonably safe to handle and store under the flysheet of your tent.

Paraffin In camping stoves this is always burned as a vapour mixed with air, under pressure. In this state it burns with a very hot flame, little affected by the temperature of the surrounding air. Pre-heating fuel is required in order to start the process, and this can be a disadvantage. If paraffin does burn as a liquid, it produces a very smoky flame which will blacken any pans with a sooty deposit. If spilled, it will not evaporate quickly and will leave a strong smell and oily deposit. Supplies are normally easy to obtain anywhere, although small quantities might be a problem. It may be carried in any strong metal or plastic container with a screw cap and is quite safe to handle.

Petrol Petrol is universally available. However, as a motor fuel

Ridge tents – left: sloping ridge tent with enclosed porch and sleeved A-pole in front (Field & Trek Trailmaker); right: transverse ridge tent with enclosed porches at each end (Saunders Base Camp).

Tents with flexible poles – left: tunnel tent with single enclosed entrance (Ultimate Pea-pod); right: dome tent with doors each side (Field & Trek Traildome).

Dome tent with extended porch (Phoenix Phreedome).

Single-pole tent – a modern Dutch design in cotton with fully enclosed cooking/storage area under flysheet; the whole of the front of the flysheet can be opened (Zwarts Egel).

Three-season sleeping-bags (packed) – the bags are filled with, from left to right: Hollofil; Hollofil with radiant barrier; ICI Superloft; down. Weights of the synthetic bags range from 3½ lb to 4¾ lb, while the down-filled bag weighs under 2¾ lb. The metre rule gives an indication of the packed sizes.

Three-season sleeping-bags – the same four bags unpacked and ready for use. (From left to right: Field & Trek Trango, Mountain Equipment Fitzroy, Mountain Equipment Firebird, Mountain Equipment Annapurna).

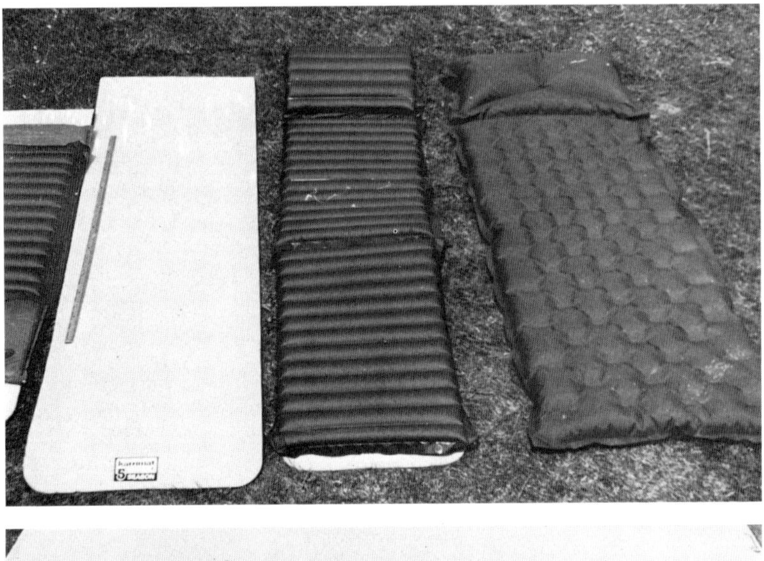

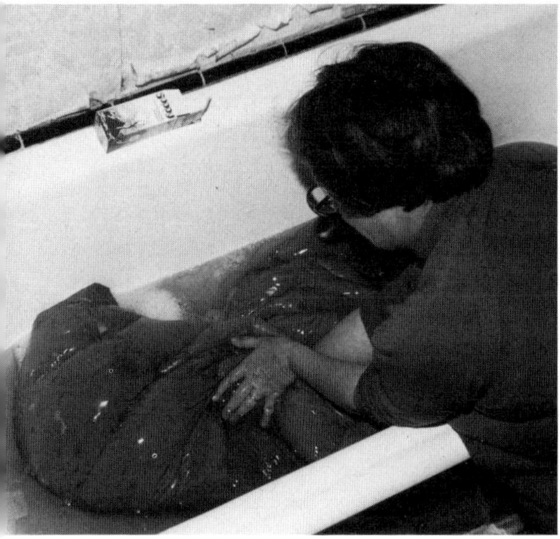

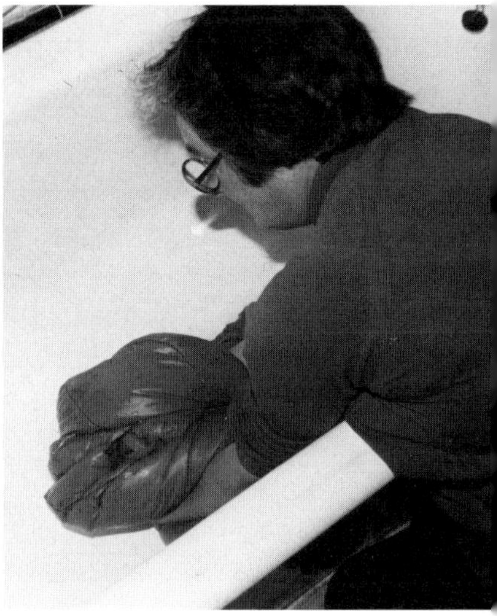

Washing a down-filled sleeping-bag:
(a) Gently press the water out with the bag lying in the bath.
(b) After allowing as much water to drain out as possible, lift carefully whilst supporting the weight in your arms.

Top left
Two bags into one – two single down-filled bags with full-length zips on opposite sides may be joined together to form a double bag (Field & Trek Winterdown).

Left
Insulating mats and airbeds.
(a) from left to right: long laminated closed-cell foam mat (Karrimor 5-season Karrimat); three lightweight airbed units linked to form a mattress with pillow (Tatteljee Button Beds). Full-size lightweight airbed (Semperit Lufthaven).
(b) single airbed unit (Tatteljee Button Beds) and self-inflating foam-filled mattress (Thermarest) lying on top of short closed-cell foam mat (Karrimor 4-season Karrimat).

Liquid-fuelled pressure stoves – left to right: petrol stove with pump and rapid ignition system (Coleman Peak 1); compact lightweight petrol stove (Optimus Climber 123); small petrol stove in box with hinged lid (Optimus Hunter 8R); lightweight collapsible paraffin stove (Optimus Mini Camper 96); collapsible paraffin stove with roarer burner (Optimus Camper 00).

Lightweight gas stoves – left to right: compact lightweight burner with hose connection to resealable cartridge (Ergoflame 7000); lightweight liquid feed burner unit for cold weather use (Ergoflame 8100); compact burner unit for use with small pierced cartridge (Camping Gaz Globetrotter); collapsible burner for use with pierced cartridges, with folding base for stability (Camping Gaz S206); small screw on burner for use with resealable cartridges – note the circular base and butane/propane mix cartridge (Epigas Mini Pakker).

Multi-fuel pressure stoves – left: this lightweight collapsible stove unit will burn a variety of fuels under adverse conditions (Mountain Safety Research X-GK); right: self-contained triple fuel stove with silent burner (Optimus 199 Multifuel).

Stoves with integral stands and windshields – left to right: methylated spirit stove set with lever for adjusting air inlet (Optimus Trapper 81); stove with refillable gas cartridge and piezo igniter (Primus Pro-Adventure); methylated spirit stove set with kettle (Trangia 27K). All the above sets come complete with cooking-pans, lids and pan grips.

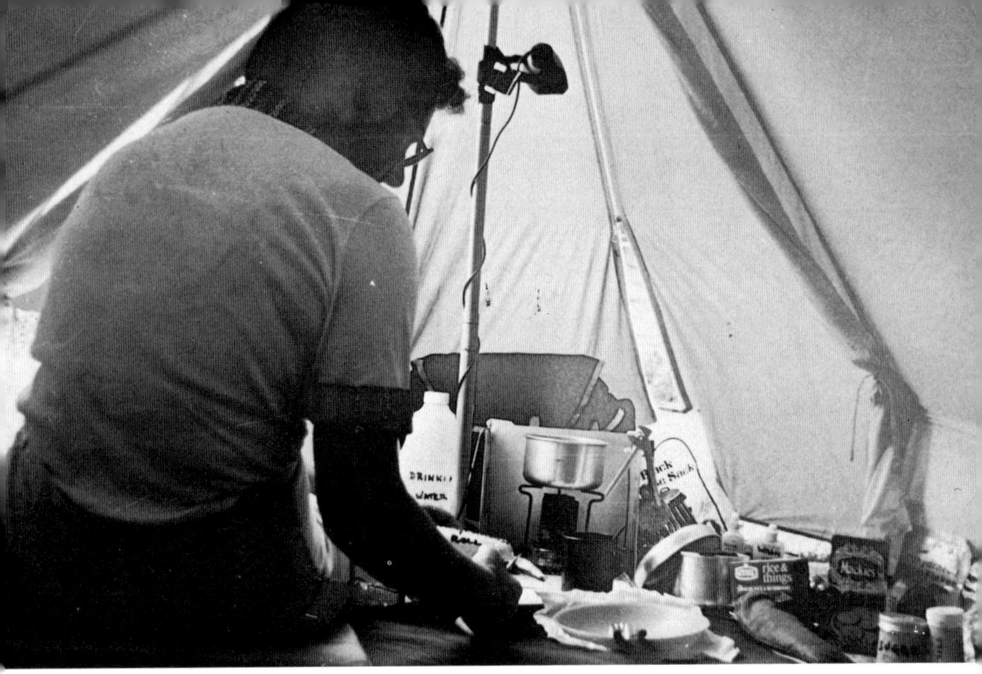

The lightweight kitchen – everything is positioned close to hand in the shelter of the front porch. The paraffin pressure stove is placed clear of the inner tent groundsheet and protected by a folding aluminium windshield, near the opened flysheet door.
Note the food-containers, rubbish bag, water-bottle and pan-grip hanging on the windshield. A battery headlamp hangs on the tent pole, and the doors of the inner tent are tied back safely.

The lightweight larder – a selection of packaged foods and drinks, all of which will keep without refrigeration until opened. Many of the items shown can be found in ordinary supermarkets.

it contains additives including lead compounds which make it unsuitable for use in stoves. Ideally, special additive-free petrol should be used, but this is not easily obtainable, especially in small quantities. In this country, 2-star petrol is often used instead, although the additives do tend to clog small burners rather more quickly than lead-free petrol. A convenient alternative is the so-called 'Coleman Fuel' sold in camp shops, which is lead-free petrol specially formulated for use in camping stoves, and comes in screw-topped metal cans of a convenient size.

Petrol is burned in stoves in the form of vapour under pressure and, when operating correctly, should burn with a clear, hot flame. The presence of additives may cause a more smoky flame, but the cold-weather performance is good. Some people object to the smell of petrol, but if spilled it will evaporate quite quickly, leaving very little smell or deposit.

If purchasing petrol other than the special Coleman Fuel, there may be difficulty in obtaining small quantities, and usually a metal can must be produced. The fuel should be carried in a metal can with screw top, although there are now special plastic containers designed for carrying petrol. These are the *only* plastic receptacles which should be used. Petrol being very volatile, great care must be taken when handling or storing it and when opening containers which have been in the sun, because of the possible pressure build-up. If travelling with a motor vehicle, it is often possible to obtain small quantities from the fuel tank for use in a stove. However, note that a car will usually be using a higher grade of petrol than two-star, with consequent increased risk of burner trouble. Also, the fuel used in two-stroke engines such as those used on mopeds is mixed with oil, so is *not* suitable for stoves.

Gas

The gas used in camping stoves is known in general terms as 'LPG'. This means 'liquid petroleum gas' and does *not* mean 'low-pressure gas' as we have seen in print elsewhere. Simply, it is highly flammable gas compressed into a liquid so that it occupies less volume and is convenient for storage and use. If the inlet to the container is opened, the liquid inside boils and produces gas. The amount of gas will be about 250 times the volume of the original liquid, and less than two per cent of the gas, mixed with air, will produce a flammable gas/air mixture. If a leak occurs in the container, or the inlet valve is opened with the container tilted, it is possible for a jet of liquid to be ejected. This will be very cold and may even remain as liquid for a while.

The LP gas used for stoves can be either butane or propane. Butane is the more usual but it will not vaporize below about 0°C (32°F) at sea level. In practice this means that it may prove difficult to operate at temperatures below about 5°C. Propane, on the other hand, will vaporize down to about −44°C (−47°F). It liquefies at a higher pressure, so requires stronger containers than butane. Under normal conditions both gases burn effectively in suitable burners, but as the gas is used up in the container, the pressure drops and the flame becomes less efficient, although this effect is not significant with propane. Gas is clean and simple to use, and recently the problem of operation at low temperatures has been largely dealt with by the introduction of containers filled with a mixture of propane and butane.

Single-burner lightweight stoves operate from one of two types of container, both of which are disposable, not refillable. One type is fitted into the stove and then pierced by a hollow spike integral with the burner head. The canister cannot then be removed from the burner until its contents have effectively been used up. The other type of disposable gas-container has a valve built into it, making it resealable. It can thus be attached or detached with gas still inside. Each type can be obtained in various sizes, and nominally the screw fitting on the resealable types is standardized so the cartridges from different makers can be used on different burners. The different types and makes are fairly widely available, but certain sizes and makes may not be always obtainable in some countries. Unusual sizes may be a problem. Storage and handling of the gas canisters should present little difficulty, but disposal of empty containers can be a problem, as there is always a residue of gas in a supposedly empty can.

Later in this chapter we will summarize the comparative costs of the various fuels we have mentioned, together with a list of names of fuels in different countries.

Stoves

Methylated spirit stoves

The most common type of stove using methylated spirit burns the fuel in liquid state in a small, simple burner which is not pressurized in any way. It fits into a combined windshield and pan support, giving a very stable assembly. The pan support is so designed that the cooking-pans which are supplied with the stove fit into the support, allowing the heat from the burner to surround the sides and base of the pan. In this way there is very little wasted heat. Air enters the windshield/support structure through holes near the base, and passes up on all sides of the burner. Control of the flame height is achieved by a combination of air control and flame control, the details differing in different makes of stove.

Diagram 17

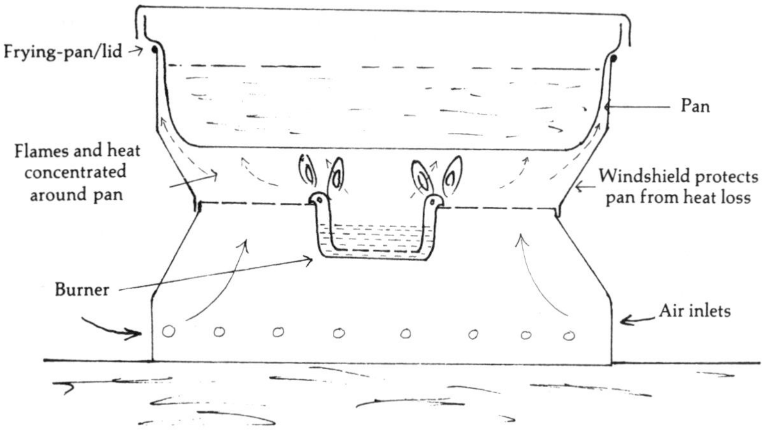

Methylated spirit stove and pan set

In one version, the air inlets are positioned on one side of the stand, the holes being turned to face into or away from the wind to vary the burning rate. In addition, a moveable flap can be used to cover or uncover the top of the burner. Another version of this type of methylated-spirit cooking-set employs a lever-operated shutter to control the flow of air passing through and around the burner. This type of stove has the merit of having very little to go wrong. The control of the burning speed is not too precise, the lever-operated shutter being rather better, in our experience, than the type requiring turning to or from the wind.

One problem with both types is that, when a pan is removed from the stove, flames from the burning fuel can appear above the surrounding windshield/pan support. To extinguish the burner requires a metal cap or other object to be placed directly over the burner, which can be rather tricky at times.

Care must be taken not to overfill, and if more fuel has been put in than is needed for the cooking operation in hand, the remainder is likely to be wasted. Practice and experience will enable the user to estimate the correct amount of fuel to use. Care must be taken to allow the burner to cool sufficiently before adding fresh fuel. Burning the fuel in its liquid form produces a fairly heavy coating of soot on the base of any cooking-pan, although this varies considerably depending on the additives in the fuel. The stoves of this type which are available are normally sold as complete sets, with burner, windshield, pan support, pans and lid, all packed together for carrying. It is also possible to obtain a small kettle to fit inside.

Liquid-fuelled pressure stoves

Paraffin stoves It is interesting to see that some of the most reliable paraffin-burning stoves follow a design which has been almost unchanged for well over half a century. The principle of operation is simple. Liquid paraffin is forced under pressure through a heated burner tube and emerges as vapour from a small jet or nipple. The vapour mixes with air and burns with a very hot blue flame which, because of the pressure, will withstand quite a lot of wind whilst still

Diagram 18

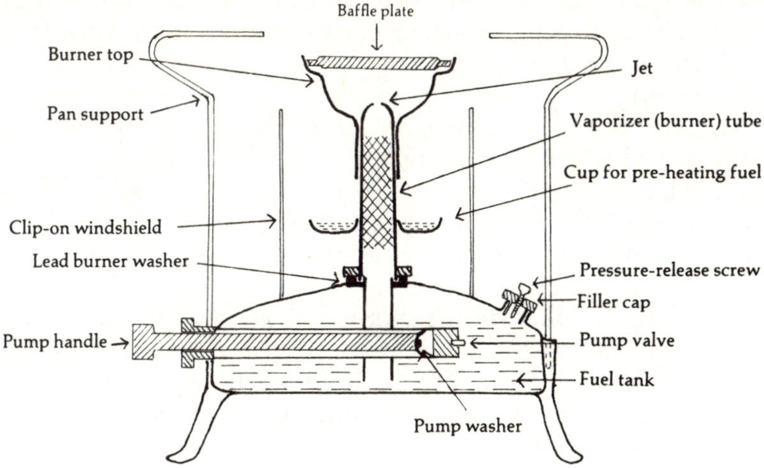

Paraffin pressure stove

remaining efficient. Cold weather has little effect on the efficiency once the flame has been established. Because the stove burns vapour/air mixture and not liquid fuel, the consumption of paraffin is low, so leading to a very economic device. With this basic design there is little to go wrong provided a few simple precautions are taken as regards care and maintenance. A slightly more complicated version employs the same system but with the addition of a regulating valve to adjust the flame and hence the heat output. Naturally this type is heavier and more expensive than the simple version. When used correctly and kept clean, paraffin stoves of this type can be free from objectionable smell and need not deposit soot.

One common feature of all the paraffin-burning pressure stoves is the need to pre-heat the burner to produce the vapour necessary for efficient operation. Until this is really hot, no pressure should be applied to force the liquid fuel through the jet, otherwise you will have a flaring smoky flame, and at the worst drops of burning fuel.

The secret of successful stove operation is to follow a simple drill. After making sure the fuel tank is full but not over-full, check that the air-release screw on the tank filler cap is open, so that no pressure build-up can occur. Put sufficient methylated spirit or paste or a broken-up solid fuel tablet into the pre-heating cup to heat the burner. Light the pre-heating fuel, watch it, and when it has nearly burned out, close the tank air release screw. Watch again and you will probably see a small yellow flame flicker above the jet. GENTLY give one or two strokes on the pump, and if all is well you will hear a hissing sound. As the last flames from the pre-heating fuel die away, this hiss will change to a gentle roar, and you are in business. Give perhaps half a dozen more strokes on the pump and place your pan on the pan supports. As the stove heats up, pressure will build up in the tank, maintaining the flow of paraffin to the burner, so you will probably not have to pump again. The steady roar is the sign that all is going as it should, with a hot blue flame which soon makes the burner top plate glow red.

If this steady roar falters or does not materialize, quick action is required. When lighting up, the most likely trouble will take the form of a sudden flare of yellow sooty flame. The immediate action must be to slacken the air-release screw, thus dropping the pressure in the tank. Without pressure there can be no flow of fuel to the burner, and with no fuel the flame will die down. The next action must be to think – what is the cause of the trouble? The most likely cause of a flare-up when lighting is that the burner was not hot enough when the fuel was allowed to flow. The flaring was caused by liquid paraffin, not vapour, issuing from the jet. The remedy then must be to allow the stove to cool down, add more pre-heating fuel and start all over again. Remember to make sure the air-release screw is well open, and do not add pre-heating fuel to a hot burner.

If trouble still occurs, or the flare-up happens after the stove has been running correctly for a while, the usual cause is either fuel running low in the tank or a blocked jet. Turn the stove off by releasing the air screw, *allow to cool* and check the tank. If empty, fill it about two-thirds full and start the whole sequence again. If fuel shortage is obviously not the trouble, the small hole in the jet could be blocked by soot if the stove has been running on reduced pressure, for example when simmering. Otherwise it is probably due to dirt in the fuel. Whatever the cause, clear the hole by carefully inserting the end of a cleaning needle of the correct size for the stove you are using. Just once into the hole, straight in and straight out again, should be sufficient. Be careful not to enlarge the hole size, or you will always have trouble with flaring and uneven burning. It is possible, with a certain amount of luck and practice, to clear a jet whilst the stove is still burning; the flame may re-ignite immediately you remove the needle, but have a lighted match ready just in case. The usual difficulty with a stove on the ground is to see what you are doing, so it may be better to release the pressure first, then restart. The best cure for blocked jets is prevention. Always filter your fuel through a filter funnel, and every time you put your stove away after a trip, empty the tank. Occasionally swill it out with clean fuel before re-filling with filtered paraffin.

Reference has been made to a similar type of paraffin pressure stove in which the flow of fuel is controlled by means of a regulating valve. The main points in operating these stoves are the same as for the simpler versions. We prefer to light the pre-heating fuel with the tank filler cap open slightly to ensure there is no pressure build-up. There is no separate air-release screw on these. When the burner is hot, before the pre-heat flame dies away, close the cap, open the valve and gently pump as before. Once the flame is established and pressure has been increased with the pump, the height of flame can be regulated with the valve. This valve incorporates a jet-cleaning needle, which operates when the valve is turned fully anti-clockwise, beyond the fully open position. The needle must never be used to extinguish the stove but merely be turned momentarily to clear the jet, then returned to its former position depending on the height of flame required. The stove is extinguished by turning the valve to the off position (fully clockwise) which cuts off the flow of fuel. Pressure in the tank should be released after use by gently opening the fuel filler cap.

With all these paraffin pressure stoves it is an advantage to use a clip-on windshield around the burner. This helps the pre-heating process and shields the flame from side winds. A final operating tip is that, if you should have forgotten your pre-heating fuel, it is possible to use a little of the paraffin from the tank. This is made easier to light if you place a small piece of tissue paper (toilet paper will do) in the cup and let the paraffin soak into it.

Petrol stoves A group of petrol-burning stoves on the market follow very much the same principle as the above-described paraffin stoves, and most of the remarks apply equally to the petrol variety. The operation is the same, in that the liquid petrol from the fuel tank is burned after being vaporized by passing through a heated jet and being mixed with air. The main difference arises from the fact that petrol is more volatile than paraffin, which means that it vaporizes much more easily and is easier to ignite. All petrol stoves have a control valve, although in this type of stove there is usually no pump, the petrol being forced from the tank to the control valve by pressure caused by the pre-heating of the burner.

Pre-heating can be carried out by allowing a small quantity of petrol to run out of the jet into the pre-heating cup, but this produces a smoky flame with fumes. It is preferable to use methylated spirit or paste or solid fuel, as in the case of the paraffin stoves. One very important difference in procedure is that the fuel tank cap *must* be closed securely during this operation, because otherwise petrol vapour can issue from it and become ignited. During the pre-heating, the valve should be closed, then just before the pre-heating flame dies down, the valve should be gradually opened, causing the fuel to ignite at the jet. After lighting, the flame is likely to take several minutes to reach full strength, as the tank pressure is built up by heat from the burner. This will be accelerated when a pan is placed over the burner.

After a period of running, the tank will become quite warm, and the heat output from the stove will build up. In some versions there is a heat shield between the tank and burner to keep this under control. The flame height is controlled by means of the regulating valve, which also includes a cleaning needle as in the paraffin versions with a valve.

Two important points need noting. In these petrol stoves, there is a pressure-relief valve built into the filler cap. This cannot be operated by the user but is a safety valve in case of excessive pressure build-up in the tank. If the tank does overheat or has been overfilled, and this valve operates, petrol vapour will be forced out from the valve. This vapour can ignite if it is directed near the burner while the latter is either operating or still hot, so position your stove in such a way that any released vapour will be directed out away from the inside of the tent and has free passage away from the stove. The second point to note is that, after extinguishing the stove with the valve, you should allow it to cool down well before opening the filler cap to release tank pressure. For operation in cold weather, it is possible to buy a pump unit to fit into the tank of one of the small petrol stoves. This can be used to force petrol out for pre-heating, also to increase the tank pressure to obtain a hotter flame.

A different type of petrol stove for lightweight campers is rather more complicated, although very efficient. It is fitted with a pump, a regulating valve and a special arrangement for aiding rapid ignition. To operate, the tank is closed and pressurized by means of the built-in pump. A valve is opened to allow fuel to enter the burner, which is then lit. After a short period the starting valve is shifted to the running position, when the flame should be established and burning with a blue colour. In very cold conditions the burner may be pre-heated with burning paste. The height of flame is regulated with a valve, again with a built-in cleaning needle. Different makes of stove may have slightly different operating procedures, so the maker's instructions must be studied. After shutting down with the valve, the lighter valve must also be set to 'off' and the stove allowed to cool down before releasing the tank pressure.

Operating problems We have dealt with some of the troubles which may occur with pressure stoves, both paraffin and petrol, as a result of blocked or dirty jets. Another general type of fault concerns lack of pressure in the fuel tank. If a pump is fitted and it is obviously working but pressure falls, causing the flame to die away, there must be a leak. Check that the filler cap is screwed down tightly, and in the case of paraffin stoves, check that the air-release screw is fully home. A very small particle of grit in this screw seating could be the cause of the trouble. If still no cure, check that the burner is screwed tightly into the tank top. The next suspect point might be the lead packing onto which the burner seats when screwed onto the tank. After long use this can become compressed. Make sure all traces of the old washer are removed, if necessary making use of a small screwdriver or similar probe to dig out all particles of the soft metal from the threaded socket in the tank. Be careful not to damage the screw thread, and do not let particles of lead drop into the tank interior. Position the new washer carefully and screw down the burner onto it evenly and firmly.

Depending on the model you have, a leak may occur at the joint between the burner and the tube which fits into the tank, at the point where the cup for the pre-heating fuel is fitted. Two spanners are needed to unscrew the burner from the tube, and a new packing washer should be placed in position, having removed all traces of the old one. Screw together again firmly and evenly but do not over-tighten. This joint should not normally be unscrewed when packing the stove.

Another possible place where leakage of air can occur is in the pump assembly itself. If you pump pressure up, then watch the pump handle, you may see it slowly move back out from the closed position. This is the clue that the valve at the bottom of the pump tube is leaking, so allowing air to come back out of the tank, forcing the plunger out as it does so. This valve is a very small assembly, and to remove it requires a special long key. You will probably not have such an article with you, but an emergency cure can be tried. The trouble may only be a particle of grit in the valve seating. Empty the tank of fuel, pour a small quantity down the pump tube and replace the plunger. With the tank filler cap off, pump hard several times. This may clear the trouble.

These methods have been used to deal with loss of pressure from the tank, but supposing you cannot obtain any pressure? The first suspect must be the pump washer, provided you have checked that all filler and air-release screws are tight. If the pump plunger slides in very easily without encountering any resistance, the chances are that the pump washer is at fault. Remove the plunger and examine the washer and its attachment. The washer is usually a cup-shaped leather piece held onto the end of the plunger by a metal washer and nut, often with a small spring. It is possible that the screw has become loose, and your washer may even be left behind in the tube with the nut and metal washer. Hook or shake them out, and refix the leather to the pump plunger if necessary, then make sure the leather is not dry and hard. A slight smear of grease – butter will do in emergency – or even a soaking in paraffin, followed by a gentle working between the fingers, should restore the washer to its required condition. Ease it carefully back into the pump tube, making sure the leather is not folded back on itself, and you should find it works quite well.

Just one other pump problem which may occur, and which can be a little puzzling, is when you find you cannot force the pump in at all, or only a little way, after which it springs out again. This is due to the little pump valve being stuck in the closed position. Not a very common occurrence, but one we have seen on a brand-new stove. The emergency treatment for this, if you have no valve remover, is, again, to empty the tank of fuel, pour a little down the pump tube and, with the filler cap open, force the plunger down hard several times. With luck it will suddenly free itself as the pressure forces the fuel through, and after a few quick strokes to make sure all is well, you can refill and carry on cooking.

General features To summarize the situation with regard to liquid-fuelled pressure stoves, we can say that the paraffin-stove types which do not have regulating valves are, as far as lightweight stoves are concerned, all of a type which can be dismantled for carrying. The fuel tank can be carried with fuel inside, the aperture into which the burner is screwed for operation being closed by a screw plug. Assembly of the stove requires removal of this plug, and the burner is then screwed into position with the aid of a spanner provided with the stove. Pan supports, burner top plates, windshield and pre-heating fuel cup are all to be assembled for use, although the whole process need take only a minute or two. Care is required in positioning these stoves as they may be unstable on uneven ground. Some of the paraffin and all the petrol stoves under consideration have regulating burners, and with the exception of certain very small stoves, all are contained in metal boxes with hinged lids. Little or no pre-assembly is called for, and this type is normally quite stable in operation. A certain amount of control can be exercised over the flame with the non-regulating burners by releasing some of the air pressure in the tank. This is done by opening momentarily the air-release screw, then tightening it again. Burning for a while on reduced pressure can soot up the jet, which may necessitate using the pricking needle to restore correct operation.

The paraffin and petrol pressure stoves are very efficient even in cold and windy weather, especially when used with a windshield. In general we have found paraffin stoves rather more efficient and less trouble than petrol stoves.

Gas stoves

The smaller, lightweight gas stoves almost exclusively use disposable containers of gas. It should be noted, however, that in a number of cases adaptors are available to run the stoves off heavier, refillable gas-containers.

It has already been explained that disposable gas-containers are of two types, each of which is available in different sizes, and the dimensions and screw fitting with the resealable valve are standardized in most countries.

The gas stoves themselves are available in two basic forms. One comprises a burner unit which fits directly onto the gas cartridge, whichever type is used, and the other is fed with gas through a short length of hose, which has a suitable fitting for the type of cartridge in use.

In general the type of cartridge and fitting has little affect on the efficiency of these stoves. The main factor apart from the gas used is the design of the burner.

We shall be going into safety precautions in some detail later, but at this stage it cannot be emphasized too much that no changing of gas cartridges should be carried out in or near

Diagram 19

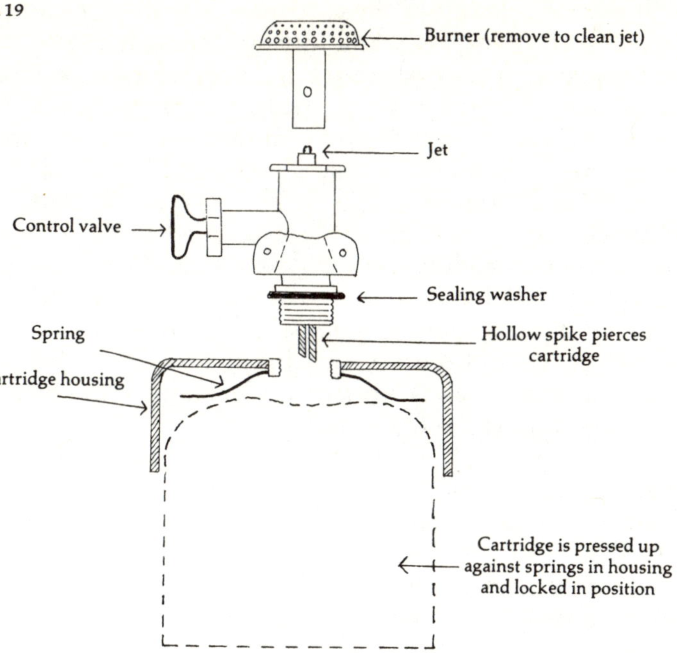

Gas stove with pierceable cartridge
(Details of cartridge housing are not shown)

the tent or near any other stove or light, and no empty or apparently empty gas cartridges should be left lying near the tent or other stove or light.

The basic type of stove using the gas cartridge which is pierced by a hollow spike has a simple burner with control valve, together with some arrangement for holding the cartridge in position. Details vary with different makes, but the principle is the same. The procedure for all makes is very similar.

First, the burner unit is checked to see that the spike is not damaged and that it is retracted away from the cartridge holder. Check that all sealing washers are in position and in good condition. Turn the control valve off. Next, the new gas cartridge is placed in position in its holder and locked against the spring pressure. In this state, the hollow spike is still clear of the top of the cartridge. The next thing to do is, holding the cartridge and fittings upright, to screw the burner steadily down. As the burner is rotated further, the spike will penetrate the cartridge, indicated by a hissing escape of gas. It is very important that you do not stop at this stage, but continue to screw down steadily until the seal is completed around the spike. The gas escape should now have ceased completely. If you carried out the operation quickly and steadily, very little gas will have been wasted, but you should be prepared for a sudden chilling effect from the rapidly expanding gas, which may come onto your hands. It will not harm you. Check carefully by listening or smelling that there is no further leakage before setting the stove up in position for cooking.

One feature of most of the stoves using this type of cartridge is that they tend to be high in relation to their base. This makes for instability when a cooking-pan is placed on top. Most stoves are supplied with some form of clip-on base, or one can be purchased as an extra. We would say that such a base should always be used. An additional safeguard is to peg this base down to the ground. A very few manufacturers provide holes in the bases for pegs, but most do not. It is a simple task to pierce three or four holes into which small pegs can be inserted. We also recommend that some form of windshield is always used with gas stoves because the flames are not as fierce as those with liquid-fuel pressure stoves and can easily be affected by wind.

When your cooking-pan is ready, light the stove – the flame can be regulated by means of the valve. If your stove has been moved or shaken in any way, wait a minute or so before lighting, or you may experience a flare-up. If this happens, close the valve to the off position immediately, wait, then try again. Be careful when lighting with a new cartridge for the first time, as there may be a sudden rush of gas. This will soon drop to a steady flow. Very cold weather, near freezing, may also give you problems with flaring, also with unstable or low flame. Try warming the cartridge in your hands first.

The procedure for using the resealable type of cartridge is very similar. The burner fitting will have a control valve, which of course must be turned off before going any further. The base of the burner will have a threaded socket which screws onto the threaded boss on top of the gas cartridge. Within the burner socket there is a fixed metal pin. This enters the hole in the top of the cartridge boss and forces down a spring plunger inside, so operating the gas valve in the cartridge. As before, it is important to check that all sealing washers are correct and that neither the burner attachment thread and pin nor the thread on the cartridge are damaged or dirty. Then, holding the cartridge upright, screw the burner steadily down. Again, as the pin operates the valve, there will be a brief escape of gas, which should cease as soon as the burner is fully screwed home. Some burners are supported entirely on the threaded boss on the cartridge, but others have a screw ring which can be run down outside the burner socket until it bears on the top rim of the cartridge. This is a much safer arrangement. Again the same comments apply as regards stability and the use of a stabilizing base and windshield. Operation of this type of stove is also exactly the same as for the type using pierced cartridges.

The major advantage of the resealable cartridge as compared with the pierced type is that the resealable type can be removed from the stove unit for convenient packing

Diagram 20

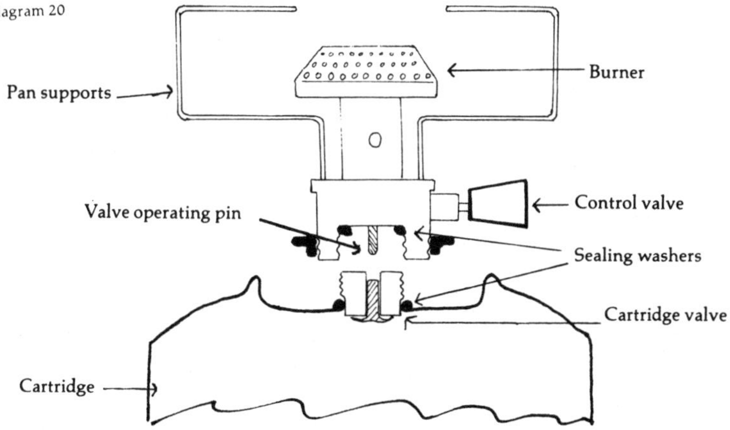

Gas stove with resealable cartridge

before all the gas has been used.

Cartridges filled with a mixture of propane and butane gas are at present confined to resealable versions because of the need for a stronger container to resist the higher gas pressure. They can be interchanged with any butane resealable cartridge of similar size, so giving greatly improved performance when cold.

Dealing now with stoves which obtain their gas supply through a short length of hose, the only type of which we are aware that is currently available is a very small, lightweight burner unit to which is attached a short hose terminating in a control valve. The valve also includes a fitting which can screw onto one of the standard resealable cartridges. Adaptor units are available to accommodate a pierceable cartridge and screw fitting, but we do not normally recommend these. With a hose-fed burner, it is very important to keep the hose away from the hot burner. Always check the hose for damage before use, and check also that all sealing washers are intact.

Two points to watch with this type of stove are, first, to make sure the burner unit is firmly settled on the ground, if necessary pegging it down. Second, make sure the gas cartridge is upright and that it, too, is firmly based. It can be held steady by pushing three pegs into the ground, forming a sort of cradle, but do make certain it is not too near the hot burner. Particularly in cold weather, gas can collect in the hose, perhaps in liquid form, and this may cause flaring when you light up. After use, when disconnecting the hose, you may well find traces of gas in it, so be prepared.

Before leaving the subject of gas stoves, we must mention one way which has been devised to overcome the poor performance of butane stoves in cold-temperature conditions. This is the so-called 'liquid-feed' model, in which a pre-heating tube is incorporated in the burner. The resealable cartridge (the only type possible with this stove) lies on its side in normal operation, with the burner unit beside it, rigidly screwed onto the fitting. To light, the whole stove with cartridge is stood on end and lit. The small amount of residual gas at the top of the cartridge burns, heating the tube. After a few moments the stove is placed back on the ground and continues to burn, the liquid gas in the container being vaporized as it passes through the heated tube into the burner. Be prepared for flaring on lighting up, and note that gas consumption is rather higher than with the normal burners.

To sum up the situation as regards gas stoves for lightweight camping, it can be said that they are generally easy to use, and clean. Efficiency drops with wind and low temperatures, but this latter problem can be overcome to a large degree by using propane/butane mix, which we feel is a far better answer than to use the liquid-feed butane burner. Heat output will also drop as the gas in the cartridge becomes used up and the pressure gets less. Windshields should always be used. Finally we would have no hesitation in expressing our preference for resealable gas containers rather than the piercing type.

Multi-fuel stoves

The idea of a stove which can operate on whatever fuel you have available has obvious attractions, especially for those who travel around here and abroad. Not only would it help if you ran out of one fuel, it would be very useful if you planned a trip to a country where your normal fuel was unobtainable or scarce. One universal stove sounds ideal. If such a stove is also capable of producing a high heat output over long periods using very cheap fuel, the ideal begins to sound just a little impossible.

We know of two stoves which may not be ideal but which do accommodate more than one fuel, albeit they are liquid fuels. The first stove looks very much like a normal paraffin pressure stove with regulating valve, assembled into a metal box with hinged lid. This type has been in existence for a very long time, was very efficient and also existed in a version intended to burn petrol. The manufacturers have now introduced a modified burner to enable the stove to run on either paraffin or petrol, and with a small adaptor, it will operate on methylated spirit. This versatility is achieved at some reduction in efficiency, but the idea seems promising. This particular stove is rather large and heavy for backpacking or cycle use but is worth considering for motor-cycle, canoe or car campers.

The second multi-fuel stove was developed for use by climbers and others who may want to obtain adequate supplies of water by melting snow without the need to carry large quantities of expensive fuel or large, heavy stoves. The system comprises a burner unit which is connected through a rigid metal pipe to a pump and control valve which screws into a metal fuel-container. The latter is not supplied as part of the stove but is a metal fuel bottle in which the chosen fuel is normally carried. It is important that you use only the make of bottle specified in the stove instructions, as it is subjected to quite high pressure in use. A lightweight windshield and heat-reflector enables the stove to function in adverse conditions, and it is claimed to operate on a variety of fuels, including paraffin, petrol (both leaded and unleaded), diesel oil, cleaning fluid and white spirit, but NOT methylated spirit. The stove takes some getting used to but certainly seems very efficient, especially in capable hands. We feel it is rather difficult to maintain and too vulnerable to damage but can prove very useful in the conditions for which it was designed. Essential spares should be carried if travelling away from 'civilization'.

Comparison of Performance, Fuel Consumption and Cost of Typical Stoves and Fuels

Figures have been given for representative stoves in each category, based on tests carried out in the open air, with a light breeze and air temperature of 31°F (–1°C). In each case, half a litre of water was brought to the boil in a covered pan. The stoves were in a sheltered position, but without additional windshields. The estimated fuel consumption and comparative costs were calculated on the basis of two days' cooking.

	Time in minutes	*Fuel used in ml or gms*	*Estimated fuel for two days*		*Cost compared to paraffin*
			Volume ml	*Weight: gm/oz*	
Pressure Stove					
Paraffin	5	16 ml	250	195/7	1
Petrol	$7\frac{1}{2}$	12 ml	180	$133/4\frac{3}{4}$	1
Coleman Fuel	$7\frac{1}{2}$	12 ml	180	$133/4\frac{3}{4}$	4

Methylated Spirit Stove	10	30 ml	450	360/12¾	8
Gas Stove					
Butane	16	16 gm		240/8½	13
Propane/Butane	6	7½ gm		110/4	7½

NOTE 1 Relative consumption and cost will vary widely with varying conditions of temperature and wind, also with height above sea level.

NOTE 2 Results are for average use with typical stoves. Different makes and models will show different times and fuel consumption.

NOTE 3 Times were recorded from immediately after lighting the stoves. Heat output will vary with warm-up, and with reduced gas pressure.

Hints and tips on stove usage

Know your stove. Learn how it works and practise at home before going out.

Carry a few essential spares such as washers, also cleaning needles for the jet and a spanner if needed.

If your stove is supplied in a metal or other box, think if you really need it. Try packing the full fuel tank in double plastic bags, and all the other bits and pieces including pre-heating fuel inside other plastic bags.

Matches should be packed in small tins. Carry at least two boxes, and as emergency ignition carry a small disposable gas lighter.

Windshields are essential. The folding sort made of thin aluminium sheets hinged together weighs next to nothing. Make a couple of thin wire spikes to push into the ground and hook over the top of the windshield to prevent it blowing over. Such windshields are easily made and are better than the sort made from canvas with wire supports. If you do use the latter type, don't believe that they can be made effectively fire-proof. Better take care with your stove.

When you are setting up a paraffin pressure stove, release the air screw first before unscrewing the tank plug, or you will find paraffin all over the place. When you unscrew the plug, do not put it down. It 'parks' either on the end of the pump handle or on a threaded bush provided for the purpose on the tank. This keeps it clean and stops it from getting lost.

Cut away any long grass or weeds around the stove. It is a good idea to stand the stove on a mat made of two or three thicknesses of cooking-foil. This will protect the grass and also keep the stove clean. Do not stand it on a flat board, as it will slide about.

Some methylated-spirit stoves are rather difficult to fill from a fuel bottle. Use a small container such as an empty 35-millimetre film can as a measure and filler. Learn how much fuel is needed for various jobs and mark your measure.

Spirit for pre-heating stoves can be carried in small plastic screw-top bottles with nozzles, such as those used for contact lens fluid or other substances. A very small quantity will last several days and is more convenient than carrying a large metal can.

Liquid fuel can be carried in a variety of containers, but make sure they have secure screw caps. Always mark fuel bottles clearly with their contents. Wrap them in multiple plastic bags when carrying, unless you carry them in bottle cages on a cycle. Some of the metal bottles made specially for fuel can be fitted with pourer spouts or screw caps to reduce spillage. You may carry a small plastic or metal funnel. Always store fuel bottles outside the tent.

Always use clean fuel. If you cannot filter the fuel into your bottle before starting, carry a funnel with a filter inside. It is worth the little effort.

When pre-heating a stove, do not place a cold pan on top until the pre-heating fuel is finished and the burner commences to roar. Otherwise you will find that the paraffin or petrol vapour coming from the jet will condense again, causing fumes.

Allow plenty of ventilation when using a stove. Paraffin and petrol can both produce unpleasant fumes when the stove is turned off, or if for any reason the flame goes out. Remember, heat goes up. If you have to move the stove, take hold of it by the base, with your hand held low down. When using gas in resealable cartridges, normally use butane but carry one small propane/butane mixture cartridge for use in the morning or if very cold. It can be taken off when using the stove during the day and be replaced by the butane cartridge, which is cheaper.

Safety with stoves

Treat your stove with respect, but do not be afraid of it. No stove caused a fire until someone lit it.

Study the manufacturer's instructions carefully.

Position your stove well clear of the side or roof of your tent if cooking under cover. Never cook inside the inner tent. Position the stove where it will not get knocked over by people entering or leaving the tent.

Never leave a stove running when you are asleep.

Keep your head well back when handling a stove, and keep long hair away.

When using liquid fuel stoves:

Use correct fuel.

Do not overfill.

Always close the fuel-container and remove it from near the stove after use.

Never fill the stove near another flame or when smoking.

Never fill a stove when it is running or still hot.

Wipe up all spilled fuel from the stove and ground.

Do not use too much pre-heating fuel, and close and remove the container before lighting the stove.

Mark fuel-containers clearly and never store near the stove.

Never leave a stove with pressure still in the tank when not in use.

If a flare occurs, release pressure immediately. If flare continues, hold stove by its base and lift outside. Do not throw, as burning fuel may spill.

When using gas stoves:

Use the correct type and size of cartridge.

Store unused cartridges well away from the stove.

Never fit or change a cartridge near another flame or when smoking, and always change cartridges outside the tent.

Never unscrew a pierceable cartridge when still containing gas, and never unscrew any cartridge when the stove is burning or hot.

Always unscrew the burner head to retract the hollow spike before inserting a new pierceable cartridge.

Always check all sealing washers before fitting a new cartridge.

Always check the hose, if there is one, for damage.

Do not lubricate control valves unless you have the correct lubricant.

Keep cartridges upright (unless liquid-feed type) and do not shake.

Check for leaks with soapy water, never a flame.

If a flare occurs, turn off the valve immediately. If still in trouble, hold the stove by its base and place outside, well clear of the tent.

Do not keep the stove inside the inner tent at night when you are asleep.

Store used cartridges well away from the tent and any flame until they can be disposed of safely. Remember there is always a trace of gas in them.

Fuels for camping stoves are known by different names in different countries. In some, paraffin is known as petroleum, and petrol is known as gas. It is therefore essential to know the local name for the fuel you are using, in order to avoid what could be serious accidents. This chart will assist those visiting Europe and the USA.

Camping Stove Fuels at Home and Abroad

GREAT BRITAIN	Paraffin	Petrol Unleaded petrol White petrol	Methylated spirit Meths
USA	Kerosene	Gasolene Gas White gas (Coleman Fuel)	Denatured alcohol
FRANCE	Pétrole Pétrole à brûler	Essence Essence filtrée blanche	Alcool dénaturé Alcool à brûler Alcool méthylique

GERMANY	Petroleum Paraffinöl	Benzin	Spiritus Brennspiritus
HOLLAND	Petroleum Lampen-olie	Benzine (normale) (Coleman Kampeer-benzine)	Spiritus Brand spiritus
SWEDEN	Fotogen Petroleum	Bensin Vit bensin	T-sprit Röd-sprit
ITALY	Olio di paraffina	Benzina	Alcool denaturato Spirito da bruciare
SPAIN	Parafina		Alcohol metilico

Pots and Pans

Now that we have dealt with the stove, we need the necessary pots and pans with which to cook.

First, let us say that with cooking-pans, as with most other things, cheap ones are a waste of money in the long run. If you buy pans of very thin metal, they will be light in weight but you will find that your food is continually getting burned. Cheap pans often have sharp angles and complicated clips and folding handles. These all make them more difficult to clean, and the handles are often not strong enough to hold a full pan safely. Avoid sets of nesting 'paint-pot' billies with wire-bail handles which can jam and get hot in use. Pans with attached handles, whether folding or not, are often said to be specially for campers and hikers. Avoid them! A frying-pan with a fixed or folding handle is dangerous. If it does not overbalance and fall off the stove, it will surely get knocked off, and at best you will have lost your food. At worst you may land up with bad burns or scalds and maybe a blazing tent. In addition to all that, the folding handle on a frying-pan has a habit of scratching and damaging the inner surface when packed for carrying.

Our preference is for good-quality aluminium pans of a reasonable thickness, well made with rounded, turned-over rims and rounded corners between the sides and bottom to make for easy cleaning. No clips or sockets for handles, as these make cleaning difficult. We use separate pan grip handles which clamp onto the rim of the pan but do not remain in position when the pan is in use.

Our pans are made from spun aluminium, and range in

size from 0.7 litres up to 1.7 litres, all perfectly plain and which nest one inside the other. The complete set comprises four pans, but they can be bought separately. Frypan/lids can also be obtained to fit, also available separately. The complete set weighs about 22 ounces. For frying we do not use the lids, but use a very good-quality non-stick pan, again perfectly plain with no handle attached. Do not confine yourself to just the smallest pan or pans, but have one slightly larger than you think you need. It will help to make the cook's life easier, and if you have a set, you can always leave the larger ones at home if you really want to go light.

An additional luxury you may fancy is one of the small kettles of the type supplied with some of the methylated spirit stove and pan sets. These kettles are very neat and can be bought separately. The smallest size will pack inside some of your pans.

Make a simple bag with a draw-string to contain the whole set. You should never have to carry dirty, sooty pans, but if you do – it helps.

The lightweight kitchen

With the tent pitched, the kitchen can be established. We normally arrange the stove, surrounded by its windshield, to one side of the entrance, just inside the flysheet porch. This leaves room for people to get in and out of the inner tent. The cook sits on one side of the tent door. Position the stove so that any controls such as regulating knobs, air-release screws or pump handles are readily to hand. Cooking on just one stove is not a magical art, although at times it may look like a juggling act. It really just requires a little thought, especially to determine the sequence in which you carry out certain operations.

First of all, let us say that the lightweight camper has no need whatsoever to rely only on frying as a means of cooking. Frying does have its place, and, by using a good non-stick pan such as we have described, it is surprising how little fat is really needed. The one thing to be careful about is spitting fat. Keep clear of the tent and flysheet, and beware any rain or condensation dripping into the pan. This is where an aluminium plate is useful as it can be laid over the top. Your main problems are how to get everything ready at the same time, working on just one burner, and how to make the most economical use of your fuel if you have to carry it all.

We suggest that the golden rules for the lightweight camp cook are: first, never light the stove until you have a pan ready to put on it; second, never have the stove running with nothing on it; third, avoid as much as possible having to put out and relight the stove during a series of cooking operations (not quite so important if you are using gas); and last but not least, always wash up all pans and utensils as soon as you have eaten. Then you can sit back and relax.

Last thing at night, before retreating into your shelter, make sure you have filled the water-bottle or container, and fill a pan for the morning brew. That is much easier than trying to get ice out of the water-bottle! At the same time, check your stove, and if necessary refill it with fuel. Then place everything safely ready for use.

The lightweight cook

Here are a few ways in which you can organize this all-important cooking task so that you may make the best use of the minimum but adequate facilities at your disposal.

Look carefully at the packets of convenience dehydrated meals before buying. Some require one pan and, perhaps, twenty minutes' cooking. Others require two or three pans, with various components of the meal taking fifteen or twenty minutes each – not very helpful if you have only one stove. Think about the size of pan required. Some convenience meals now available are packaged in foil sachets and require heating in boiling water for five minutes or more. They come in one- or two-serving sizes and, the double-size packs do require quite a large pan if you are to immerse the whole of the sachet in boiling water. One answer to this is to work the contents of the envelopes down to one end before standing them in your largest pan. The results seem just as good.

A little pre-planning can turn out a very good meal using either 'boil-in-the-bag' or non-refrigerated foil-packed meals. For example, a 'boil-in-bag' meat or fish dish can be placed in the boiling water and surrounded by freeze-dried peas from a packet, and perhaps tinned potatoes can be added just before everything is ready. Watch the times required and add items accordingly. The result can be a really first-class meal with little effort and as a bonus no dirty pans to wash up!

Talking of washing up, make a habit of refilling the pan as soon as you serve out the food. A small spot of washing-up liquid in the pan, and back on the stove – the washing up almost does itself as you eat. With some boil-in-the-bag dishes, you can use the same water the meal was boiled in for washing up, so saving on fuel. The possibilities are endless.

Of course, you will not want to eat convenience and dehydrated food all the time. They have their place and are easy to carry and store. Keep some for at least one meal in case you cannot get to shops. But be prepared to use fresh food when possible, but on one stove, how do we do it?

Start with the things which take longest to cook, such as potatoes and carrots. Cut up or slice these very small and start them going first. When they are nearly cooked, take the pan off and place it, with a lid tightly on, to one side. Maybe you can wrap the pan in a towel to keep it hot. Then cook the meat, which may be fried chops or something similar. When ready, cover the frying-pan and stand it on top of the vegetable pan to keep hot. Finally, peas or something which only takes a few minutes if of the packet variety. While you are serving the vegetables, the meat can be brought back to heat, then everything is hot and on the plate ready for you.

To keep something hot whilst cooking something else, it is possible to make use of the idea known as 'tower cooking'. In this, the first component of the meal is cooked, and the pan is then stood on top of the pan containing the next item to be dealt with. Either stand the top pan right on the underneath pan, so acting as a lid, or stand it in an up-turned lid on the lower pan. Of course you must take extra care that the tower does not overbalance, but this can be a very useful method.

A large pan with a well-fitting lid can be used for braising, in which meat and vegetables are cooked together with a small amount of water. With suitable seasoning, and vegetables chopped or sliced up small, the meat can be partly cooked first in a small amount of fat, then the other ingredients and water added – watch out for spitting if you add the vegetables and water to hot fat! If necessary, weigh the lid down. It is a good rule always to place a lid on a pan in which you are boiling water, to save heat and so save fuel.

Eating

Some years ago we were talking to the manager of a well-known camp shop about some of the dehydrated foods then available for backpackers. He agreed that it was very necessary to have hot food when one was cold and tired, then remarked 'but it would be nice if we could enjoy it!' How right he was, for several reasons. We need to choose the right food to eat at the right time and, by choosing well and by cooking well, to ensure that we also enjoy it.

The right type of food

In order to function properly, the body needs sufficient quantities of the right types of food, but the balance of these types must also be correct. Food consists of protein for tissue growth and muscle repair, fats in small quantities to provide warmth, carbohydrates to produce energy, minerals such as calcium for healthy teeth and bone tissue and iron to produce red blood cells, fibre to provide roughage and keep our insides working properly, vitamins which are essential to our good health, and water. Let us go into a little more detail about each.

Proteins take about four hours to be absorbed by the body, so producing energy at a much slower rate than do carbohydrates. These are assimilated easily and are quickly converted into energy. However, if we have too much carbohydrate, the surplus is converted into fat. Fat is important as it helps to provide warmth, but again, if we have too much and do not work it off, it is stored by the body and we are carrying extra weight which we do not need. It follows that, if we need to use our energy early in the day, we need to have eaten a breakfast containing a high proportion of carbohydrates in order to give us that energy quickly. Muesli breakfast cereals are ideal for the purpose; there are many different brands on the market, or you can make up your own if you prefer. Other carbohydrate foods include bread, rice, potatoes and other vegetables, sugar and fruits.

Protein foods include eggs, meat, cheese, fish and milk. All contain some fat as well as the vital minerals that we need in our diet. The approximate daily requirement for a balanced diet is sixty per cent carbohydrate, twenty per cent protein and twenty per cent fat. A table of food values is given in Appendix IV.

Of the vitamins, it is important to have sufficient Vitamin B as this is needed by the body to convert the carbohydrate intake into sugars (for energy). It can be found in such foods as yeast extracts, wholewheat bread, liver, lean meat, and all fruits and nuts. Vitamin C, since it cannot be stored or produced by the body, must be taken in daily. The best sources for this vitamin are fresh citrus fruits and green salad vegetables, although stewed fruit and tinned fruit will contain about half as much. If you know you are going to be short of Vitamin C, it is easy to obtain it in tablet form. These tablets should be taken with you if you are planning a long trip where you are relying on dried foods.

Calories

A calorie is the unit used to measure the heat-producing power of food. One gramme of carbohydrate and one gramme of protein each give 4.1 calories. One gramme of fat will give 9.3 calories. The average adult needs a thousand calories per day just to keep his body functioning when at rest. When you take an activity such as backpacking or cycling, you are obviously going to need many more; in fact your requirement may well be within the region of five to six thousand calories and will certainly be four thousand plus. So you will see from these figures the amount of food you need. You will also have to ensure that your fluid intake is sufficient to replace that lost by physical exertion. You may lose several pounds of body weight, as well as valuable mineral salts in this manner.

On a weekend trip, it does not really matter too much if

the balance of your diet is not quite correct. However, on longer trips involving physical exertion it is necessary to ensure that you have all the right quantities of each of the constituent foods.

Dehydrated foods

Food is very much a personal thing: we ourselves are not 'fussy' eaters, but we would hesitate to recommend some foods to our friends which others have told us are 'first class'. Virtually all of the specially prepared backpackers' foods on the market today contain all the necessary ingredients for a properly balanced diet. Nevertheless, one does not always wish to buy these foods, as some of them are very expensive. The AFD (accelerated freeze dried) foods are the most expensive of all and have a shorter storage life than ordinary dehydrated foods, which are much cheaper. However, they are very quick to prepare, often only needing the addition of boiling water to make them ready to eat, so they are ideal as emergency foods. Some are designed to be made up in the foil sachet in which the food is packed, but this does not always work too well. The bag gets too hot to handle and can split open when you least expect it. It is also difficult to reconstitute food which gets stuck down in the bottom corners of the bag. The remedy is to mix the food as directed and then transfer it to a cooking-pan to finish the job properly.

Many of the foods available are improved by the addition of suitable herbs or spices, and it is worth experimenting with some before setting off on your trip. Some backpackers we know carry small quantities of herbs and spices in miniature resealable plastic bags. The weight is negligible but makes all the difference to the food you eat.

The ordinary dehydrated foods, besides being cheaper than AFD foods, take longer to prepare. So long as you choose wisely from those that are available, however, they are very good and can form the basis of excellent meals. They can be obtained in both small and large packs and include meat and vegetable dishes as well as some fruits. Catering-size packs are particularly economical and can be obtained from many outdoor shops, large supermarkets and cash-and-carry stores. Once they are opened, we have found the contents keep quite well if stored in screw-cap jars in a cool place. Some foods are available by mail-order only, although the firms marketing them are often to be found at country shows and similar exhibitions.

Desserts are something which some people never bother about. However, they do offer the opportunity of supplying part of your fruit ration. Various packet desserts are available from supermarkets. We have recently found a 'fruit topping' in a plastic packing which can be used as a pleasant fruit dessert. Instant whips and custards are also very useful, especially those designed to be made up with water only. Dried fruits, can be eaten in their dried state or be left to soak and stewed.

Ordinary packet soups can provide the basis for a good meal, as do some of the 'instant' sauces now available. Easy-cook rice, savoury rice with added vegetables, pastas etc can all be used to give good variety.

Meat can be a bit of a problem, but salami keeps very well and can be chopped and added to your meal base. Rolls of chicken and ham sealed in aluminium foil can be purchased at many supermarkets – discard the box in which they are packed and write directly on the foil with a felt pen stating the contents. These will keep, unopened, for long periods. We also recently discovered some 'long-life' packs of sliced beef, pork etc in our local supermarket. They were very expensive but would make a pleasant change.

Drinks are available in packet form in many varieties. Fruit drinks are produced in sachets and can be made up either as concentrated fruit juice or in a weaker state for a refreshing drink. Milk drinks such as Horlicks and drinking-chocolate are also available as 'instant' drinks in individual sachets. 'Cuppa soups' and 'Souper mug' are ideal for very cold days. If you fancy a milk shake, try 'Two Shakes' – a powder flavouring which can be stirred into milk.

Storing perishables

Most backpackers will use dried milk, but there may come a time when liquid milk will need to be carried. The long-life variety is probably best, as it will keep well, although it must be used up when opened as you would use fresh milk. Carry long-life cartons inside a strong plastic bag for safety. Margarine and other fats can also present a problem. We use a standard 250-gramme tub of margarine – not a low-fat spread as you cannot cook with it. This is put inside a round plastic box with screw cap for transport, and the space between pot and tub helps to keep it in reasonable condition. When it is very hot, we keep it in a little water in our washing bowl, with a wet 'J-cloth' draped over the top. When storing such items under the flysheet, remember to move them at night so that the sun will not shine on them first thing in the morning.

If you fancy a little wine on your trip, small sachets are occasionally available from family provision merchants, and wine in light alloy cans is available in some supermarkets.

The important thing is to enjoy your food. If you do not, you will not eat well, and you could find yourself faced with problems on a long and strenuous trip. Eat the right kind of food in the right quantities, prepared so that it is palatable, and you will be a long way towards enjoying your camping trip.

5 Clothing and Footwear

Selecting the garments

In temperate climates, there is a wide variation in temperatures throughout the year. The lightweight camper is likely to be outside in all weathers and must therefore be well prepared in order to remain dry and comfortable. He will not be able to carry vast quantities of clothing to allow for weather changes, particularly if he is backpacking or cycle camping. He will have to carry a selection of garments which can be used in different combinations to suit the weather conditions which he encounters. He will also have to take into account any activities he plans to undertake – such as climbing or canoeing – and plan his clothing accordingly. The answer is to plan a wardrobe in which some clothing, at least, will be able to do 'double duty'.

The first layer

Underclothing is very much a personal choice. However, there are some useful points to remember when selecting these garments for use when camping. Many people prefer cotton next to the skin, but this can get very damp with perspiration caused by exertion. This, in turn, can cause the body to become chilled.

Nylon underwear cannot be recommended, as the nylon does not absorb moisture.

Over the last decade, there has been a tremendous increase in the number of manufacturers of thermal underwear. Despite its name, it is quite suitable for use in summer as well as in winter, and there are varying types and grades of thermal fabric used to produce garments for different applications. Thermal underwear is designed so that the perspiration generated by the body can wick through the garments next to the skin, thus allowing both the body and the undergarments to remain dry. These garments are made from a variety of different fibres – polypropylene, polyester/viloft, chlorofibre and polyester/viscose amongst others. They are obtainable from both specialist shops and high-street stores. The big advantage of thermal wear is that it dries quickly when washed, or if it should inadvertently get wet. Therefore it is ideal for the lightweight camper.

What comes next?

For many people, a T-shirt will serve as both underwear and outer garment, particularly in warm weather. In cold weather, however, it can be used as an extra layer on top of a vest or singlet. It can be made of pure cotton, polyester/cotton or some kind of thermal fabric. Have the T-shirt reasonably loose, so that a layer of air can be trapped between it and the undergarments. This trapped air will act as an insulator and will keep you warm when necessary.

In winter the T-shirt may be replaced with a soft wool jersey. This should not have a high collar but should be of a simple round-neck or crew-neck style. Long sleeves may be preferred at this time of year; they can always be pulled up to the elbows if necessary.

Most people will prefer to wear a shirt over the T-shirt or jersey. This can be made of all wool, a wool/cotton or wool/acrylic mixture or entirely from man-made fibres. Whatever the choice, the shirt should be loose enough to be worn over normal underwear, and extra T-shirt or jersey, and should button through to the hem. Breast pockets with button closures are very useful for holding a handkerchief, compass and whistle, and possibly a tube or packet of sweets. Cuffs should be buttoned or have Velcro closures but should not be tight. The shirt can be worn either tucked into the waistband of trousers or breeches or loose over the top like a jacket.

Trousers or breeches?

The advantage of trousers is that one can wear additional warm clothing under them. If breeches are worn, then the extra layer can only be worn down to the knees, which can be a nuisance in very cold weather. However, there is no doubt that breeches are very comfortable and are favoured by many people. Their big advantage is that they fit rather more closely than trousers, and when walking in long grass or high bracken they do not get soaked around the ankles. Trousers are often made with tab fastenings at the ankles to stop them flapping around, but they will still get wet in such conditions.

Breeches are ideal for cycling – there is no loose fabric to get caught in the chainwheel. Salopettes – a sort of stretchy overall trousers and top combined – are favoured by some. They fit close to the body and give a lot of freedom of movement. Whether you choose trousers or breeches, make sure they have enough pockets. Good backpackers' trousers will have two side pockets, at least one hip pocket – for money etc, which should have a buttoned or zipped closure – and a map pocket which will be either on the front of the trousers above the knee or on one hip. Some trousers and most breeches will also have a hammer loop. Most will have good waist adjustment and belt loops as well. Breeches should fit well over the knees, so that when the knee is bent, no gaps appear between the lower edge of the breeches and the top of the stockings being worn. The lower edge should have comfortable adjustment, with Velcro or buckle fastening, and a gusset should be incorporated. These garments should always be made from wool or a wool mixture. NEVER WEAR JEANS – once wet, they cling to the legs and do not dry easily, and can be the cause of hypothermia, especially in windy conditions.

Outer garments

It will be seen from the garments we have discussed so far that any adjustment to the amount of clothing being worn will be made to the top half of the body. In addition to the basic clothing, a windproof anorak is needed. This may be made of windproof cotton fabrics, such as Ventile or Grenfell cloth, or may be made of one of the newer man-made materials. Some people prefer to use a fibre-pile jacket, which will not be windproof unless it has a windproof shell or lamination. A new development is a fleece fabric said to be as warm as fibre-pile but more windproof.

Others may prefer to use a light down or polyester-filled 'sweater', rather like a duvet jacket but not so thick. Oiled wool sweaters are also popular to wear over a shirt and under a waterproof. In very cold weather a duvet jacket will also be useful. Fibre-pile trousers are a useful addition to a fibre-pile jacket. The suit thus formed can be worn as extra clothing in bed if necessary, and it makes comfortable, dry spare clothing to change into if one gets wet. A light tracksuit performs the same function in warmer weather.

Features to look for

To be really effective, *you* must feel comfortable in whatever outer garment you choose. Anoraks should be loose-fitting enough to wear over a sweater, but not so loose as to let the wind get underneath the hem. Many anoraks have a drawcord at waist and/or hemline. Some are designed to pull over the head, but the majority these days are made in 'jacket-style', with a double-ended zip which can be opened from either end for ventilation. This may have a 'storm flap' either under or outside the zip. Windproof cuffs are a 'must'; they can either be made from knitted tubular fabric or consist of an extra piece of fabric inside the bottom part of the sleeve, with elastic in the hem and a stud or Velcro for adjustment. Good pockets, placed so that they will not get in the way of a rucksack hip belt, are also necessary. A map pocket is essential. This may be external or may be concealed under the zip. A hood is also essential. This can be attached to the main body of the anorak or may be detachable or sewn on beneath the collar to 'tuck away' between the outer and lining materials when not required.

The alternatives to an anorak – fibre-pile or fleece jacket, down or polyester 'sweater' – should also have at least hand-sized pockets. A small internal pocket for a wallet can be very useful and should be secured with a piece of Velcro so that there is no chance of anything falling out when removing the garment.

Oiled sweaters are often given a showerproof finish, so they can be rather useful in misty conditions when a full set of waterproofs is not really necessary. The greatest advantage of the alternatives is their flexibility in providing layers of warm clothing.

No lightweight camper will have the capacity for carrying all these different types of garment. Choose the clothes that will offer the greatest versatility for the activities you plan, so that the maximum use is obtained from each item of clothing and the various combinations thereof.

The layer principle

The whole idea is to use the clothing in various layers to suit the conditions encountered, as is illustrated by the following story:

A group of young people were out on a practice expedition in the West Country. They were properly equipped and should have had few problems if they had followed the training they had received. They were walking over rough moorland and carrying full camping kit, climbing gradually with the wind in their faces. The party became quite warm because of their efforts, and most of them gradually removed outer garments as they warmed up, to give their bodies a chance to cool down. Unfortunately, one lad was rather reluctant to remove the outer layers. He reasoned that, with the cold wind blowing, he would catch a chill. He became soaked from perspiration on the inside of his garments. At the crest of the hill the party stopped for a rest and a snack, sheltering in the lee of some rocks and replacing some of their clothing as they had been taught. The lad who had kept his outer garments on started to shiver, but despite putting on a waterproof, there was no improvement, and after discussion the party decided to contact their supervisor for advice. They had to walk another three miles over rough terrain to reach a telephone box in order to do so, by which time the boy was showing signs of hypothermia. He was eventually taken back to base, having learned his lesson the hard way.

It is essential for anyone wishing to enjoy outdoor activities to realize that these layer principles are necessary. It *can* be a nuisance to take off a sweater and stuff it in the rucksack, especially if it is raining and you have to remove your waterproof in order to do so, but once you are used to the procedure, you will do it automatically.

Waterproof clothing

In this country, one cannot go anywhere without waterproofs. A variety of garments are available to suit all kinds of activities, and in a vast range of different waterproof materials.

For walkers, the most popular type of garment is a long jacket, or cagoule. Jackets are usually made with a double open-ended zip, which has a storm flap to cover it, plus two good hip pockets and a hood, which may have a stiffened visor to protect the face in foul weather. A cagoule is a long, smock-like garment, which is pulled on over the head. There is often a short zip and gusset at the neck, a 'kangaroo' breast pocket for a map, and a hood similar to the one on a jacket. These garments are made in nylon of various weights. The walker is likely to settle for a five-ounce proofed nylon, preferably with a polyurethane coating, or he may prefer a four-ounce or seven-ounce neoprene coated nylon. All these garments have a big disadvantage – condensation. Some manufacturers have attempted to minimize this problem by lining the garments with a lightweight fabric, but this is not always successful, especially in a person with a high metabolic rate. During activity the human body loses as much as $2\frac{1}{2}$ pints of water by perspiration. If the body is enclosed in a completely waterproof layer rain will be kept out but the moisture from the body will be kept in. Apart from the discomfort caused by damp inner garments, this moisture can condense on the inner surface of the waterproof garment, and in conditions of severe cold or wind it can give rise to body chilling. What is required is a material which will resist the penetration of rain from outside, yet will allow the passage of moisture-laden air from inside. If such a moisture-permeable waterproof fabric does not *repel* water, a layer of water on the outer surface will seriously interfere with the release of this moisture. Add to these requirements the need for durability in use and laundering, and its suitability for making up into garments, dye fastness and so on, and we finish up with a pretty formidable specification which has led to much research.

Moisture permeability

One way of obtaining moisture permeability combined with waterproof characteristics is to use a 'microporous' layer in which the pores, although much larger in diameter than the particles of water vapour, are many times smaller than even droplets of misty rain. In effect, the layer acts as a kind of one-way valve, allowing moisture-laden air to be propelled out by the warmth of the body whilst still keeping out the rain. At the time of writing, there are two manufacturers claiming to have products which meet these requirements.

One version is 'Gore-Tex' fabric, in which a microporous polytetrafluoroethylene (PTFE) membrane is laminated between outer layers of woven or knitted nylon, polyester or polyester/cotton fabrics. The surface of the PTFE film exhibits water-repellent properties, and the pores in the membrane act as the 'one-way valve' described above. The other material is 'Entrant', in which a variety of nylon, polyester or polyester/cotton fabrics are treated with a microporous coating of polyurethene, which penetrates into the thickness of the material, forming a secure bond. Additionally, the surface and internal pore structure are given a water-repellent treatment. Both of these materials have a further advantage in that the extremely small pores provide considerable protection against wind penetration, an important requirement for any outer garment.

To complement your waterproof jacket or cagoule, over-trousers will be required. These should be plenty big enough to pull on over walking-boots, and most trousers designed for walking will have a long zip on the outside leg to facilitate this. A gusset should be stitched behind the zip to prevent water penetration. Trousers made from coated, non-breathable fabrics may be made with a wide band of net at the waistband to facilitate ventilation. However, since the advent of breathable materials, the majority will prefer to invest in a waterproof jacket and trousers made from these fabrics.

There is another fabric which, whilst not actually breathable, does help to cut down the problems of condensation. This is a plastic-coated knitted nylon fabric, rather more bulky than other proofed nylons but nevertheless very flexible and comfortable to wear. Occasionally it is available with a towelling backing fabric. Because of its bulkiness, it does not pack down very small, so it is more suitable for garments used for sailing than for backpacking etc.

Seams

Seams are probably the most vulnerable part of any waterproof garment. Well-designed waterproofs will have the minimum number possible, and these will be properly sealed to prevent water seepage. Many will have waterproof tape specially welded to the inside of sewn seams. Others will be sealed with a chemical sealant. Both these processes are extremely labour-intensive and are therefore a major factor in determining the cost of the garment. Other waterproof garments, which would be perfectly adequate but for the lack of sealant on the seams, can be treated with special sealants by the purchaser, and in fact many manufacturers recommend this procedure.

It should be noted that the above comments refer to waterproof garments for all types of outdoor activities. The needs of cyclists and canoeists are the same when it comes to keeping dry, but the style of garments required will be a little different from that best suited to the needs of backpackers and walkers.

Cold-weather clothing

Earlier in this chapter we discussed the general needs of the lightweight camper with regard to clothing. In very cold weather, it is essential that good insulated clothing is carried for additional protection. Many manufacturers are now offering dual-purpose garments for such conditions. Down-filled and polyester-filled duvets and thick fibre-pile fabric jackets are still popular, but the advent of new insulating materials has made the choice of cold-weather clothing much broader.

To enable the lightweighter to keep his weight low in such conditions, a number of manufacturers have produced insulated shell garments. These have a proofed outer shell, normally of either Gore-Tex or Entrant fabric, and a good insulation layer between this outer shell and the lining of the garment. The insulation inside may consist of Hollofil, 'Thinsulate', or 'Libond'.

Some of these insulated garments consist of two separate items of clothing which may be linked together with zip-fasteners to form one unit, or each part may be used individually. This means that each individual can work out numerous combinations to suit the prevailing conditions for the cost of one garment. Other garments are simply waterproof shells lined with fibre-pile fabric or, occasionally, down.

Flexibility

The following combinations for cold-weather camping can be suggested for use with a basic layer of thermal underwear, wool jersey, wool shirt and trousers/breeches.

1. Insulated waterproof shell garment plus light polyester-filled duvet jacket or waistcoat.
2. Waterproof shell garment plus winter-weight polyester-filled or down-filled duvet plus lightweight pile suit.
3. Waterproof shell garment plus thick pile suit, plus windproof anorak.

As previously mentioned in this chapter, the advantage of carrying a pile suit is that it makes an excellent set of spare clothing, for use in the sleeping-bag, if necessary. We are back again to this subject of flexibility, which is so important. We tend to use our waterproof shell garments as the windproof layer over a thick pile jacket with a light polyester-filled waistcoat under it. This combination seems to work well for us, as we can carry summer-weight sleeping-bags and use the pile suits inside them, thus cutting down on our overall weight.

Care of clothing

Clothing for lightweight campers can be expensive. If you want your gear to last you well, it will pay you to look after it. Clothing should be kept clean, and the manufacturers' instructions concerning laundering should be adhered to. Garments made with down filling should be washed with special down cleaner. Gore-Tex fabrics and Entrant need extra care, and there are special cleaning products available for laundering these. If you have a garment which uses more than one type of fabric and filling – for example, a down-filled jacket with a 'Gore-Tex' shell, use a low-lather, bio-degradable product to clean it.

Head, hands and feet

We have already said in Chapter 3 that more than thirty per cent of body heat can be lost through the head. It is the most vulnerable part of the body because it is so exposed to the elements. Nevertheless, one of the easiest ways of regulating body temperature is to put on or remove headgear. For most walkers, this will take the form of a woollen balaclava hat which can be altered to form a simple woollen cap. Many people prefer a simple woollen bobble hat, but the balaclava style is preferable as it can be pulled down to protect the ears and a good part of the face as well. This style is also popular amongst cyclists. In hot weather, a cotton bush-hat or sun-hat is well worth taking with you. The brim should be wide enough to protect the neck from the sun's rays, remembering that these will affect you more easily when you are high in the hills or on the water.

In fine weather, hands are not likely to cause any problems, except that, if you plan to do any climbing, you will naturally be carrying gloves among your other equipment. However, in cold or wet conditions the hands can quickly become very uncomfortable, and it is necessary to protect them. The problem is that you will need to use your hands – for example when undoing your rucksack, pitching your tent and so on.

Working with gloves on is not always easy. We have found that a pair of thermal gloves are the most comfortable and convenient. They are thin enough to be able to feel your fingers through the fabric so that you can do reasonably 'fiddly' jobs whilst wearing them, and they also dry very quickly when wet. Some people may prefer to cut the ends off the fingers of their gloves, thus making mittens which will protect all but the very ends of the fingers. A pair of waterproof overmitts can then be worn over them. These mitts may have some kind of thermal or fibre-pile lining for extra warmth. In winter, some people prefer fingerless mitts made from fibre-pile or wool instead of gloves. These allow the fingers freedom of movement within the protection of the mitt. Mitts may be windproof in themselves or may be covered with a shell made of windproof fabric, and in turn can be covered with waterproof over-mitts.

Cyclists will also need to keep their hands protected, and many will prefer to use track-mitts available from specialist suppliers.

We now come to the question of feet. Apart from proper foot care, which we cover in Chapter 8, it is necessary to wear the right kind of sock and the right kind of boots or shoes for the activity you are planning and the time of year in which you are out, as well as for the terrain over which you will be travelling.

Most people will be comfortable in socks. Ladies should not attempt to wear tights as they can restrict the circulation and cannot easily be removed if blisters start to form. There are all kinds of different socks available, and much will depend on personal choice.

If your feet perspire freely, you will undoubtedly feel more comfortable in wool or cotton socks, or a mixture of the two fibres. Man-made fibres have improved enormously since their first introduction, and it is now possible to buy socks which are made from them, or from a mixture of natural and synthetic materials, which are comfortable to wear. The advantage of socks which include some man-made fibres is that they are more hard-wearing than those made of natural fibres alone. Some people find socks made of a synthetic fabric towelling very comfortable.

Socks should always be free of darns or holes if they are used for walking, and they should be washed carefully to prevent them from becoming stiff and hard. They should be changed frequently for comfort, so plenty of spare pairs are needed. Special walking-socks are available and these normally have the feet lined with a loop-stitch (towelling effect) for comfort. This helps to cushion the feet against the pressures of walking. Some people prefer to wear two pairs of socks, especially inside a pair of boots. We have found the best combination is to wear a pair of wool/nylon socks (seventy per cent wool) next to the skin and a pair of thick grey 'raggsocks' over them, the latter being turned over the top of the boots to prevent the entry of small stones, twigs etc. When wearing lighter boots in summer, we sometimes wear just one pair of loopstitch socks. When wearing training-shoes, we find ordinary wool/nylon socks satisfactory.

If you wear breeches, you will need to make sure that your socks are long enough to completely cover any exposed leg, remembering that when you bend your knee, more leg will be uncovered! It is possible to buy extra-long stockings which come above the knee, and these are ideal to wear with breeches.

Whatever you decide upon, remember the whole purpose of wearing socks: they are intended to provide both insulation and padding, to help absorb perspiration and to ensure that your feet remain comfortable. Two pairs of socks will trap air between the two layers and give added insulation. They will also reduce friction on your feet and help to prevent blisters. However, the two pairs must not be so tightly fitting that there is no chance of air circulating between the two. Tight socks also restrict the circulation, and this will result in cold feet. They must be big enough not to restrict the circulation, but not so big that they wrinkle and cause discomfort and, eventually, blistering feet. So you have to be sure that your *socks* are really comfortable, even before you get down to choosing your outer footwear. Fibre-pile socks are useful. These can be used as bed-socks as they are loose fitting and do not restrict circulation. They are also ideal for use in the tent as 'slippers'.

Choosing your footwear

This is perhaps the most difficult and important decision for the backpacker. There is a very wide choice of both boots and shoes available, made in a wide variety of materials. Gone are the days of the simple choice between leather boots and leather shoes. Modern footwear is made of all types of materials, including plastics, leather, nylons, suède and various proprietary fabrics such as Gore-Tex fabric and Cordura. The problem is, how do you choose from all this?

Boots

Boots have been available for years now. Heavy boots suitable for mountaineering weigh around four to five pounds a pair, and they are still obtainable. They are mostly made from leather, with welt-sewn soles, which have a mid-sole made from leather or rubber, or both, and some kind of stiffener between the mid-sole and the outside sole. This latter sole is almost always a Vibram sole, designed to grip the ground. The one big problem with these Vibram soles is that they are slippery on wet rock. The uppers of these boots are normally made from one piece of leather, so there are no seams to let in water or to rub a sensitive spot on the feet. They also have a 'bellows' tongue which prevents water from seeping inside. The boots will literally last for years, and they can be resoled by a specialist shoe-repairer when the need arises. We have had our own boots for more than ten years and have had them resoled twice during that time. They have been well worth the money originally spent on them. However, heavy boots like these do have some disadvantages. In summer, when the weather is hot, they are not very comfortable for walking in. However, they are ideal for winter walking on moorland and in the mountains. This

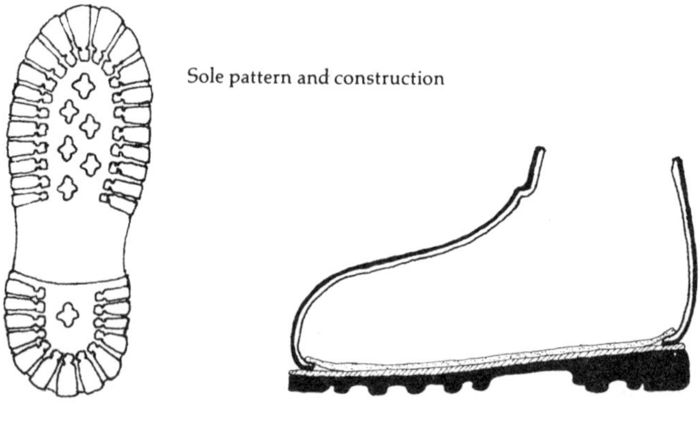

Sole pattern and construction

Vibram-soled mountain boot

Diagram 21

particular type of boot is more likely to keep your feet dry than any other kind of boot, with the possible exception of a wellington boot.

For some years now, manufacturers have been producing lighter-weight leather walking-boots, with bonded-construction soles. These are made from light-weight leather or suède (not always a one-piece upper), and they are not so stiff as the heavy walking-boots. They often have a soft 'cuff' around the ankle for extra comfort, and, like the heavy boots, they generally have a 'bellows' tongue to prevent water from seeping inside. These boots weigh around $2\frac{1}{2}$ to 3 pounds. The big advantage of both the above types of boots is that, being leather, they can be treated with one of the proprietary wax dressings and will thus keep your feet dry in the majority of conditions.

However, let us face the fact that you are sure to get your feet wet at some time or other, especially when walking in long, wet grass or in boggy terrain. At the very least your boots will be damp inside from the perspiration produced by your feet. Wet feet will not harm you if you keep walking, provided that your socks are not chafing. If this occurs, it would be wise to change into a dry pair before carrying on. If the boots are properly treated, however, there is no reason why your feet should not stay reasonably dry and comfortable too.

More recently there has been a big upsurge in the production of new 'lightweight' boots, with claims that they are lighter and better than anything ever before made. They are made from various materials, and weigh between two and three pounds, which is not very different from the lightweight leather boots described above. Although some of these boots are claimed to be waterproof, there are some on the market which are definitely not so; consequently they have to be treated with special sprays to make them waterproof.

The soles of the new-style boots have a pattern of studs and cleats, which achieve a good grip and tend to clog up with mud less than the old mountain pattern soles. They are also very flexible. These boots were developed because walkers were finding the heavy boots very uncomfortable

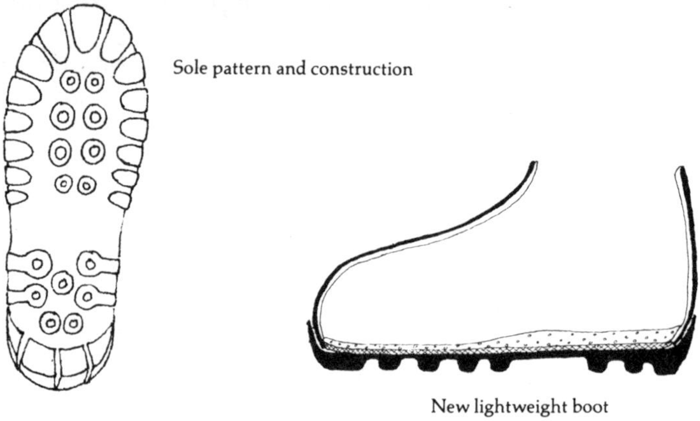

Diagram 22

after a long day out. In fact, many were turning to the use of training-shoes for walking because they were much lighter and more comfortable, even if they did let in the water. Some, but by no means all, of the new lightweight boots are built on the training-shoe principle and are just as comfortable to wear. The advantages definitely outweigh the possible disadvantage of damp feet. Another advantage is that fabric boots, in particular, do not need 'breaking in'. It must be remembered, however, that in conditions of snow and ice, the heavier, older-style mountain boot will be necessary, particularly if crampons are needed.

What is most important, whatever style boot you decide on, is that they must be fitted properly. By far the best way to get a well-fitting pair is to go to a specialist retailer who is prepared to spend time fitting them for you. It is useless to buy a boot with a narrow last if you know you have broad feet. A specialist fitter will measure your feet accurately and will only bring boots for you to try which he is fairly certain will fit properly. Always take your own walking-socks with you when you buy boots. If you wear two pairs as a normal course, take both pairs. When you have tried your boots on, walk around the shop for a while to get the 'feel' of them. They should not be tight, and you should be able to wriggle your toes inside with comfort. If you try the boots first with the laces undone, push your foot right forward as far as it will go, and if you can push your forefinger down the back of the boot behind your heel, your boot should be about the right fit. If that is the case, tighten the laces so that they are looser over the toes than at the ankle. Your heel should be well back against the heel of the boot before you tighten them. You should now have plenty of space to wriggle your toes.

But what if you have no specialist shop near you? The answer is to buy boots from a specialist mail-order supplier. They give specific instructions for ordering in their catalogues, and these should be followed to the letter. If the boots do not fit after following their instructions, they will change them provided that they have not been worn out of doors and have not been treated with any form of dressing or compound.

Shoes

We have already mentioned that the development of the newer-style boot came from the needs of walkers for something with the comfort and lightness of a training-shoe. For summer walking, or indeed for walking anywhere where the ground is not too rough, shoes can be perfectly adequate. Some will undoubtedly prefer 'trainers'. Others will prefer a more conventional shoe. The best type of shoe will have a good fastening across the instep to prevent the feet from slipping around too much inside. Either laces, buckles or the newer Velcro'd tabs are ideal, provided that the shoe itself is giving reasonably firm support to the foot. Avoid gym shoes and rubber or plastic shoes for walking, as they make the feet sweat. For cyclists, shoes should not be too wide, and if toeclips are used, it is advisable to wear properly designed cycling-shoes. However, many lightweight campers who are also cyclists favour training-shoes because they are also comfortable to walk around in on the campsite. Canoeists will inevitably be getting their feet wet, but some protection is necessary, and most choose to wear gym shoes as these come to no harm in the water.

Wellington boots

Wellington boots are very useful, but the biggest problem is their weight and bulk. There are two versions which do merit some consideration, however. One is the Scandinavian close-fitting wellington with studded soles suitable for rough ground. It is possible to buy special studs to fit these for giving extra grip on icy ground. Provided that these are worn with thick socks inside, it is possible to walk quite long distances in them and still be comfortable, and, of course, your feet will remain dry. The other type of wellington boot is an 'over-wellington'. This is a lightweight moulded rubber boot, which is very flexible and has a thin sole. The whole thing is designed to pull on over a pair of ordinary shoes or trainers, yet a pair will fold very small to slip into your baggage. They are absolutely ideal for cyclists and others who wear shoes, but who need to keep their feet dry in camp.

Gaiters

One effective method of keeping both boots and legs dry and free from mud is to wear a pair of gaiters. These are available in a number of styles and fabrics. The simplest are basically an elasticated tube of either canvas or proofed nylon which is slipped on over the feet and pulled up to the knees, but it is now much more common for zips to be fitted to gaiters so that they are easy to get on and off. Zips may be fitted down the back, but it is more convenient when they are at the side, or even down the front of the gaiter. They should be protected with a flap to prevent rain from entering, and all gaiters should have a strap or lacing under the instep to hold them in place.

The 'overboot' style is more sophisticated and, as its name implies, is designed to be fitted onto the boot itself. This is done either by a wire fitting round the welt of the boot or by a tight-fitting rubber 'rand' which fits over the sole of the boot. These are fitted to the boots before you put them on your feet. Some of these 'super' gaiters are lined with insulating material, making them particularly suitable for use in severe conditions.

Most modern gaiters are made of strong rucksack nylon

or 'Cordura' – a nylon fabric with the feel and wearing properties of canvas – although plain canvas gaiters are still available. Some have the leg section made of Gore-Tex fabric for extra comfort. Gaiters, of course, are ideal for wearing with breeches to keep the legs dry.

Care of boots

Good footwear is expensive. Boots should be treated before use. Leather boots should be treated several times with a good wax dressing. Remember that some boots will have been impregnated with grease during manufacture and may resist a wax dressing in the initial stages. Continued application is necessary after each use, so that it will gradually soak into the leather. Boots should be washed immediately after use with clean, cold water and should be scrubbed clean of mud and peat. They should be allowed to dry naturally at room temperature, and never near a fire, radiator etc. Wet boots should be stuffed with newspaper and allowed to dry away from direct heat. When the newspaper becomes wet, change it for some fresh, dry paper. When the boots are dry, apply more leather dressing and store in a well-ventilated dry place. Fabric boots should be washed and dried in the same way as leather boots, but they should then be treated with special fabric proofer. This can be sprayed on both the inside and outside of the boots. Several coats may be applied, and the process can be repeated as necessary.

6 It's the Little Things that Count

So far in this book we have discussed in detail the points to look for when choosing your major items of equipment. There are, however, many odds and ends that help to make life much easier for the lightweight camper. Some might call them 'accessories', but they are rather more than that. Some are essential items, such as your torch, whilst others are non-essentials which are convenient to have with you and which add to your comfort. Some of them need cost very little – or even nothing at all!

The kitchen department

Many of the 'odds and ends' will be used in the kitchen department. Windshields for the stove, for example, can be made from pieces of thin aluminium sheet, joined together with piano-hinge, or may be made from cloth supported by wire pegs made from cleaners' coat-hangers. Glass-fibre curtain fabric is ideal; look in the remnants box in your local department store.

A chopping-board is very useful – not of course the heavy household type but a small piece of plastic laminated board which can be slipped into the rucksack pocket or other suitable place. We have two, which we find extremely useful, both for preparing food and for standing hot pans on.

Food-containers do not have to be especially purchased. Plastic bags can be used for some dry foods, but do make absolutely sure that they will not split. We prefer to use small plastic or aluminium screw-cap containers. These may often be obtained from your local pharmacist simply by asking. If you can make a friend of the canteen cook at work, you may be able to obtain some empty bulk spice-containers. These, although rather large for the single person or weekender, are useful for longer trips to hold such things as sugar or milk powder and are ideal for families too.

Small 35-millimetre film containers are useful for small quantities of jam or marmalade, and we even know one intrepid camper who carries a small tot of whisky in one!

It is possible to buy re-fillable tubes from specialist shops. These are open at the bottom end and are sealed by means of a special slide-on plastic peg. They should, naturally be used only for foods which can be squeezed out of a tube.

Many lightweight campers do not bother to take plates or bowls because they eat from their cooking-pans. Since there are usually two of us using one set of pans, we prefer to take plastic plates which are lighter than metal, the slightly flexible variety being much easier to pack. An aluminium plate can be useful if you need to keep food hot. Do not use metal mugs, as you cannot drink from them until the liquid inside is almost cold! Plastic mugs are almost 'taste free' nowadays and are much the best type to use. You can mark useful measures on your mug by scoring lightly on the outside with a sharp point and marking over this with a permanent-ink felt pen.

Cutlery should be kept together in a small bag, to prevent loss of small items. We each have a brightly coloured bag, just large enough to hold knife, fork, spoon and teaspoon, pot grab, wire handle (for ladle) and baby tin-opener, and a small bamboo butter-knife which we use as a cooking spatula. One carries a crown-cork opener, and the other a campers' corkscrew. The ladles we mention are French. One has holes, useful for serving vegetables, etc, and the other is a normal ladle used for liquid foods and coffee.

A plastic bottle of the variety used for 'Five Pints' and similar dried milks is very useful for carrying a drink for the journey. It fits very well into a normal cycle bottle cage and costs nothing.

Water-buckets can be a bit of a problem. The lightweight canvas buckets of old are no longer available, although buckets made from PVC can be purchased from specialist shops. The 'water-bag' is a comparatively new innovation and is an excellent piece of equipment. It rolls up very small, yet holds two gallons of water. It also has the advantage that it can be partially filled and carried in the top of the rucksack without fear of leakage. If you want to save money, a 2.5 litre plastic squash bottle (round) will fit into larger rucksack or pannier pockets. A small, square squash-container can be converted into a useful bucket by cutting away the top part immediately round the pouring spout, but leaving the handle intact. This makes it easy to use when getting water from a stream. The bucket can be packed full of food and takes up no extra space in rucksack or pannier. Matches are always packed in a tin – we always carry more than one box – and a small disposable gas lighter is also useful. Folding pocket scissors (not the first-aid pair) are convenient in the kitchen for opening cartons of milk or hot sachets with boil-in-bag meals. Partly used cartons can be kept closed by means of plastic clothes pegs of the 'gripper' type. These are also useful for pegging back flapping door panels. Washing-up equipment is necessary unless you want to risk upset stomachs. We use cut-down Spontex dish mops and carry concentrated liquid in a plastic bottle formerly used for contact-lens fluid. These, together with a nylon pot-scourer, are packed in a small waterproof bag. 'J-cloths' are used in place of tea towels.

Washing-kit

Personal washing-kit must be mentioned. Obviously everyone will have his or her own preference, but we carry a small bar of soap in a plastic box, facecloth, camper's toothbrush which packs into its own handle, toothpaste, mirror, small hairbrush and comb, small roll-on deodorant, and, for Pat, a small battery razor. All these, with possibly a small box of talcum powder, are packed in waterproof bags, one for each person. Towels are an obvious necessity, and for weekend trips a guest towel is quite sufficient. However, if there is the chance of a swim, a larger one is taken. A 'travellers' towel' weighing less than two ounces is obtainable and can be quite useful.

We do not use a bowl for washing up dishes, this being done in the cooking-pans. However, a small plastic bowl for personal washing can be improvised from the bottom of a one-gallon squash or liquid soap container. Unlike a canvas basin, it does not collapse when filled with water. Yet another idea is a one-kilo margarine or ice-cream tub.

Torches, lamps and candles

Torches and lamps are again a matter for personal preference. Many backpackers favour candles but unless they are in special candle lanterns or securely fixed inside a cooking-pan we would not recommend them. Torches are safer and in most instances give a better light. An excellent headlamp is available mounted on a firm elastic webbing band which is adjustable to fit round the head. The lamp itself can be angled to shine on your book, stove or what you will. It uses four HP7 or equivalent batteries which are the same type as those used in many small radios and razors. In this way batteries can be interchanged, those too weak for a lamp often being adequate for a small radio.

Your torch may be hung from a small plastic hook pushed onto the tent pole, such hooks being sold in packets of five or ten in camp shops – sometimes among the frame tent accessories. Cyclists will find removable battery headlamps ideal for use in the tent at night.

Gas, paraffin or petrol lamps should not be considered for use inside a lightweight tent because they give off far too much heat in addition to fumes which may damage the proofing. There is also the fire risk.

Essential oddments

Maps are, of course, essential for any traveller, and you will obviously choose those most suited to your needs. Keep them in a plastic bag or map case to protect them from the weather, or alternatively spray them with one of the new aerosol sprays specially designed for protecting maps and documents. A compass and whistle should be carried by all who walk in the hills. Choose a reliable compass of the 'Silva' type and a good referee's or police-type whistle.

First-aid kit is dealt with fully in Chapter 13, and it should always be carried. Do not forget, however, that your tent or your clothes may need some first-aid treatment. A small mending-kit made up to suit your own requirements should include at least a needle and thread, some self-adhesive repair tape and a couple of alloy rings and tent rubbers.

Some little luxuries

A small radio, very useful for weather forecasts, can be a real companion if you are 'holed-up' due to bad weather, or during long winter evenings. Do use an earpiece if you can, as sound travels far at night, and your companions or neighbours may not share your taste in music!

A camera, for recording the high spots of your travels, is rather nice to have. You do not need a big one, or an expensive one. A small 35-millimetre camera or an instamatic will record your journey on film.

Binoculars are something of a luxury because the lightweight ones are very expensive, and the heavier ones, although often cheaper, take up too much room. A monocular might be considered as a substitute. If you like bird-watching or looking closer at distant views, you will probably find it worth saving up for a pair of lightweight binoculars.

A book is another way of whiling away the time when you are 'holed up'. If you want to read a lot during the dark evenings, make sure you have enough spare batteries!

Another luxury which is worth carrying if you can find the room for it is a small back-rest. This can be made very simply from a wide piece of webbing, with cords threaded through the ends which are then looped round the feet. A somewhat primitive idea, but it does work. Another idea is to make a small canvas 'chair' which is placed directly on the ground but has a back-rest supported by two pieces of wood joined in the centre with a wing nut. Even more luxurious is a small inflatable chair, supported by light alloy struts which are held in place by webbing and studs. The whole thing rolls very small and can easily be packed inside a rucksack or saddlebag. The struts can be removed and the chair can then be used in conjunction with a button-bed to make a mattress for sleeping on.

The necessary evil – money

Without money you cannot travel very far, even if you are

'under your own steam', because of course you have to eat. Take sufficient cash with you to tide you over the first few days, especially if a weekend is included. Carry your cash on a money belt or somewhere secure, so that you do not lose it.

If you are only going to be passing through towns at times when the banks are closed, a cashcard for use in automatic machines is useful. For young campers without a cheque guarantee card a Post Office savings account can be helpful. Otherwise young people will need to carry all their funds in cash. This should be safely stowed on different parts of their person, so the risk of losing it all at once is minimized.

7 How Shall We Travel? Where Shall We Go?

Few options available to the traveller offer as much flexibility and freedom as camping. There is so much variety of scenery and so much to see in the historic towns of the United Kingdom, whilst depending on personal inclination and finances the overseas possibilities are endless. The lightweighter is ideally placed to take advantage of these opportunities.

Beginning at home

Believe it or not, eighty per cent of our land is countryside. This is criss-crossed with rights of way of all kinds, from the smallest narrowest footpath to wide green tracks. Don't forget that there are other 'ways' besides roads and tracks. The rivers, canals and lakes of the United Kingdom also offer many opportunities for exploration. You are free to travel where the will takes you – provided you can do so without wilfully breaking the law!

Means of transport

First, before deciding where to go, how shall we travel? Some will have their own transport; others need to rely on friends or to use public transport. Ever since 'Beeching' the rail services have suffered continual cut-backs, and in many areas small stations are closed on Sundays, making it extremely difficult for the weekend traveller to get home. Bus services are suffering the same fate, so that in many rural areas there are no buses at all, let alone on Sunday.

So what is the lightweight camper to do? If he has a car, he can get to his chosen area with little difficulty. By choosing minor roads and camping *en route* he will avoid the hassle of motorway driving. Motor cyclists, too, will have no problems reaching their destination. Some of the smaller 'step-through' machines can be ridden for quite long distances; you do not always have to have a powerful machine. Mopeds can be very useful for short-distance travel and are easy to ride and cheap to run. The bicycle is a favourite with the lightweight camper. He can travel further than the walker yet still go at a slow enough speed to enjoy the fresh air and surroundings. He can use lanes or bridleways and may even indulge in a little 'rough stuff' riding over mountain tracks.

The walker probably has the edge over all these, as he can reach areas where no one else can go, from mountain ridges to riverside paths. Because he may have to make use of buses and trains, he will almost certainly encounter travel problems. In some areas the Post Office runs a minibus – called a Post Bus – which travels a route around villages collecting the mail but also providing a very useful passenger service. In other districts special services by either minibus or small coach run where no other public transport exists. Such a service is the 'Mountain Goat' bus service operating over some of the Lake District passes. Details of transport facilities in the area you intend to visit can be found in the small book entitled *The Bed, Breakfast and Bus Guide*. This is updated annually and lists the names, addresses and telephone numbers of transport operators in different counties.

An ideal way of exploring the waterways is by canoe or small boat. Miles of inland waterways, including rivers and their estuaries, together with coastal waters, await you. There may be problems of access, and a permit is often required, particularly for inland waters.

Those who are interested in riding may like to try lightweight camping with horse or pony; the difficulty here will be to find suitable accommodation *en route* for your horse!

When conditions permit, camping combined with cross-country skiing is possible, but this should be attempted only by those who have thoroughly mastered the art of making their way across country on skis and are thoroughly proficient and equipped for winter camping in the snow. The skiing looks easy, but believe us when we say you ought to start young if you want to try this mode of travel!

There are just a few points we should mention concerning using cars. Let the car do the work for you, and if you are new to lightweight camping, try touring with the car. Another idea is to take your cycles on the roof. Pitch the tent and tour the area without kit. However, remember the extra height when trying to enter car-parks or pass through automatic toll barriers. Often there are height-restriction bars which are not always obvious until the last moment, so be warned! An enjoyable backpacking trip in an unknown area is possible by garaging your car by prior arrangement near your starting-point and saying goodbye to it for a week.

Rights of way

At the start of this chapter we said this country is criss-crossed with rights of way. These are paths or tracks with right of access on foot, by horse-riders or by cyclists; in some cases also by motor vehicles.

Since the creation of the National Parks in 1949, much has been done to improve the footpath situation in this country. The National Parks and Access to the Countryside Act laid definite obligations on every local authority, insisting that they survey and map all public rights of way in their own areas, classifying them as footpaths, bridleways or 'roads used as public paths'. These latter are often known as RUPPs. After (often) long delays, the Definitive Maps were produced by the Highway Authorities. The showing of a path on the Definitive Map is conclusive evidence that it is a right of way; the map also defines its status as a footpath, bridleway etc. A footpath is available for use by pedestrians only, a bridleway by pedestrians, horseriders and pedal cyclists, and RUPPs carry all rights of way including access for motor traffic, although the highway authorities are not obliged to keep them in a usable state of repair. Likewise bridleways do not have to be kept in a usable state for cyclists.

The Countryside Act of 1968 laid down that the Definitive Maps had to be revised every five years to maintain the information up to date. Unfortunately local authorities have found difficulty in keeping to this schedule. The Act also imposed the duty upon local authorities to provide signposts at every point where a right of way leaves a metalled road. The County Council maintains any bridges, but landowners must maintain stiles and gates. No person has the right to alter the route in any way without going through the proper procedure as laid down by law.

The Countryside Commission is responsible for recommending routes for long-distance paths. It has produced a useful booklet on waymarking, resulting in the adoption of standard signs in many areas. A yellow arrow indicates a footpath, and a blue one a bridlepath. The small 'acorn' sign is familiar along the official long-distance paths.

The law relating to footpaths in Scotland is quite different to that of England and Wales. In Scotland a right of way is 'acquired' where a route between two public places has been used by members of the public without let or hindrance over the 'prescriptive period', currently twenty years. Therefore, if a route has not been used for such a period, it will cease to be a right of way. It also means that a new right of way can come into use provided that the public have used it without let or hindrance over twenty years.

The showing on the map of a footpath is no guarantee that a right of way exists. Even if a path is shown as a public right of way on the Ordnance Survey map, it may be very difficult to find on the ground!

Paths and parks

Backpackers will in all probability think first of our long-distance paths. Some are highly over-used, causing problems with erosion and headaches for the conservationists. These problems are growing all the time and will become even more serious if money is not forthcoming to help local authorities to improve the situation.

With a little careful planning, you can work out routes of your own covering areas of your choosing and places *you* want to visit. Start simply. A walk along the North or South Downs in spring or autumn will be especially rewarding, but do not confine yourself to the 'official' ways. The bridlepaths may be muddy, but hopefully the footpaths will not be too bad. It can be really hot on the Downs in summer unless a breeze is blowing, and solid chalk underfoot can feel like concrete road surfaces, which are not too grand to walk on. Do not think only of the well-known long-distance footpaths. There are many other lovely routes such as the Peddlars' Way in Norfolk which follows an old trade route from Hunstanton on the coast to Thetford in the south of the county. This can be linked up, via the ancient Icknield Way, with the Ridgeway, so making a marvellous long walk for an extended holiday. Other possibilities are the Two Moors Way across Dartmoor and Exmoor, the Dales Way in Yorkshire, the Viking Way and the Wolds Way in Lincolnshire. Further south are the Saxon Shore Way following the *old* coast of Kent from Gravesend to Dungeness, and the Weald Way linking the South and North Downs.

The National Parks have much to offer, but in peak holiday times it can be very difficult to find somewhere to stay. The lightweight camper can often persuade a cottager to allow him to pitch for one night in his garden or smallholding. Even this may be difficult in some areas, so to be sure of a pitch arrange it in advance if possible, even by telephoning ahead early in the day. However, genuine walkers and cyclists are seldom turned away even from sites which are stated to be full.

Interesting routes for cycle campers may often be found in some of these areas which contain networks of bridlepaths in conjunction with country lanes. The same applies in designated 'Areas of Outstanding Natural Beauty'.

The Cotswolds, Malvern Hills and Shropshire are all areas within easy reach of many cities. Special Cycling Weeks are organized in the New Forest each year, with camping sites and forest tracks opened for riding when normally they are closed to cycles. The conversion of old disused railway tracks into bridlepaths is increasing, and old drove-roads, originally used for driving cattle or sheep to market, provide ideal ways for both walkers and cyclists. Many of these drove-roads are now classified as RUPPs and may offer good riding for motor cyclists or moped riders. However, animosity exists in some areas between motor cyclists and walkers and landowners. To avoid this, riders of motor cycles must think of others and ride at a reasonable speed, avoiding damage to the path surface and annoyance to others. Definite steps are being taken in some places to prevent the use of these paths by motorized vehicles. We ourselves walk, cycle and ride mopeds, and we know that feelings run high on both sides. If users of these paths abuse their freedom, they may very well find them closed for ever, so the lesson must be 'be reasonable and you will be tolerated'.

Scotland and Ireland have some fine country for both walkers and cyclists. Campsites are available in the Forest Parks, otherwise permission from landowners or tenants is often available for the asking. There is usually not much objection to campers camping 'wild' out of sight of roads or houses provided they are genuine lightweight campers, and are discreet and follow the normal practices of good camping.

Many folk fight shy of going to Northern Ireland because of the 'troubles', but Ulster is a beautiful area with some fantastic scenery. To mention just two areas, the wild coast of Antrim in the north and the Mourne Mountains in County Down are ideal for walking and cycling.

Beach walking is a fascinating pursuit for many people, offering miles of coast and estuary paths where one will hardly see another soul, whilst the coastal paths of Pembrokeshire and the South-West Peninsula are marvellous walking routes, although somewhat hair-raising in high winds!

For the motorist using lightweight camping gear, endless possibilities exist to set up a 'base camp' from which to explore on foot or in the car, whilst moped riders can enjoy the country lanes and remain well within their capabilities as regards range. Suggestions for them may include Kent and Sussex, East Anglia, north Hampshire and Wiltshire, the Vale of York or Cheshire.

Finding the way

The key to your routes will be your map. The Ordnance

Survey Routemaster maps will probably be most useful for motorists and motor cyclists on tour. Special features include tables of distances, telephone and local radio services in the area covered, and a great deal of general tourist information including campsites. Walkers and cyclists will find the 1:50,000 Landranger Ordnance Survey maps better for their purpose, with paths and bridleways which are rights of way clearly shown – footpaths by a line of *red dots*, bridlepaths by *red dashes* and a combination of *dots and dashes* in red for roads used as public paths. Any other path marked in black is not necessarily a public right of way. Much information and explanations of the various signs and symbols used will be found printed in the margin of the map sheet or inside the cover, and this repays careful study.

Special editions of maps covering popular areas are the 1:63,360 Tourist series, although we consider these to be too detailed and of too small a scale to be of great use to walkers.

The Bartholomew 1:100,000 National map series, successors to their old Half-Inch Cyclists' maps, are preferred by many cycle tourists.

If walking in wild or open country, the Ordnance Survey Pathfinder maps, at a scale of 1:25,000, are much the best. These are the so-called Second Series editions at this scale and are gradually replacing the First Series maps. The new sheets are based on modern surveys, include rights of way information and cover twice the area of the original sheets. They offer really detailed information such as fences, walls, guide-posts and even isolated trees, thus providing an invaluable aid to the walker in establishing his position. The Outdoor Leisure maps to the same scale cover some of Britain's most popular recreation areas and are packed with useful information for serious walkers and climbers and for families on less energetic holidays. All these special maps include details of camp sites and picnic areas.

Travelling on the water

We have already mentioned the problems of access on the waterways. The fact is that, unless there is a public right of navigation in existence, you cannot just go where you wish. The right of way on a waterway belongs to the owner of the river bank – hence the problems frequently encountered by canoeists when face to face with fishermen! When a right of navigation does exist, it may sometimes be necessary to obtain a special permit before taking your craft on the water. Also remember that you need gain access to the water from a public place. If you must cross private land to do so, permission must be obtained. Once on the river, if a public right of navigation exists, you are in exactly the same position as a walker on a public footpath – you cannot be asked to leave.

Canals are a different matter. Most canals are accessible to canoeists, and provided they obtain a permit from the Waterways Board, they will find miles of water available for peaceful canoe touring.

Remember, however, that on canals or rivers you do not automatically have the right to use the banks. On canals there is nearly always a towpath along one side or the other. On rivers this is not the case, but where there is a right of way on the water, that right extends to the right to moor, to anchor or to ground the vessel should it become necessary. This means you can pull the canoe up on the bank to repair it, and no one can object. It also means you may come ashore to walk downstream to inspect a rapid, for example, and if you decide that particular stretch of water is unnavigable, you may portage the canoe along the bank until past the obstacle, after which you must re-enter the water. This right does not extend to permission to camp. The position on tidal waters is different. Unless the water is owned by the Crown – for example, a naval base – you have a legal right to canoe. Apart from Crown-owned waters, the only exception is where commercial companies hold licences for salmon netting.

Maps and charts

Probably the best maps for inland waterways are contained in the Nicholson/Ordnance Survey *Guide to the Waterways*, published in three volumes and covering the whole of England. For the Norfolk Broads, Hamilton's Charts will tell you all you need to know, while for coastal waters and estuaries suitable charts are produced by both Imray and

Stanford and should be available through map and chart dealers. Ordnance Survey 1:50,000 maps are also useful.

Going overseas

Abroad, there is endless scope, ranging from backpacking in the USA to trekking in Nepal, from cycle touring in Holland to mountain walking in Norway, from canoeing in Sweden to walking the network of '*Grande Randonnée*' footpaths in France, and much more besides.

Careful preparation is necessary before venturing overseas. We consider it essential to hold an International Camping Carnet issued to their members by clubs which are affiliated to the FICC. Such clubs can also help with advice and information regarding camp sites abroad, as can the various National Tourist Offices in this country.

A number of useful addresses are given in the Appendices, and we will only add our advice to try to learn at least a few words and phrases of the local language before you go. Local people will appreciate your efforts, and your own enjoyment will be increased.

8 Backpacking

Any situation in which you find yourself without a vehicle will require you to carry your gear in the most comfortable and convenient way. Normally this means on your back, with your hands free and unencumbered. Although carrying kit on the back can be called 'backpacking' we usully think of the word as meaning walking with all you need during the day, camping for the night, then moving on. The variations are, of course, endless.

Preparing yourself

For backpacking your body is your vehicle, and it must be in good condition, your feet particularly must be looked after. Carrying a heavy pack will impose a great strain on them – its weight presses down, causing movement in the bones of the feet, thus causing them to swell. In hot weather they will also sweat profusely, causing great discomfort inside your boots unless you are careful. Prepare your feet properly before setting out, and your problems will be minimized. You may still get a blister or two, especially when first starting, but go out with no preparation and you are asking for trouble.

Your body too must be kept fit. The first thing to consider is your normal daily life. If you are in a sedentary job, travel daily to work by car, perhaps have a hasty snack lunch then come home to a large meal and an evening watching the telly, you are not going to last long if you suddenly decide to try backpacking! Go off one weekend with about thirty pounds weight on your back with the intention of walking for twenty miles or so in one day and you'll never make it! You will have to build yourself up to a proper state of fitness.

Conversely, if you are on your feet all day and every day but not standing still all the time, and if you walk to work and eat sensibly, you are going to start with the advantage that at least your feet are used to the weight of your body.

How, then, can you prepare yourself for a backpacking trip which you hope to enjoy? For a start, walk whenever you can. No matter if it rains, put on waterproofs and go. You will have to get used to the rain if backpacking. If you get breathless, take it slowly at first. Check if you are overweight. If so, try to get your weight down to an acceptable level by sensible eating, without fancy methods of dieting. Once this is done, you will feel much fitter in yourself. At weekends try longer walks without kit for a start. Do not think that backpacking is solely for the young; we know many who started in middle age. If you are reasonably fit you will come to no harm. If you do suffer from chest complaints or any other illness which makes you doubt your ability, but you still want to try, ask your doctor for his opinion. The same applies to women who are pregnant: ask the doctor for advice. You will probably find he will not object if you keep the weight of your pack down and do not go to extremes.

Once you feel you are reasonably fit, purchase a pair of boots if you have not already done so. Then walk in them to break them in. Put them on as described in Chapter 5 and wear them around the house, including going up and down stairs. Once you are sure they fit well, get some dressing into them and go for a walk outside. First go for a short distance – say about a mile – preferably on a road rather than on grass. This will be harder on your feet but will be better for breaking in the boots. When you get home, take a look at your feet. If there is any sign of redness or of a blister forming, watch out! Before your next walk, even if a short one, harden your feet. Each night before going to bed, wash and dry the feet thoroughly, then take a little surgical spirit in the palm of the hand and rub it into your heels, massaging the ball of the heel as well as the back by the Achilles tendon. Treat the soles of your feet in the same way, also along the sides near the big toe. Then dust the feet with a good foot-powder. Gradually increase the distances you walk in your new boots until you can manage about eight miles without discomfort.

Carrying it all

To carry your kit you require a rucksack, the choice of which must depend on performance and comfort as well as the size of your bank account.

Choose a sack which is big enough to pack everything inside. If some items such as the tent or sleeping-bag must go on the outside, they must be packed in a good-quality stuff-sack and securely strapped in place. Never go out looking like a tinker, with pots and mugs dangling on your back. Apart from looking untidy, there is a risk of losing them or getting caught up in overhanging bushes or branches.

Load-carrying in comfort

The main objective behind all the variations in design of rucksack is simply to enable you to carry comfortably and easily all you require. If you are not comfortable when carrying your load you will not enjoy the experience.

The simplest type is the frameless sack in which the bag containing the load is slung from the shoulders and hangs against the wearer's back. Although convenient for day use, carrying such things as a waterproof, lunch, pullover etc, it cannot really be considered for backpacking. If heavily loaded it will drag down on your shoulders, and where it presses on your back it will become very hot and uncomfortable. To overcome these problems, designs have been developed using some form of rigid framework to hold the sack away from the back and to distribute the weight more efficiently.

Some thirty years ago virtually all rucksacks were of the old A-frame style, wide at the base, with the whole of the weight taken by the shoulders. Occasionally they were fitted with a waist strap to prevent the sack swinging around. This was the style used by the commandos during World War II, and many were sold cheaply afterwards to people keen to take up camping. Unfortunately they were heavy, and the whole design was completely wrong for the human body.

Such a loaded pack caused the wearer to walk with his spine bent to distribute the load more evenly, the consequences of which were uneven stressing of the spinal pads or discs.

On the other hand, if the discs are stressed evenly, they are capable of carrying a tremendous weight without ill effects, and this can be achieved by allowing the load to bear directly down the spine, which is maintained in an upright position. Modern rucksack design has, by the use of rigid external or internal frames associated with carefully designed and positioned hip belts and shoulder slings, achieved very great improvements in load-carrying ability. Up to seventy per cent of the load is transferred from the shoulders to the hips, allowing a reduction of fatigue as the shoulder and stomach muscles can be greatly relaxed. The load is moved closer to the centre-line of the body and allows the wearer to walk with the spine in a more natural upright position. This also improves balance, important when climbing or walking over rough ground. A well-designed framed hip-loading system has the further advantage of improved ventilation of the back.

At this stage it must be emphasized that the success of the hip-loading idea is dependent upon choice of the correct size of rucksack, a subject into which we will go further. Before doing so, the matter of external and internal frames will be considered.

External and internal frames

A simple and flexible system of support for a rucksack is achieved by using a rigid frame to which the carrying-harness and hip belt is attached. The load is packed into almost any suitable type of bag, ranging from a simple stuff-sack to a very sophisticated rucksack, and this is secured to the pack frame. In this way, it is possible to choose a good frame and harness to suit the size of the wearer, with a cheap sack for the kit. Later a better pack can be obtained for use with the same frame. This is a particularly sensible arrangement when equipping young people who are still growing, as the external frames are usually capable of adjustment over a certain range of sizes.

The development of internal-frame systems which still

Diagram 23

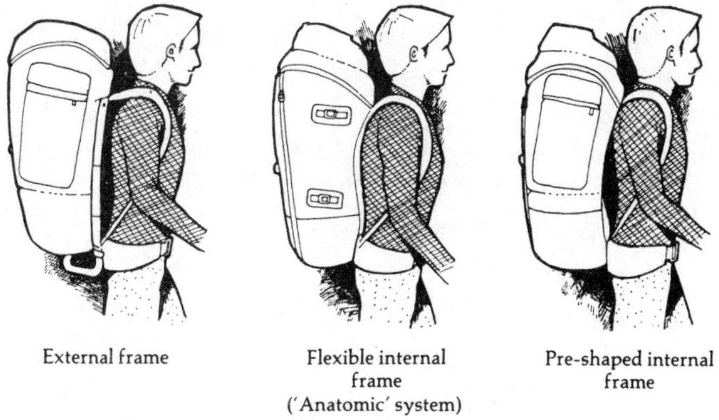

Hip-loading rucksack systems

make use of the hip-loading idea has opened up a whole new range of possibilities in the choice of rucksack. The frame is rigid and fits inside the main sack. Being pre-shaped and with suitable padding, it enables the pack to sit closer to the body at the top of the back (depending on the adjustment of the shoulder harness) and at the hips, while allowing adequate spacing and ventilation elsewhere. Balance and stability are good, and with good design they are extremely comfortable to wear. Without the projections of an external frame, the internal versions are rather more convenient to handle when travelling by bus or train, or when packing in the boot of a car. Two points should be mentioned, however. First, the rucksack/frame combination is a complete entity, unlike the external frame system, so there is less flexibility in choice of combinations of frame and sack. Second, the possibilities of adjustment for size are limited, and in general they tend to be more expensive than separate frame and pack combinations. Finally a word about the so-called 'anatomic' system. This is a variation of the internal frame idea in which the frame is flexible. The result is that the sack hugs the back, leading to improved stability at the expense of ventilation. The system is intended mainly for climbers rather than for long-distance backpacking.

Diagram 24

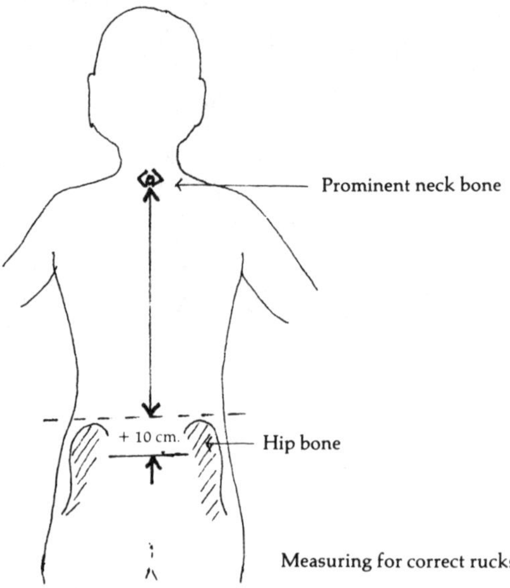

Measuring for correct rucksack size

Choosing the correct size Before going any further, we must deal with this very important subject. We are referring to 'fit' – the size of pack frame to suit the wearer – and not size of the pack itself. First, the size of wearer requires explanation. A tall person does not necessarily require a long frame. It depends entirely on the length of your back.

There is really no substitute for a personal fitting by the trained, experienced staff of a specialist retailer, but where this is impossible there are specialist retailers who will supply sized rucksacks through the post. They give advice on what size to order and will be willing to exchange unsuitable goods provided they are unused.

It is impossible to measure yourself accurately, so get a friend to help. Feel the back of your neck and you will find a prominent bone. Get your friend to measure from this bone down your back to a point level with the top of the hip bone. This latter point can be located by placing your hands on your waist and feeling for the prominent rounded shape on each side. The measurement must be taken to a position down your spine level with the prominent hip bones, then add about ten centimetres (four inches). This will give the correct size of frame reasonably accurately.

To check the size of your rucksack, fill it with a reasonable load and slacken the shoulder slings. Put it on so that the hip belt sits with its top edge just above your hip bone when the hip belt is fastened. Tighten the shoulder slings until the sack or frame is close to the back and feels comfortable. The top harness attachment point should be level with the prominent bone at the back of your neck, or no more than five centimetres (two inches) below it, and a good proportion of the weight will be transferred to the hips.

Most external frames from top-quality manufacturers come in more than one size, each size having adjustments to fit two different back lengths. Over the range the differential between sizes is normally about five centimetres (two inches). The non-adjustable types, normally internal-frame versions, are mostly available in three different sizes with a similar differential.

External frame construction

The frame itself is usually made of light but strong alloy tubing, with side members bent into a shallow S-curve. The cross tubes which space the sides apart are also curved to avoid pressing into the back. The frame joints may be either welded or made with plastic compression joints and screws. Whichever method is used, it is essential that the frame is rigid, and this should be checked before buying. Satisfactory welding of alloy tubing is a highly specialized technique not always used on cheap frames, which often suffer breakage at the joints. Screw compression joints are satisfactory if kept tight, and are easy to repair in the event of breakage. Normally they should not be dismantled and reassembled too often, as the plastic plugs can become loose, although an occasional adjustment for size is possible. Some frames have additional diagonal bracing to increase stiffness, and very tall frames often have the top cross tube bent or curved down to provide clearance for the wearer's head. The main variations are the 'ladder' type with side tubes curved as described above, or the L-shaped version where the frame is bent out to form a platform below the sack. In some cases this provides space for a separate stuff-sack below the main sack. The L-frame is easier to stand on its base for packing and unpacking, but the ladder-frame is best dealt with by standing it up and supporting it by means of a cord and tent peg. The tube ends of both types should be protected by plastic caps. A fairly recent development is the external frame made from moulded plastic material. This is supposed to be quite strong, and if moulded in one piece there should be no problems with joints. The main advantages are low weight and versatility with regard to attachment points for harness, hip belt, sack or stuff-sack.

Slings and belts

The comfort of your pack depends not only on correct fitting but also on the supporting harness. Shoulder straps must be padded and wide enough to prevent their cutting into the top of your shoulders. At the same time they must taper where they pass under the arms to the lower attachment points. The buckles for adjusting sling length should be easy to operate with the loaded pack on your back, and when you are wearing gloves, but they should not slip of their own accord. If your shoulders are narrow or sloping, or if you are wearing nylon outer clothing, problems may be caused by the slings slipping off the shoulders. Many rucksacks have an adjustment to allow the straps to be moved sideways to suit the width of shoulders.

The hip belt should be padded similarly. Probably the best padding for both belt and slings is closed-cell foam stitched inside the webbing straps, as it will not become saturated with rain.

For comfort and adequate support the hip belt should be at least ten centimetres (four inches) wide at the back and across the hips, and should be attached to the frame or sack in such a way that some swivelling movement is possible. The hip belt length must be easily adjustable when fastened, and an easily accessible quick-release fastening is essential. An external frame should have backbands of webbing or nylon mesh, tensioned by turnbuckles or lacing, to hold the pack away from the wearer's back, but when trying on a loaded pack make sure the fastenings do not dig into your back.

The load-container

We have stressed the importance of size in connection with the fitting of the rucksack to the wearer. Now we will consider the capacity of the container for the load, in other words the sack itself. Most manufacturers quote capacity in terms of litres of internal volume, referring to the main sack excluding pockets. However this can only be used as a rough guide; more important is the practicality of packing the items of equipment into the spaces provided, which is a different matter entirely.

One large sack – or a divided one? Choice of the sack will depend partly on personal preference and partly on the intended use. The main sack can have one single compartment or two divided by a horizontal partition. The single compartment allows more flexibility in packing, and if you are unfortunate enough to have to evacuate your tent in a hurry, especially in the dark, it is very much easier to stuff everything in. On the other hand many experienced backpackers prefer two compartments as they like to keep bedding and clothing separate from cooking-pans, the tent and other items. However, it is not always possible to get bulky sleeping-bags with synthetic fillings into the lower compartment, which should in any case have a zip-fastener of adequate length going round to the sides; even better is a zip opening both ways from the centre. Another 'must' is an aperture in each corner of the dividing-floor next to the wearer's back to allow long tent-pole sections to be packed vertically inside.

Front opening for easy packing Another variation of pack is the 'front-opening' or 'zip-around' style in which the opening is on the front. The sack is laid on its back for packing, just like a suitcase. The zip-fastener should have two pullers moving from each side to meet in the centre at the top when closed. For extra security there are often additional straps across the sack, and it is essential that the zip be well shielded from the weather. This type is popular with people who travel on public transport as often a carrying-handle is fitted at the top and provision is made for stowing the shoulder harness and hip belt out of the way when required. It follows that internal frames are used with this type.

Closures Whatever type of sack you choose, it must have an effective flap to protect the contents. Lack of this is invariably a fault with cheap rucksacks. On top-loading models the top flap should be 'contoured' or shaped so that it fits over and around the inner closure of the main sack, even when fully loaded. It should also be large enough to permit items such as wet flysheets to be laid under it with no risk of falling out. Beneath the outer flap an inner closure, either the top edge of the compartment or, better, an extended sleeve or 'snow lock', should be provided with a cord lace which can be drawn up tight and secured with a cord lock. The outer flap must be able to close right down and released to accommodate anything underneath such as the tent flysheet. Long web straps with easily operated buckles are necessary to hold everything in place but must be capable of being released with one hand when necessary. Similar buckles will be needed on the slings, while, as already mentioned, the hip belt must be fitted with a quick-release buckle.

Pockets Pockets are essential for the backpacker, although for climbing they can prove dangerous. The ideal solution is to have detachable pockets which are used when walking to base camp, then left in the tent whilst climbing. Cheap sacks seem to have too many pockets, none of which are large enough to be of any use. We certainly prefer at least two which are able to accommodate a stove and spare fuel, which are thus kept away from clothing, food and bedding yet are easily accessible without opening the main flap. At least one pocket on the top flap for waterproofs, maps and other items needed in a hurry is recommended. The total number and position of pockets is largely a matter of choice, but all must have good closures well protected from rain.

External fittings Rings or special slotted patches should be provided through which can be passed straps to secure external loads such as insulating-mats or sleeping-bags should that be necessary. Some packs are provided with straps and loops for carrying an ice-axe and may also have attachments for securing crampons. This latter facility should have a leather patch to protect the sack from damage from the metal spikes. Any such fittings must be strongly stitched and/or riveted to the main sack, and reinforcing-patches provided. Specialist sacks can also include such features as tunnels behind the side pockets with fixing for carrying skis in a vertical position.

Materials Durability, strength, weather-proofing and weight are all to be considered when selecting the material from which to make a rucksack. Materials are given many names by manufacturers, but for simplicity we can group them into three types of fabric, namely canvas, smooth nylon and 'texturized' nylon. Canvas is hard wearing but can be unpleasant to handle in cold conditions. It is heavier than equivalent synthetic materials and is not so waterproof. Nylon materials do not absorb water as canvas does, and good-quality nylon with a good coating will be more waterproof. The 'texturized' nylons have an appearance and feel similar to that of canvas combined with the advantages of the synthetic fabric. Resistance to wear by abrasion is good. The important thing to remember with all nylon-coated fabrics is that, although they are waterproof in themselves, the rows of stitching provide a potential place for leakage. The seams should therefore be sealed before use, although most manufacturers do not do this themselves as it is a labour-intensive hand operation.

Packing it in

Packing a rucksack is quite definitely an art; some are much better at the job than others.

From what has already been said about how the human body reacts to carrying a load, it will be seen that ideally the load should be positioned so that the weight acts in a line directly down through the spine to your feet on the ground. To approach this ideal, the centre of gravity of the load should be kept high and as near to your back as possible; in other words all the heaviest items should be concentrated in a small space near the top of the pack, adjacent to your back, while all the other lighter items are disposed elsewhere. Unfortunately heavy items tend to be large and of awkward shapes; also some items may be required *en route* while others are not needed until after the tent is pitched, so the whole business needs rethinking.

Many authorities on the subject try to define what is called the vertical 'zone' method of packing, or the 'horizontal' method. The former method divides the space in the main compartment of the pack into three zones. The first is nearest the wearer's back and should contain the heaviest items, the next extends the whole height of the pack, down the centre, and is for the medium-weight items, while the outer zone furthest from the back is for the rest. In contrast, the so-called 'horizontal' arrangement divides the sack into three horizontal areas, with heavy items at the top, medium in the centre and the lightest articles at the bottom. In fact, neither method can be followed exactly, but they can be used as a guide. Whichever way you pack, one thing is, in our view, essential. That is to make use of waterproof plastic bags or sacks in which to pack things, as no rucksack is completely proof against driving rain. This is most important in the case of your sleeping-bag and spare clothing.

Our own procedure normally is to make sure that all items such as sleeping-bags are compressed as small as possible in their own stuff-sacks. Items such as pan sets are in their own separate bags, to keep them together and to protect other things. Closed-cell sleeping-mats may be folded (if of the thin three-millimetre type) and placed down inside the pack next to your back, or they may be rolled loosely, placed vertically in the sack and allowed to expand to act as a liner, leaving packing space in the middle. Otherwise the thicker mat may be rolled tightly and secured under the flap or strapped underneath.

We then place a plastic dustbin-liner or similar large plastic bag in the rucksack and push bulky but light articles into the bottom, making sure the corners are filled with spare clothes, socks, sheet sleeping-bag liner or similar items. Spare pullovers should be near the top in case of need.

Diagram 25

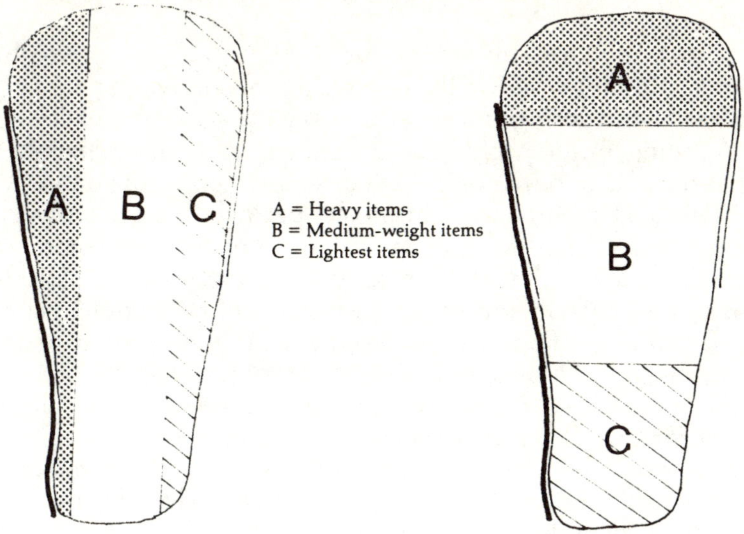

Vertical Zone method of packing

Horizontal Zone method of packing

'Zone' methods of packing

Details must vary with individuals and their own kit, but the main principles are the same – everything protected by plastic bags, inside liner for the main sack, light, bulky articles at the bottom and heavy things at the top near your back.

The stove and spare fuel always goes in the same outside pocket, just in case of leakage, and we always put these into double plastic bags. Of course this is assuming the use of liquid fuel, but we follow the same procedure with gas if we use it. Toilet kit, plates, cutlery – all in their own separate bags – can be placed in outside pockets so they are ready to hand when needed, and the same applies to the first-aid kit, small trowel, drinking-mug and water-bottle. One golden rule is 'never pack an empty space!' There is always something small such as a coffee-or sugar-container which can go in your mug, or the cruet in your pan set. When packing nesting pans, particularly if they are of the non-stick type, place sheets of kitchen towel, tea-cloth or 'J-Cloth' between them to prevent rattles and damage to the surface.

Much modern equipment and clothing is light in weight but is still bulky, so we have a space problem when packing. When considering food, some saving can be made by discarding outer packing and cartons, although remember that the instructions for use are often printed on the outside.

The next to the last thing to be packed will probably be your tent. Whether carried by one person or shared, it should be packed at the top as it is relatively heavy. Also it must be accessible without opening up the whole pack. Under the top flap is ideal provided there is no risk of its slipping out. Pegs should be in a separate bag to protect other items from damage or dirt. An outside pocket will be ideal for this. Poles are best packed in their own bag and can be either slipped down the back of the pack, inside, making sure you do not push sharp ends into your sleeping-bag, or strapped securely outside. In this case it is advisable to have loops on the pole bag through which straps can be passed. If you have nesting poles which pack into a very short bundle, the best place is across the top of the inner sack under the flap. Separate bags for the flysheet and for the inner tent are a good idea, as then the wet flysheet can be kept away from the rest. Load-sharing between two people is easier with this arrangement.

The last thing to be packed will be your outer waterproof garments, in a top pocket or under the top flap, ready for use.

Small things such as maps, compass, guide-book and notebook can go in your jacket pocket or in a map pocket on the pack. A camera requires a safe but accessible place. Devise your own system so you know where everything is when required.

If unable to carry your gear for various reasons, a possible alternative is to pack your equipment in suitable bags secured to some form of trolley such as a good-quality shopping trolley. With plastic sacks or bin-liners providing protection against rain, and reasonably large wheels, there is little difference from pushing a small child in a 'buggy', and there seems little in the way of ground which stops some families doing long journeys like this.

How heavy is it?

How much weight can you or should you be carrying? Individuals vary but an average man should limit his load to not more than one quarter of his body weight. He may carry more, up to one third of his own weight, but not, we suggest, in any degree of comfort. In practical terms a man should not carry more than about thirty-eight pounds, the corresponding load for an average woman being just over thirty pounds. These should be aimed at as maximum loads to allow backpacking for pleasure.

With well-designed, correctly fitted packs, the target loads we have quoted should not present many problems, although it is better to aim at lower weights particularly in summer. Weigh your kit before packing, and do not forget the food. Gradually you will find ways of replacing things with lighter equivalents, but do not overdo the idea of leaving behind things you did not use last time. First-aid kit and waterproofs are essential, although we hope we never have to use them! A number of things, whilst not strictly essential, are nice to have for your own comfort and enjoyment – which is what this is all about. You are not taking part in an endurance test or commando survival exercise.

If two people are sharing, the problems are very much simpler because much of the equipment is very much the same for two as for one, and the tent and cooking equipment are carried by two people. However, let us assume you are going solo. The following list is just a guide to average weights of essential groups of items, and it is not intended as an itemized check list. Add to these the weight of your food and water and all the other 'odds and ends' such as torch, toilet gear and so on, and you will see how quickly the weight builds up.

Sleeping-bag	3 lbs
Tent	5 lbs
Stove with fuel	2 lbs
Pans	10 oz
Insulation pad	1 lb
Spare clothes	2 lbs
Waterproofs	2 lbs
PLUS Rucksack weight	3 lbs 4 oz
TOTAL	18 lbs 14 oz

Putting on and carrying your pack
With a reasonably heavy pack which is comfortable to wear, you still have to master the art of getting it on and off your back without help from anyone else. Picking up and

Diagram 26

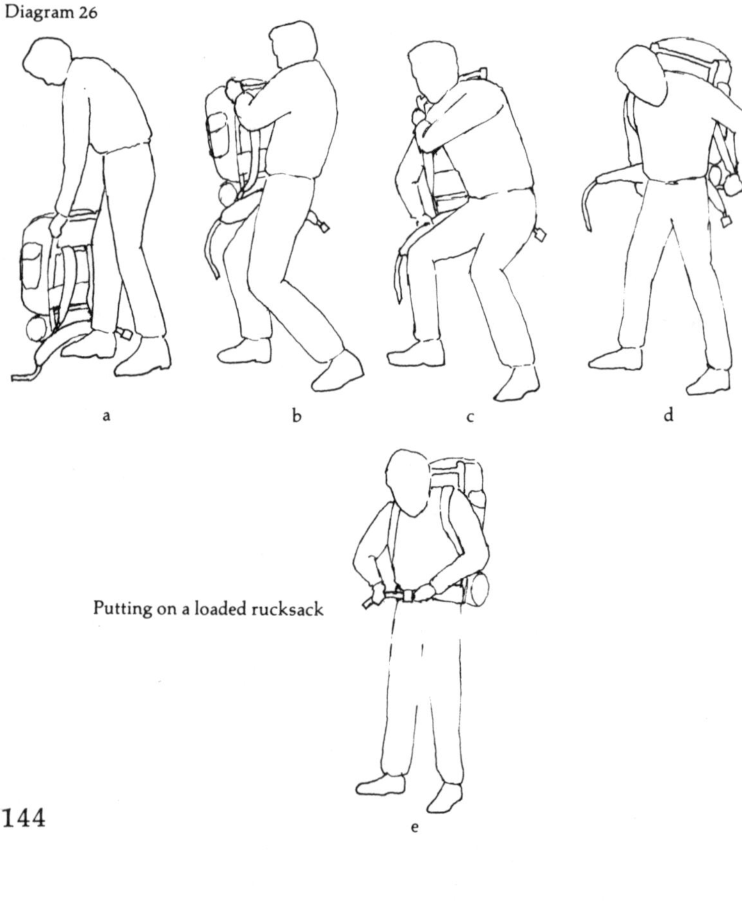

Putting on a loaded rucksack

Top left
Outer jacket – full-length zip is covered by a studded flap, the hood and roomy pockets making for a serviceable wind- and shower-proof garment (Field & Trek Windfall).
Right: Synthetic fabric sweater – the synthetic fleecy fabric, although thinner than fibre pile, is more windproof and is lighter than conventional woollen sweaters (Mountain Equipment Thermo Fleece).

Fibre-pile jacket and trousers – elasticated waist and cuffs, knitted ankles and single-ended zip on jacket eliminate cold spots (Field & Trek Slimline).

Top
Rainwear – left to right: mountain jacket in Gore-Tex fabric, with extra length, ample hood with wired visor, protected zip, pockets and cuffs; matching overtrousers have zipped gusseted lower leg openings (Berghaus Lightning jacket and Oxford overtrousers); lightweight jacket in PU-coated nylon with protected zip, hood and matching overtrousers (Craghopper Rambler); cheap suit in 3 oz acrylic-coated nylon with pull-on jacket with detachable hood and matching overtrousers; neoprene-coated nylon jacket with taped seams, wired hood and protected zip, with matching overtrousers with gusseted zip leg openings (Field & Trek Alpine).

Centre
Cold Weather clothing – left to right: duvet jacket with outer layer of Entrant fabric over Hollofil insulation. The hood is detachable (Mountain Equipment Super Fitzroy); lightweight duvet jacket with Hollofil insulation, ripstop nylon outer, detachable hood, two-way zip and extra length (Field & Trek Tarn); duvet jacket with Hollofil insulation in polycotton outer cover, with detachable hood and high zipped collar (Phoenix Northeaster); down-filled duvet jacket with nylon covering, protected zip and detachable hood (Mountain Equipment Lightline).

Bottom
Combination jacket – the outer jacket is of wind-resistant material and has four pockets and integral hood which will pack into the collar. It may be worn alone or with the inner jacket. The inner jacket with two pockets and collar is insulated with Thinsulate and may be worn either alone or zipped into the outer windproof garment for use in winter conditions (Berghaus Gemini).

A selection of boots – left to right: lightweight boots with polyester/suede uppers and moulded soles with stud and cleat pattern (Karrimor KSB 3S); lightweight boots with one-piece leather uppers and rubber soles with stud and cleat pattern (Berghaus Bionic SL); close-fitting Wellington boots with studded soles for rough ground and separate metal screw-in studs for use in icy conditions (Nokia Bogtrotters); traditional lightweight leather boots with new pattern stud and cleat soles (Berghaus Sella 107); heavy leather boots with moulded Vibram soles suitable for mountain walking and rock-climbing. These will take crampons (Berghaus Bronzo).

Sitting in comfort – left to right: canvas back support with folding wooden struts; inflatable lightweight seat with collapsible alloy support (registered design by Tattlejee of Holland); webbing band with adjustable cord around feet.

Backpacking with the family.

Winter pitch.

Right
A well-packed cycle – a modern set of bicycle bags including front and rear panniers and a bar bag, mounted securely on carriers (Karrimor Kabriolet range).

Left
A selection of rucksacks – left to right: large-capacity two-compartment sack with flexible internal frame and fully adjustable back length to suit different users (Berghaus AB75); medium-capacity sack with single main compartment and flexible internal frame (Berghaus Delta 55); large-capacity single-compartment sack with rigid pre-shaped internal frame, available in three sizes (Karrimor Jaguar 6); large-capacity two-compartment sack on rigid external frame with padded hip belt (Karrimor Senior 2 unit).

Right
The cycle in camp – pitched and ready for the night, with the bike locked, the saddle covered and the machine held upright by guylines to pegs.

Ready for the road – two cycles packed with gear for winter touring.

Travelling on two wheels – a bicycle, moped, motor cycle and lightweight motor cycle, all with full camping equipment packed ready for the road.

Travelling afloat – a two-man Canadian canoe.

Canoe packing – stowing waterproof bags aboard a single-seater kayak.

Starting young – even the smallest backpacker can carry her share!

Equipment for youngsters – good equipment is essential, and clothing, boots and rucksacks are available in children's sizes. Note the balaclavas to keep heads warm.

A weekend club meet – lightweight campers on a farm site.

A lightweight club rally.

handling loads the wrong way can lead to trouble with your back, so it is worth learning the trick.

Stand the pack upright on the ground with the shoulder harness towards you and the slings slackened off. With the knees slightly flexed, grasp the top of the harness with both hands, lift the pack and balance it on your right thigh. Still holding the sling in your left hand, slip your right arm into its sling and, taking the weight on the right shoulder, lift the pack onto your back. Now your left hand is free so you can finish putting the pack onto your shoulders by passing the left arm into its sling. Lift the pack up so the hip belt rests on the hips with the top edge of the belt just above the hip bone. Fasten the hip belt buckle and tighten the belt. Finally tighten the shoulder slings so that the whole load is comfortable. When carrying the pack, keep the hip belt tight and adjust the shoulder slings to maintain a comfortable 'carry', slackening them a little if necessary to control ventilation of the back. In this way the hip loading can be varied to give some relaxation. The slings can be slackened when going uphill to allow the top of the pack to move away from the head, and as the body leans into the slope this keeps the centre of gravity of the load above the hips and legs. Conversely, when going downhill tighten the slings to bring the pack nearer the body to improve your balance.

Taking off the pack is the reverse to putting it on, with control being maintained so the loaded rucksack does not drop heavily onto the ground. Finally remember when getting into a bus or train that your pack is wider than you are. You may have to get it off your back quickly, but do remember to unfasten the hip belt before slipping the slings off your shoulders!

Caring for your pack

Your rucksack is an expensive and vital part of your gear, and one which will be subjected to more than its share of wear and tear, so it will repay looking after.

When new, the seams should be sealed with one of the products sold for the purpose, and this treatment should be repeated at intervals, depending on how often the bag is used. If you sew labels or badges to your pack, treat the stitching with sealant.

Dust and mud should be removed from the fabric and webbing by brushing. Cleaning with a solvent may affect the proofing. If damp, the complete pack must be hung up to dry, particularly if canvas is used. Leather strengthening patches or straps should be treated with a leather-preservative. Although normally nylon and other synthetic materials are not affected by contaminants, a number of cases have been known of bags being harmed by battery acid when carried in mini-buses. In this case the bag should be immersed immediately in cold water to dilute the acid.

Finally, keep a careful watch on all straps, buckles, rings and stitching at points of strain, and make any necessary repairs before trouble gets serious. Failure of a pack or frame when on the hills can be disastrous.

Starting off

Now you have body and feet in good condition, boots well broken in and a properly fitting pack with your equipment safely stowed, you are ready to start your trip. Do not be too ambitious at first and make sure you know where you are going. Much of the 'know-how' of backpacking is similar to that for other ways of lightweight camping and travelling light, but as a backpacker you have two special things to think about. You are walking, and you are carrying a large object on your back.

If starting on public transport, give yourself plenty of time, especially at holiday times, when buses and trains can be crowded. Take care when waiting in public places, as pickpockets can easily slit pockets of rucksacks without your knowing.

Normally we do not recommend hitch-hiking, but if you do it, remember that pack frames can damage car seats. Do not wait where it may be dangerous or illegal for a driver to stop, and always remember that the driver who picks you up is doing you a favour – treat him accordingly.

If part of your journey is along busy roads, beware of traffic, and if there is no footpath, walk to face the oncoming traffic.

Under way

Once at the starting-point of your walk, get your map out and get your bearings. Do not start off at a fast and furious pace but take it easy. If you allow one hour for every $2\frac{1}{2}$ miles measured on the map and add an hour for every 1,500 feet you climb, you will find that pace quite enough. In metric terms this is one hour for every four kilometres on the map plus one hour for every 450 metres climbed. Plan a stop after the first hour for a 'breather', but stop before if your feet are uncomfortable. If there is simply a 'hot spot' or red patch on your foot, apply a piece of 'Moleskin' or Micropore tape to the area; put your socks on again, ensuring there are no rucks or creases, boot up and go on. If the skin has broken or a blister has formed, the wisest course is carefully to release the clear fluid from the blister by pricking it with a needle sterilized in a match flame. A piece of darning-wool threaded in the needle and drawn through the blister will soak up the remainder of the fluid. Then apply a medicated Elastoplast or similar dressing to either the blister or the broken skin area. Rest for a while if you can before going on.

Carry on steadily but only for about ten miles in all. This will occupy about four hours, which is enough for the first time. Do not leave it too late in the afternoon before you look for a pitch for the night. A recognized campsite will save your having to worry about drinking-water and sanitary arrangements. Alternatively you can ask permission at a farm, but if you cannot find anyone to ask, be discreet in choosing a pitch out of sight of roads or buildings. Find a sheltered spot near a hedge or wall, but not under trees. Pitch the tent tail to wind in a position unlikely to get waterlogged. If possible, plan for the early morning sun to dry the flysheet.

Food and water

Food has been discussed in some detail in Chapter 4, but the backpacker will have to take particular note of such factors as bulk and weight, and the type of country he will be crossing. There is not much point in carrying weight-saving dehydrated food if you know there is going to be difficulty in getting water. You will certainly have to carry some water with you. For an overnight trip you will need at least two pints to drink. Carry a ready-prepared meal in a foil sachet which can be put in water and heated before opening. The water is then available to make your drink and to wash up. For sweet a small tin of pineapple in natural juice is an ideal way of enjoying your fruit and being refreshed at the same time.

On longer trips in water-shortage areas you will have to plan very carefully and arrange to come down into the valleys for water if necessary. In some areas public taps are provided and there is hope that this trend will continue.

When engaged in physical activity such as walking with a load, the body uses up energy rapidly, and this must be replaced. Sufficient carbohydrate should be taken at breakfast time to provide energy for the next few hours. When on the move, stops should be made every three hours or so for food with a high proportion of readily digestible carbohydrate. The main consumption of protein and fat should be left until the evening meal. This will provide the fuel for the body to burn during the night to keep you warm.

Good housekeeping

Your tent is your home, and a good housekeeping routine will make your life much easier. With limited space you must keep your things dry and may have to cook safely even if it is raining or blowing outside. This means you must plan exactly where to place everything to hand. Ideally you should be able to put your hand on anything without having to move about too much. Small items can get lost very easily in long grass if left lying around.

Arrange things so you do not have to reach across the stove for pans or water-containers, do not place hot pans directly on the ground, and never sit in the front of the tent with the stove between your legs: if there is a mishap, you will not be able to get out safely.

After laying out your bedding well back from the entrance, keep spare clothing and other unwanted articles packed away.

Preparing for the night
Check the tent, adjusting guylines as necessary and making sure all pegs are secure. Close the outer door, take off your boots and lay them carefully on their sides near the door, making sure water cannot drip into them. Avoid wearing your day clothes at night. Check that nothing is pushed against the tent wall from inside, fold your clothes and spare clothes for a pillow and relax in your sleeping-bag.

Up in the morning
You will wake early, probably to the sound of birds and with the sun shining on the flysheet. Brew up, shake out the bedding while you have breakfast and wash up. If the tent is dry, air the sleeping-bag on top before packing. If this is not possible, turn the bag inside out and spread it inside the tent for a while. It is often a good thing to get on the move early – it is the best time of day for walking. If the weather is wet, pack up everything into its bags and containers inside the tent, and get as much as possible into the pack. A last quick brew-up and you can pack the inner tent while the stove cools down. Finally, close the top flap of your pack, place it outside, don your waterproofs and get down the flysheet. Pack this and the poles and pegs, check all is secure and – last but not least, a quick look round the site for any signs of your stay. Flattened grass but no litter.

The end of the trip
When you reach home, unpack everything, wash out empty food-containers, pans etc and air your bedding. Even if you had a dry pack that morning, the tent needs airing. You will then be half way to being ready for next time. Finally, think over what you took with you and what you did. Maybe your kit checklist needs amending. If this was your first time out backpacking, you will find the next trip even better. Do not be afraid to try new ideas or reject things you found not so good. Remember, it is *your* comfort and enjoyment that matter.

Backpacking in the hills
In the United Kingdom, we have some superb areas of wild country. Many of our National Parks include such areas and

offer good opportunities for camping high up in the hills. The lightweight camper, properly equipped, is ideally placed to enjoy these areas: he will be able to stay out when the non-camping walker has to return to the youth hostel or farmhouse in the valley. By camping out and setting off early again next morning, he will be able to take advantage of the shorter days in spring and autumn.

Equipment for hill-camping

The importance of proper equipment must be stressed. Much of what is available today is quite suitable for use in the hills, but we have to say that some of the kit which is fine for normal backpacking, cycle camping etc in lowland areas is not sufficiently robust for use in high country. This is particularly applicable to tents. The best tent for the purpose will have a good flysheet with a fully enclosed bell end at the front. It will have a sloping ridge, so that it is lower at the rear end. The inner must have a good 'tray'-type groundsheet, and there must be ample separation between inner and outer, so there is little chance of the flysheet touching the inner tent in a strong wind. Sleeved A-poles give good stability, and pull-out guys at the sides assist in separation. Some tents have double zips on bell ends, which are most useful as these allow for easier access and variable windward shelter when cooking; they may also have access to the rear bell end of the flysheet from the inside, enabling what might otherwise be wasted space to be used as a storage area. The mountain tent with sleeved A-poles at both ends, will be more expensive but if well looked after, should last a long time.

A-poles, of course, add to the weight of your tent. But they give that extra stability which is needed in the hills.

Over the last few years, there have been considerable developments in dome tents, tunnel tents etc. These are extremely stable when used in mountains, as their flexible poles are subjected to far less strain than upright or A-poles. Dome tents are also remarkably roomy inside. Their big disadvantage is that they are impossible to erect single-handed when a strong wind is blowing. All the main poles have to be inserted before the tent is secured completely to the ground, and in windy conditions it can act like a parachute or hang-glider! They are popular, but it is necessary to have a second person at least to help with pitching in such conditions.

For the hill-camper wishing to travel really light, one of the small 'Gore-tex' tents available on the market might suit. These single-skin tents are very light in weight and are ideal for the solo camper, although it has to be said that some of them are very cramped and are really only suited to the odd night out.

Once you have settled the question of tentage, check your other kit. Take a survival bag: these, made from bright orange heavy-gauge polythene, are very useful even though you have a tent. They can be used as an 'under-groundsheet' to protect the tent groundsheet when pitching on rough ground, as well as serving their real purpose should the need arise.

It is essential, even in summer to have a woollen hat of some kind. Of course, you will never be without good waterproofs that will protect you from driving rain with wind behind it, and your boots must be strong and waterproof.

It can be much colder at night in the hills, so you must ensure that your bedding will be warm enough, and that you have sufficient insulation beneath you.

Using your map and compass

Carry a good compass of the 'Silva' type, and good Ordnance Survey maps. The best scale to use when walking in the hills is 1:25,000. Always be prepared for recent changes on the ground, such as new plantations, changed boundary fences and so on. Make sure that you can use both your map and your compass. Whatever edition of the map you use, there is always an explanation of the use of the grid lines for giving accurate references to any place on the map. The Silva compasses comprise a compass, protractor, bearing sight, straight edge and ruler all in one.

Diagram 27

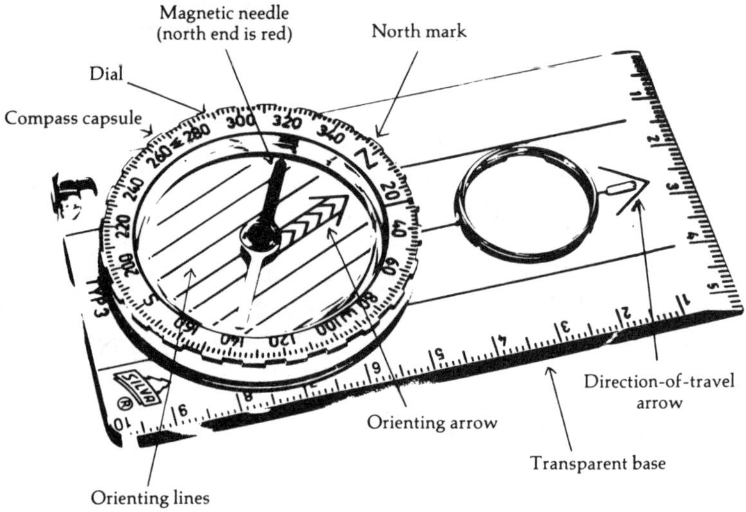

The 'Silva' compass

When you start off you want to be able to find a route from your starting point to your destination. Perhaps you can see a landmark that you know you have to pass? If it is open moorland and you are able to walk cross-country, all you need to do is to point the 'direction of travel' arrow towards your destination and, holding the compass level, turn the dial until the north mark on the rim is opposite the red end of the needle and then walk in the direction the arrow is pointing. Every hundred yards or so, check that you are still walking in the right direction. Even if you lose sight of your objective, you should eventually reach it, and you have no need to worry about bearings or magnetic variation.

Diagram 28 Staying on course

But what if your starting point is along footpaths? Perhaps you are not sure which way the path goes across a field? Or which of two tracks you can see is the correct one?

Lay the edge of your compass on the map along the line of the footpath that you must take, with the direction-of-travel arrow pointing in the direction you have to go. Turn the compass dial until the north on the rim points to the top of the map, and line up the north-south grid lines on the map with the orienting lines on the capsule. You now have a grid bearing set on your compass which has just been used as a protractor. If you lift the compass off the map and, holding it level, turn the whole instrument around until the red end of the needle points to the north mark on the rim of the dial, the direction-of-travel arrow will point almost in the way

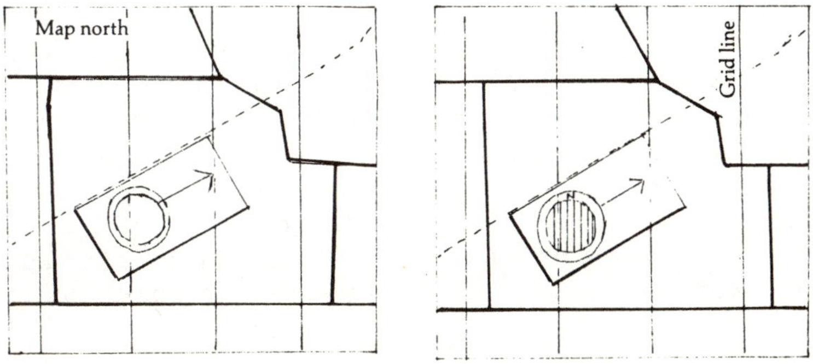

Diagram 29 Which direction?

you want to go. For most purposes this will be accurate enough.

Maps are drawn with the vertical grid lines pointing to *Grid* north, but your compass needle points to *Magnetic* north, which is not the same. In many situations, this difference will not matter, especially over short distances. To correct the compass setting, turn the compass until the red end of the needle points to the 354° mark, instead of to the north mark. This will automatically compensate for the difference, and will be sufficiently accurate for most of Great Britain. The exact figure to use at any time can be found from the information printed on your Ordnance Survey map. To make the whole business even simpler, you can stick a very small piece of adhesive tape on the bottom of the rim of the compass capsule to show the position of the 354° mark.

Diagram 30

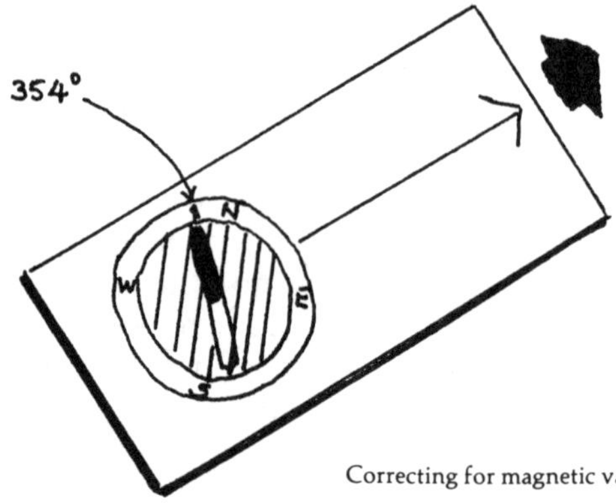

Correcting for magnetic variation

This simple method can also be used if you want to identify various features on the landscape around you. Turn the compass dial until the north mark is opposite the direction of travel line, and place the edge of the compass along any convenient north-south grid line on the map. Then, holding the map and compass together, turn them both around, making sure you hold them level, until the red end of the needle points to the 354° mark on the rim. Your map will now be set so that it lines up with objects on the ground.

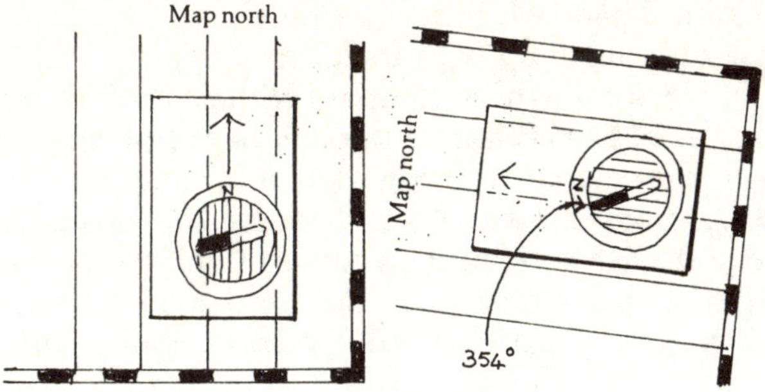

Diagram 31 How to set your map

When you are walking along following a direction indicated by a setting on your compass, it is as well to look back to your starting point occasionally to check that you are still on course. Alternatively, you may want to return the way you have come following a bearing. In either case, just leave the compass dial on its original setting, hold the compass level and turn until the *white* end of the needle points to the north mark (or 354° if that is how you originally set it). Once again, there are no calculations required, to obtain a 'back-bearing'.

Diagram 32

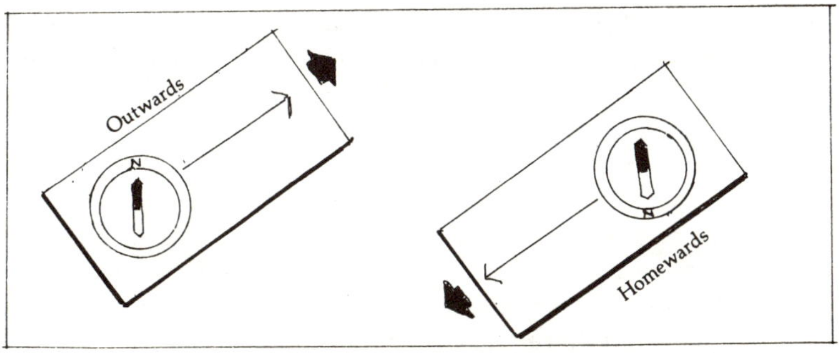

Easy way of finding a back-bearing

Supposing you want to identify one of several similar features that you can see, first point the direction-of-travel arrow at the feature and, holding the compass level, twist the dial until the red end of the needle points to the 354° mark on the rim. Then, without altering the dial setting, lay the compass on your map with its long edge just touching your position. Turn the whole compass around until the orienting lines on the capsule base lie parallel to the north-south grid lines on the map. The edge of the compass, or a line extending from it, will pass through the position of the feature you wish to identify. You will notice that, once you have set the dial whilst sighting the distant object, you do not refer to the compass needle position again. You just use the compass as a protractor to find a line on the map.

Diagram 33

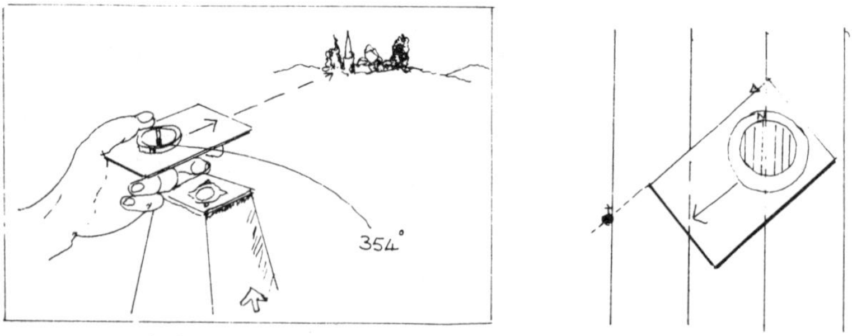

Which church can you see

This method can also be used to check your own position on the map. Normally you find yourself somewhere along the line of a road, stream, ridge or valley. Look for some feature nearly at right-angles to this line which you can identify on the map. Sight along your compass direction-of-travel arrow, and turn the dial until the red end of the needle points to the 354° mark as before. Lay the compass on the map with its edge touching the distant feature and rotate it until its orienting lines are parallel to the north-south grid lines, with the north mark towards the top of the map. Your position will be where the compass edge cuts across the line of the feature (road etc) on which you are standing. If you are still uncertain of your position, you can repeat this process using a second distant landmark. Draw pencil lines on your map along the edge of the compass leading back from the feature, and where these cross should be your position.

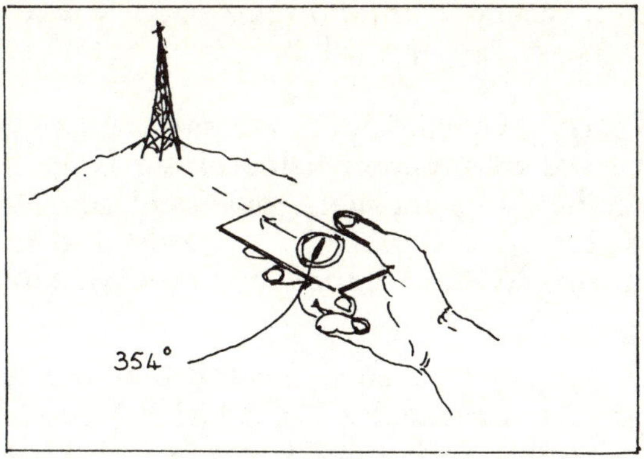

Diagram 34

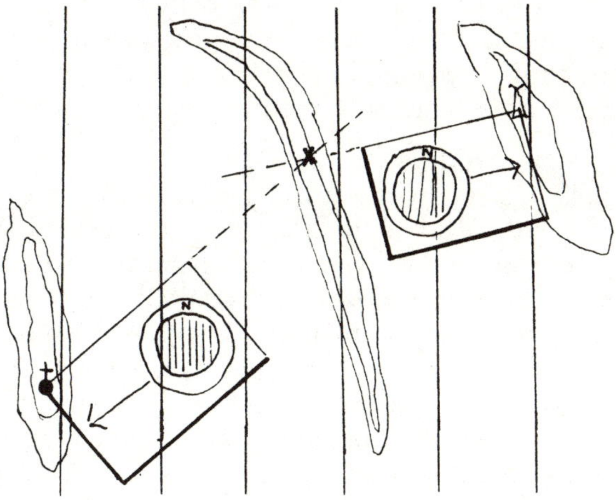

Making certain of your position

We give some suggestions for further reading in the appendices of this book, but however much you read on this particular subject, nothing will be a substitute for plenty of practice.

Always carry a whistle, but never use it unless you are in trouble or need to summon help for someone else. Your first-aid kit should be adequate, as should your knowledge of first aid. Emergency procedures are detailed in Chapter 13. Study them carefully, so that you know what to do.

Food and water

Ensure that your food is adequate and that you carry food for use in an emergency. This MUST be kept for emergencies only, and should consist of chocolate or mintcake bars, fudge, barley sugar etc. Carry some water-sterilizing tablets with you. Mountain streams are often very clear but there is always the chance that something such as a sheep carcase may have polluted the water. We ourselves would never drink untreated water. Whilst on the subject of water, it is much easier to collect it from a stream in a plastic bucket or wide-topped container, rather than a water-carrier with only a very small opening.

Hill-walking techniques

When backpacking in the hills, you will find the walking rather different. With a heavier load on your back – of necessity because of the extra gear you need – you must set an easy pace for yourself. It is not wise to be on your own in hilly country in case of a mishap, so you will have to adjust your pace to suit the slowest member of your party, and this is not easy for some people. Try to start at a slow, steady pace so that the body becomes accustomed to an easy rhythm, thus enabling it to adjust itself without strain when beginning to climb. The same speed of pace should be used on all types of ground, the length of pace being shortened as the ground gets steeper or becomes more difficult. If it becomes very steep, it will help to walk in a zigzag pattern. You should keep your feet flat and walk very deliberately, and your hands should be kept free to assist your balance. Sometimes it helps, when ascending hills, to put your hands on your hips.

By walking rhythmically, you will reach the top of the hill with plenty of wind to spare for tackling any further ascents. Make a point of having regular stops – say for about five minutes every hour. As you ascend, you may find yourself becoming over-heated, and your clothing should be adjusted to compensate for this. When descending hills, especially those with very steep slopes, keep the knees very slightly flexed. This will compensate for the jolting which may occur as the feet strike the ground and will take the weight of the body. Descending a slope when carrying a load can be deceptively more difficult than climbing up, and accidents occur more often during a descent, especially at the end of a tiring day. When crossing a stream or traversing loose scree, tighten the harness slings so that the pack is as close to the body as possible, for better overall balance.

Only ford streams if they are shallow – no higher than your knees – and you can see the bottom. You may wish to remove your socks and roll up your trousers, but put your boots back on. It is very easy to slip in bare feet, and boots will protect your feet from sharp rocks which may be hidden. Always unfasten your hip belt in case you need to throw off your pack in a hurry. Some people like to carry a thumbstick to aid them, but often they are more trouble than they are worth.

If it is necessary to cross scree do not go too fast, and lean backwards so that you can sit down if you find your legs twisting under you. This will effectively halt you, even though the scree might be moving under you. In winter, do not walk on snow-covered scree.

When picking your route, try to avoid causing unnecessary erosion. Where a definite path exists, it should be used rather than creating additional tracks.

In some areas, notably on Dartmoor, there are stretches of boulder-strewn moorland covered with bracken or tussocky grass. It is very easy to put your foot into a hidden hole, so take extra care when walking over such ground. If you should have the misfortune to dislodge a rock on a slope, warn anyone who might be further down the hillside by shouting 'Below'. This will tell them what has happened, and they can then take steps to protect themselves.

The technique when crossing large areas of peat is to move with quick steps, aiming for any tussocks of reed which you might find, for a little extra security. The top of Kinder Scout is notorious for its peaty terrain, and it is sometimes quicker to work your way round the edge rather than attempt to cross the centre. Use your map and compass with intelligence in such conditions.

If you become lost on the hills, never follow a stream down, because water always takes the shortest route, and you may find yourself tumbling down a waterfall. When walking over steep, rough ground with a group, it is an excellent idea to carry an eight-millimetre walkers' rope. This is available from specialist retailers, who will give advice as to its use. It is *not* intended for climbing but to give additional confidence and security and to keep the group together in mist or poor visibility.

Perhaps the biggest hazard of all in the hills is the risk of exposure. Caused by a combination of factors, it may result in the occurrence of further accidents, and the affected person will be quite seriously ill. The subject is dealt with fully in Chapter 13. It can be dangerous to carry on too long in the hope of finding a good spot to pitch camp. An assessment of the distance walked and that still to be covered should be made in good time. This should be about 2 p.m. in winter, 4 p.m. in summer, and, if necessary, plans should be changed, perhaps choosing a shorter route.

Camping in the hills

When in the hills, it is important to get as much shelter as possible. If feasible, camp near a stream, but not too close. You do not want to be kept awake by the sound of running water; nor do you want to run the risk of being flooded out in the event of a sudden rise in the level of the water due to rainstorms on higher ground. Try to find some shelter from the prevailing wind; there may be a small bank or hillock to offer shelter. Do not pitch under trees.

Avoid rocky outcrops, especially if there is evidence of loose rock. You may find that you need to use a steel peg to make a pilot hole for your alloy ones. If you have to anchor your guylines with rocks, take care that strong winds do not cause so much movement that they wear through and break. The technique is to place the stones or rocks on top of the pegs, not on the actual guylines.

Never pitch on poorly drained ground, even if it is the only sheltered place available. Better to be in a slightly more exposed position than washed away in the middle of the night! Find a site well before dark, and pitch your tent immediately.

Once you are organized, get your sleeping-bag out of its sack and lay it out so that it can 'loft up'. Fetch your water from the stream, making sure you get it upstream of any evidence of animal presence, and add sterilizing tablets immediately. Your washing place should be downstream of your drinking-water collection point. Find a suitable place for a latrine hole. This must be downstream, in a reasonably secluded spot, and at least thirty yards from the bank of the stream. Preferably it should also be situated down wind, but this is not always possible. Arrangements should be made with others in the group to ensure privacy.

In winter, there are long nights, and you will have to spend a lot of time inside your tent, mainly in your sleeping-bag. Make sure that you get into dry clothes as soon as possible, and if you have to go out again, put your wet things back on. Keep your feet warm by wearing fibre-pile socks. You are then halfway to winning the battle of staying warm all over. Have a really good meal at night, and keep as much of your equipment as possible in your pack, in case you have to do a quick move in the night. Keep your torch right by you, just in case. There are some 'golden rules' to be observed by those who would like to camp high in the hills, and they are, in the main, equally applicable to all backpackers. They are contained in the following 'Mountain Code', which appears on the back cover of the booklet *Safety on Mountains*, published by the British Mountaineering Council. It costs very little and should be read and carried by all backpackers.

The Mountain Code

Be prepared

Do not tackle anything which is beyond your training and

experience.

Ensure your equipment is sound.

Know the rescue facilities available in the area you are in and the procedure in case of accidents.

Know first aid.

Avoid going into the mountains alone unless you are very experienced.

Leave word of your route and proposed time of return. Always report your return.

Make sure your map and compass skills are well practised.

Rely on your compass.

Consider other people

Avoid game-shooting parties.

Lead only climbs and walks you are competent to do so.

Enjoy the quiet of the countryside; loud radios and voices do disturb.

Do not throw stones and dislodge boulders.

Do not pollute water.

Choose a climb which will not interfere with others, or wait your turn.

Be weather wise

Know the local weather forecast

Weather conditions change rapidly. Do not hesitate to turn back.

Know the conditions on the mountains; if there is snow or ice, only go out when you have mastered the use of ice axe and rope.

Respect the land

Keep to footpaths through farm and woodland. If in doubt, ask.

Camp on official sites or obtain permission of the landowners.

Dig a hole to make a latrine and replace turf.

Remember the danger of starting a fire.

Take all your litter home.

Avoid startling sheep and cattle.

Help conserve wild life

Enjoy the plants, flowers and trees but never damage or remove them.

Avoid disturbing wild life.

The following extracts from the Country Code which are not included in the Mountain Code above should also be observed:

Enjoy the countryside and respect its life and work.
Fasten all gates.
Keep your dogs under close control.
Use gates and stiles to cross hedges, fences and walls.
Leave livestock, crops and machinery alone.
Take special care on country roads.

In conclusion, heed the advice and respect the knowledge of local people on weather and other hazards. They can be relied upon to know best.

9 Cycle Camping

The basic lightweight camping equipment will be equally suitable for cycle camping as for backpacking, but the cyclist will be using roads of some sort whereas the walker may be well off the beaten track. Using roads has its own attraction if we get off the main roads and strike out along the network of very quiet minor roads and lanes which criss-cross the countryside.

By following routes along established roads, the cycle camper is almost bound, sooner or later, to come to a village or pub, so he is not quite so isolated from some sort of civilization. This means that there is not quite the same need to be self-supporting as regards food. It is wise to carry at least one good meal just in case, but normally food can be bought *en route* much more easily by the cyclist than by the walker. For the same reason the cyclist may find it easier to make use of established campsites, which will have the necessary facilities and often some kind of shop where essentials can be bought.

The problems of route-finding for the cyclist will be rather different from those of the backpacker. The cyclist will need maps of somewhat smaller scale as he will be covering longer distances, and he will need to check his position fairly quickly, but always in relation to his location on a definite road or bridleway.

When planning your route, it is useful to work on an estimated speed of ten miles in the hour, as this seems to be a good average, allowing for short stops, hills and so on.

When planning the first cycle-camping trip, a good way of trying out one's gear and machine is to choose a fairly easy route, not too far, and if there is a convenient youth hostel which has a campsite attached, that might be a very good destination. Otherwise, choose a campsite which has the necessary toilet facilities. Then you will have an opportunity to deal with any minor problems which might arise with the kit or carrying-arrangements without being committed to a long run next day.

The cycle

It is possible to spend several hundred pounds on a lightweight bicycle specially built for you. If you can afford it and that is what you want, then do so, going to a specialist cycle-builder and taking his advice, having told him what you require. For most of us, especially when starting out it will be a case of buying an 'off-the-peg' touring machine or even making do with what we have got. There is nothing wrong with that. Get out your bike and have a good look at it. If it is rideable, you can certainly go somewhere on it, and with suitable arrangements for attachment you can carry some camping-gear.

It is advisable, however, to give a bit more thought and preparation than that. First of all, make sure the machine is in good condition, wheels and steering adjusted and lubricated, position of saddle and handlebars correct for your own comfort, chain adjusted to correct tension, nothing rattling or falling off – in short, your bike is roadworthy and serviceable. Remember that the brakes will have to stop not only you and your bike but also the additional load of your kit. So take extra care in adjusting the brakes. Renew the brake blocks if necessary. Check over the tyres, renew if necessary, and pump up hard. This will make pedalling easier and reduce the risk of punctures. Pay special attention to suitable carriers for taking the bags in which your camp kit will be packed. Last but by no means least, check your lighting system, whether battery or dynamo. Check that the lights are not obscured by the bags and baggage. Then you can really have a try-out of your new activity.

If you find the idea of cycle camping to your liking, the next subject to consider will without doubt be the matter of gearing. This, to put it simply, is the way in which you can make your life easier when pedalling up hill and down dale with a loaded bike. It is probably also one subject which provokes more argument amongst experts and others than almost any other subject in the field of cycle camping.

The problem is that our bodies produce energy which is converted by a very simple and effective mechanism into forward motion along the road. The bicycle has been described as one of the most efficient means of converting energy, but our bodies work best at a constant steady rate. The object of bicycle gearing systems is to allow the body to work at this constant speed – known as 'cadence' or pedalling rate – whilst allowing the forward speed of the machine to vary with the slope of the road. Possibly your bike already has some form of variable-speed gear, but it is probable that you still found you were having to pedal far too slowly and made hard work of it up hill. You may even have had to get off and push.

Of the two common systems for changing gear, the hub type is rather limited in the number and range of gears possible. This leaves us with the derailleur system in which the chain from the chainwheel is moved from one to another of a set of different-sized sprockets – the small toothed wheels which are mounted on the freewheel hub on the rear wheel. If a large chainwheel drives, through the chain, a small sprocket, then for each revolution of the pedals (and hence the chainwheel) the rear wheel will turn more times, so the bike will be travelling faster. This is called a high gear, but you have to do comparatively more work to move the load. If, on the other hand, the sprocket is larger than the chainwheel (an unlikely situation in practice!), the reverse results, and you find yourself pedalling very fast but the bike moves slowly. This is a low gear. On the level, one should pedal at a steady rate, usually of the order of 70 to 80 revolutions per minute, and the cycle will travel at about 20 m.p.h. with no head wind. To maintain this steady rate of pedalling up a slope, increasingly lower gears need to be selected, with the bike travelling progressively slower. The effort required from the rider will remain fairly constant. When running downhill, a higher gear will still allow the pedalling cadence to stay constant.

Fine, you may say, but what gears or gear ratios do I

need? A lot depends on you and your state of fitness, but as a rough guide it is recommended that for the highest gear about 70 inch to 75 inch is suitable, while the lowest should be about 30 inch to 34 inch. Remember that this is for a loaded bike and for touring in varying country. The term '70-inch gear' relates to the size of wheel of a mythical penny-farthing cycle which would give the same result! It is at least a simple way of comparing gear ratios.

Many books are available which give tables with all the various combinations of chainwheel and sprocket sizes and wheel diameters and the resulting gear ratios, so this saves you doing the calculations. In the end it will probably be best for you to go to a specialist cycle-dealer, tell him the highest and lowest gears you require and ask his advice. The normal simple arrangement is to have five gears. With the addition of a second chainwheel and a front changer, you can have ten gears spaced between the extremes. That is the theory, but in practice you find that two are probably duplicated so you finish up with eight plus additional complications. It all depends on how involved you want to get, but we suggest you get some experience before spending a lot of money.

If you have decided to carry out some alterations to your existing cycle, or to buy one for camping, you might consider changing your brakes. For a loaded bike, the best type of brake, unless you are going to go for a very expensive model, is the centre-pull caliper brake. In dealing with packing and carrying, we refer to the method of fixing carriers to the brake bolts. At the same time you should make sure nothing hinders the free working of the brakes or the brake levers, especially when fixing a bar bag.

Since your comfort is all important and will affect your efficiency as part of the machine, care is called for in choosing a saddle. Expert cyclists will talk about how they break in their leather saddles, which then last them for years. For those of us who are perhaps not quite so dedicated, there are now available saddles which make use of modern materials and technology and are designed with the human anatomy in mind. Models are made for both men and women and can be thoroughly recommended.

Next to saddles is perhaps the matter of handlebars. The

most commonly used type for touring is the so-called Randonneur pattern, which may be described as a shallow drop version. Hardly anyone these days seems to use flat bars for touring, although there is some medical opinion which rejects the dropped handlebar as being liable to cause spinal trouble.

Another subject for discussion is whether or not to use toe clips, with or without toe straps. Certainly tight toe straps have the disadvantage that you may not be able to disengage the foot quickly if you have to stop suddenly with a loaded bike. Clips are alleged to increase the pedalling efficiency by amounts ranging from thirty to fifty per cent, depending on the expert concerned.

A touring bike should have mudguards, to prevent you and your kit from being subjected to a constant spray of water and mud; for the same reason, mudflaps are to be advised on the front mudguards. The total weight of all these is marginal. Make sure there is sufficient clearance between the mudguards and the tyres, as you will find you pick up quite a lot of mud, grass and other things when riding through lanes and onto a campsite.

The wheels may be held by quick-release hubs or by nuts. The only advantage with quick-release hubs is if you plan to carry your bike on a car roof rack of the type which takes the front wheel in a separate holder. Otherwise there is no point in having them, and if the wheels are secured by nuts, it makes them less easy to steal. The tyres should be the wired-on type with separate inner tubes. So-called tubular tyres as used by racing bikes are not to be recommended for touring. Tyres should always be inflated hard. Whether or not you need to get specially strengthened wheels with additional spokes of a heavier gauge is debatable. If your kit weight is not excessive and you ride with reasonable care on rough roads, you should not experience much trouble. However, if you weigh about fifteen stone and have kit to suit, that may be a different matter!

When deciding where to attach the clips for your tyre pump you must think also of where you can position cages for a drink-bottle and for a bottle to hold fuel for the stove. Normally these can all be positioned on the seat tube and down tube of the cycle frame, possibly with the pump along the top tube. A normal or conventional lady's frame is not really strong enough for touring with a load, but an excellent frame is the so-called 'mixte' frame in which double tubes run down from the head tube to the rear axle. Even so, especially with centre-pull brakes, problems arise over fixing things like pumps and bottle cages.

Lights and reflective devices

Good lights and reflectors make sense and are legally required. The strict legal requirement is that a cycle must carry, at night, a front lamp showing a white light and a rear light combined with a reflector, which must be red. The rear light must be at least $1\frac{1}{2}$ inches in diameter or equivalent area, and must be between 15 inches and 42 inches from the ground. The lights may not be attached to bags or to the rider but must be attached to the cycle.

There are many differing opinions as to which are best – battery lamps or dynamo lamps. Modern developments are always likely to change any situation, but, briefly, dynamo lamps give a very good light when the cycle is in motion. A good beam is important when cycling at night in the country, where you need to see your way. When you stop, however, you have no light by which you can be seen by others, such as cars coming from behind. Dynamos also tend to slip on muddy or icy wheels, so giving a dim light. Battery lamps give a good light when the batteries are new, and remain lit when you stop. Spare batteries are essential, but you then have a lamp for your tent when you get to camp. With front and rear lamps to the latest British Standard specifications, both lamps take the same type and size of battery and bulb which are universally available, so this simplifies the problem of spares.

An additional large rear reflector on the cycle combined with reflective pedals makes a tremendous improvement to your visibility at night, as any motorist will tell you. Wearing light-coloured clothing and reflective bandoliers, together with reflective strips or patches on your panniers and saddlebags, will all add to your peace of mind when riding in poor visibility during daytime as well. These items can be either sewn on or bought in self-adhesive form at what is a small price to pay for the safety they bring.

Tools and spares

Unlike the backpacker, you will have to carry a certain amount in the way of tools and spares to maintain your machine in good order. Equally important is to know how to use them. There are bound to be a few adjustments required so you should carry with you spanners to fit the various brake, saddle and wheel nuts, a pair of small strong pliers, screwdrivers to fit any screws on the machine, an adjustable spanner and tyre levers (3). A small cycle tool kit in a wallet will probably include the necessary multiple tools to fit bottom bracket lockrings, pedals and wheel-bearing cones. If your machine has any Allen screws, include the appropriate sizes of Allen key. A puncture repair kit and a small pair of scissors will complete a basic tool outfit.

Pack all the items in a small wallet of some sort, wrapped in a rag to prevent them from rattling. The rag will also come in useful for wiping off oil or dirt. Include a few things such as a small roll of adhesive tape and a short length of copper or soft iron wire, and a small container such as an empty film can with hand-cleanser, and you will be prepared for most simple problems on the road.

If you are planning a longer trip, especially to more remote areas or maybe abroad, a number of additional tools and spares are advisable. If you use cotterless cranks, a tool for removing them, also a chain-link remover and spoke key will supplement the basic kit. Carry a spare inner tube, spare brake and derailleur cables, two or three spare spokes and a small can of oil, but make sure the latter is well wrapped up and cannot leak. To complete the spares a few nuts and bolts of suitable sizes should include those for fixing your carriers. Make sure everything is securely packed and carried where it can be reached easily.

Essential items in addition to the above are spare bulbs for your lights, together with batteries if you use battery lamps. A good place to carry the spare bulbs is inside the lamp casing. There is usually plenty of room to wrap and place a spare bulb or even two, and they are then all ready to hand if needed. Wrap batteries to protect them from damp.

Correct size of cycle

Before loading up and starting to ride, some mention must be made of the correct size of frame. So far we have been assuming that you have a cycle and that it must, therefore be of the correct size for you. Perhaps that was a little optimistic. The fact is that, if you have a cycle for everyday round-town riding, you may be getting by, but if you are planning to spend several hours in the saddle pedalling a loaded bike the question of size takes on a rather different aspect. Your comfort is all-important.

A number of formulas are given in various technical books dealing with the bicycle. For a start, if you measure your inside leg and subtract ten inches, that will give you a good guide to the frame size you need. Then by adjusting saddle height you should find a position where, with your weight evenly distributed on the saddle and your heel on the pedal, your knee is slightly bent when the pedal is in its lowest position. It is also important, especially with a loaded bike, that no tilting is necessary when mounting and dismounting. To check this, straddle the crossbar with both feet on the ground. You should be able to lift the bike about an inch. The top of your handlebar bend should be about an inch lower than the top of the saddle. To find a position for the saddle in a front-to-rear direction, place your feet on the pedals and with the pedal cranks horizontal, your forward knee joint should be vertically above the pedal axle. Finally you should be able to sit with arms outstretched comfortably to grip the top of the bars. With the arms slightly bent to absorb shocks, the angle of your body to the horizontal should be about forty-five to fifty degrees. These factors are only guides, and you must determine what suits you and what is most comfortable by riding a reasonable distance.

What to wear

The cyclist who takes part in racing or time-trials will have a whole range of specialist clothing at his disposal. Much of this will be inappropriate for the cycle tourist, and in particular the cycle camper. For one thing, he is likely to be cycling in all weathers, and for another he will want to stop *en route* and perhaps walk around shops or do some sightseeing. At the end of the day, the cycle camper will come off his machine and be a normal lightweight camper, with perhaps a cool or even cold evening and wet grass underfoot.

The general principles of clothing have been described in Chapter 5, in which it was seen that the aim is to maintain the body at an even temperature. The cyclist when riding will get warm. At the same time he will be moving fast and subject to the cooling effect of the wind. Loose, floppy garments can be a nuisance, although the ultra-close-fitting gear of the racing cyclist is not necessary. The need to allow the body to 'breathe' and the ability of the clothing to absorb perspiration are important, and so is the need to provide protection from sun or wind. A factor which must be taken into account is the discomfort which badly placed seams can cause when sitting all day pedalling.

Starting with the feet, we see this problem of conflicting requirements. Cycling-shoes with plates or cleats to retain their position on the pedals in the toe clips can be dangerous to the touring cyclist who has to disengage his feet in a hurry, perhaps with heavy traffic around. Also they are definitely not recommended for walking up hill, for sightseeing or when in camp. However, shoes need to have stiff soles to help pedalling and to have lightly ridged soles to prevent slipping on the pedals. Leather or canvas uppers will allow the feet to breathe, and although trainers are possible, a better solution is the specialist shoe now being made for touring cyclists. Foot comfort is completed by wearing woollen-mixture loop-stitch socks.

Shorts may be comfortable in summer for riding, but be prepared for sunburned knees and upper legs. It may be just as comfortable to wear trousers of the tracksuit type which zip or clip around the ankles. Underneath, it is important to have seamless or flat-seamed underpants, and a visit to a specialist cycle shop may be worth while. A thin woollen shirt allows for evaporation of perspiration, and sleeves which can be rolled down to provide protection against sunburn or insects are advisable. A light sweater or track top can be carried to add on top if required, and in colder weather or in hilly country a fibre-pile jacket is useful.

Whatever you wear as an outer garment against cold, do remember that it must be long in the back. As you lean forward on the bike, it is very easy to find your clothing riding up and exposing the lumbar regions to chill winds.

Some pockets around the back are useful for a handkerchief, sunglasses or small change, but for carrying wallet, credit cards, passport and similar valuable items we prefer a belt pouch which can be slipped around to the back of the waist while riding and is quite safe.

Protection for the hands when riding is best obtained from mitts with padded palms, supplemented with fibre-pile mittens when cycling into a cold head-wind. A woollen balaclava for similar conditions, together with some form of eyeshade such as a light peaked cap, will complete this part of your wardrobe.

If you are normally riding in shorts, a pair of light trousers for wear in the evening may be useful. If you want to ride in them, the ankles can be held tight with bands of material secured with patches of Velcro – these are much more effective than metal trouser clips.

There remains the problem of what to do when it rains. The traditional cycle cape is really a nuisance, as it catches the wind and flaps about. Far better is a suit of jacket and trousers. The jacket should zip up the front, instead of being the sort that slips on over your head. It is easier to get on and off, and it is possible to regulate the ventilation. The sleeves should be capable of closing around the wrists to prevent rain from driving up the arms, and the jacket should be long enough to cover the thighs and to enable you to sit on it at the back. A short jacket can blow up and also can catch on the saddle when you are getting off the bike. A hood is mainly of use in camp, as, if worn when riding, it restricts rear vision and hearing when riding in traffic. To match the jacket, trousers must fasten around the ankles to keep them clear of the pedals or chain. A ventilated waistband is useful, and both jacket and trousers should be large enough to provide a loose fit over other clothes.

Protection for the head against rain is still best provided by a sou'wester, which is light and easily packed, allows ventilation and directs the rain away from your collar. Make sure it is secured by a tape or chinband against the wind.

A rain suit for cycling is best made of rather heavier material than those made for walking other than in really foul weather. This will prevent the garments from flattening themselves against you with increasing problems with condensation. Recently suits in the new moisture-permeable waterproofed materials have become available, in designs specially developed for cyclists, and these may solve some of the condensation problems.

Whatever outer clothing you wear, it must be realized that, in conditions of wind and rain, the cyclist can be subject to the same conditions which confront the hill walker and which can lead to chilling and exposure.

There seems very little that can be done to keep the feet dry in hard rain. Not only does the rain drive onto your legs and ankles and run down into your shoes, but your legs are also sprayed with water from the road, even when you have mud flaps. Canvas-topped cycle shoes will not matter as they will dry out, but leather shoes require dressing and will need careful drying out away from heat. Various types of spat or overshoe are available from cycle shops and may be the answer.

Although they are not really intended for riding in, we have found some very lightweight 'over-wellies' useful for wearing in camp, where there may be long grass. These will roll up very small for packing and are slipped on over your shoes. They are not intended for walking over rough stony ground but do help keep the feet warm and dry around the tent.

Carrying the kit

Practically all the normal lightweight equipment we use for backpacking can be used when cycle camping, with just one exception. That is, of course, the rucksack. A rider should *never, ever* carry a backpack. For a start, it will be uncomfortable when riding, tending to move and causing the back to sweat and perhaps become sore. Additionally, it will affect the balance and control of the machine, and if you hit bumps on rough roads, the resultant jarring of a heavy pack will not do your spine any good at all. So, the lesson is

– let the cycle carry everything.

There is a temptation to assume that by carrying things on a cycle it is possible to carry a lot more, in terms of weight and bulk. This should be resisted and the disciplines which you practise when backpacking, of keeping the total weight within reasonable limits, should be followed when awheel. Equally important is the question of packed size. You will still have to cope with a sleeping-bag and tent, with its associated poles.

The general idea to be followed when packing for cycle camping is to keep weight low for better stability – the opposite to when packing a rucksack – to distribute the load between the front and rear for equal balance, and to make sure everything is secured against vibration and shock.

For short trips of perhaps one night, and in the summer, it will not be necessary to use all the possible bags at the same time, but the following are available:

1. Rear panniers
2. Front panniers

Diagram 35

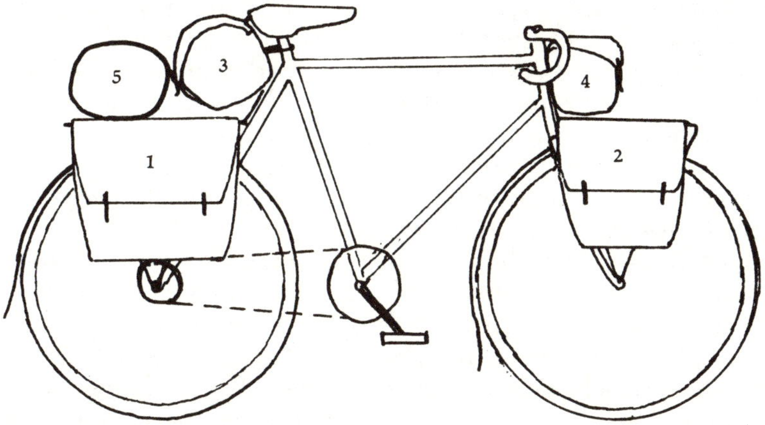

Possible ways of carrying kit on a bicycle

3. Saddle bag
4. Bar bag
5. Stuff-sack for rear carrier

Attaching the bags

When using rear and front panniers, it is necessary to have suitably designed carriers or frames mounted on the cycle to allow attachment of the pannier bags in a secure way, and to prevent the bags from swinging or interfering with the wheels when on the move.

Such carriers must be strong and light in weight. They must also be rigid when loaded and on the move. There must be arrangements for attaching and removing the loaded bags easily. The carriers must be capable of being fixed to the machine with absolutely no risk of their coming loose when loaded. There should also be provision for attaching the lights, front and rear, so that they are not obscured by the loaded bags.

For strength without undue weight, steel carriers are probably best. The steel can be nylon coated, which prevents rust. The rigidity will come mainly from the design of the carrier frame and its method of attachment to the bicycle.

Rear carriers should be attached at the top either by clips to the tops of the two rear stays or to the centre bolt of the rear brake assembly. The bottom of the carrier on each side is fixed either to the mudguard stay bolt or onto the wheel spindle. Some cycles have lugs brazed onto the frame to provide fixing points for the carrier. This is ideal but should be done during manufacture. Front carriers normally fix to the mudguard stay bolts or wheel spindles at the bottom and have a fitting to go onto the front brake bolt, between the brake assembly and the front fork crown.

Methods of attaching the pannier bags vary with different manufacturers, but it is worth checking that you can fix each bag separately, when loaded, by just lifting into position. Usually the top is hung onto the side rail of the carrier by hooks, which should be prevented from sliding in a fore-and-aft direction when riding. There must also be some means of preventing the bottom of the bag from swinging outwards, also from swinging in against the wheel. This attachment is often achieved using some form of elastic arrangement with a hook which engages with a suitable ring on the side of the carrier. Lamp brackets are positioned on the end of the carrier platform where the lamp will not be obscured by the load. Brackets on the side of the framework are not satisfactory.

A final point to check with both carriers is that it is possible to secure a bundle or bag on top by suitable straps or rubber shockcords with hooks.

Normally a saddlebag is carried by passing straps through rings on the back edge of the saddle, allowing the bag to hang down. Swinging is prevented by a strap around the seat pillar. With the larger type of bag used when touring, some additional support is necessary. This may take the form of an 'uplift' which is a metal support or frame, attached to the bag by the straps, and which then hooks into the saddle eyes or rings. A large bag may rest with its bottom on the top of the rear pannier carrier. One very effective type of rear carrier has a saddlebag support integral with the carrier in the form of an extension of the top frame which is curved up behind the saddle, and to the top of which the saddlebag suspension straps are fastened. This is much simpler than using a separate uplift. A front bag for fastening onto the handlebars can be attached by straps to the bars and by a strap to the handlebar stem to prevent swinging, or it can be attached to the bars by means of a special carrier which hooks onto the bars. Whatever method is used, the bag must be held clear of the brake mechanism.

Choosing cycle bags

So far we have dealt with the attachment of the various bags to the cycle. Requirements to be considered when choosing the bags are our next concern. It stands to reason that the material of which the bags are made should be waterproof and hard-wearing, much the same as for rucksacks. In fact cycle bags are made mainly from the same materials, canvas or coated or textured nylon. The same remarks apply regarding sealing of the seams and the stitching holes. When looking at the closing flaps of cycle bags, however, one must remember that they will be subjected to a lot of driving rain, upward splashes from the wheels and road, and wind accentuated by the movement of the cycle at speeds of perhaps up to 25 m.p.h. or more on downhill stretches. So it can be seen that inner closures with outer contoured flaps fastened with well-shielded zips are necessary.

Another point to look for in choosing cycle bags is whether they have leather reinforcing patches at points subject to abrasion from the carriers. On panniers, both front and rear, some means of stiffening should be provided inside the backs – that is, the sides which are against the cycle. This stiffening can be fixed in as part of the bag construction, or a pocket may be provided into which you can slide a piece of thin board or similar material.

Front panniers are often supplied as a pair, joined by a bridge of material which sits over the carrier. The pair of bags can be lifted off the bike and carried easily in this way. Rear panniers are preferably separate, although they are often provided with carrying-handles for use off the bike. Some types are provided with a means of linking them together to carry off the bike as a pair, although this may prove a little difficult with large, heavy bags. For this reason we do not favour the rear pannier sets which comprise two side panniers with an integral top bag which bridges the carrier, as apart from the difficulty in handling the loaded set off the cycle, it reduces flexibility in packing.

An important consideration with rear panniers, is clearance for your heels when riding. The bags need to be attached as far forward as possible on the carrier for good balance, but may then need to be shaped so they taper back away from the heels. Pockets can be fitted on the rear edge, also on the outside, and the same considerations of useful size apply as in the case of rucksack pockets. We like to keep stoves and fuel out of the main bag. Heel clearance is, of course, not a problem with front panniers so they can be made without the taper. Pockets may be provided, and it is possible to have dual-purpose panniers which may form front panniers or small rear panniers, depending on your requirements. An interesting and fairly new development is the so-called 'low-loading' idea in which front panniers are carried low down, level with the centre of the front wheel, instead of each side of a carrier fitted above the wheel. Tests have shown that this low position improves stability and bike handling.

Cycle saddlebags can be obtained in a variety of sizes, some of them having a double set of fastenings for the flap so that it may be used in a high or low position, with corresponding increase in capacity. Being high on the machine, the saddlebag should not be used for heavy items. Side pockets provide additional accommodation.

The front bar bag on the handlebars is a useful place to carry those 'odds and ends' you need *en route*, such as camera, cycle lock, maps etc. Often these bags have a transparent map case on top, either as part of the flap or detachable. This bag provides a convenient place for sunglasses, energy-giving sweets, in fact all those things which you would normally carry in the pockets of a walking jacket (or a lady's handbag). The top flap should open away from you so you can get at the contents when sitting on the saddle; this is also the best way to protect the contents from driving rain.

Finally, if you use a stuff-sack on the carrier, use one which is waterproof, has a well-shielded zip closure along its length and is fitted with loops through which securing straps can be threaded.

Packing your bags

The general principle is to pack heavy items as low and as near the centre of the machine as possible. Distribute the total load so that about two thirds is over the rear wheel and one third over the front, without too much weight in the bar bag. This is your handbag (or shoulder bag) when shopping or sightseeing.

Make sure everything is as secure as possible, with items in separate waterproof bags. Having said that, a few ideas on how individual items can be packed on the cycle may be useful. For a start, tools and spares are additional to your camp kit and should be packed so they can be reached without opening up the main bags with risk of getting things wet.

Saddlebag pockets are one possibility, and if you carry

spare spokes they may be taped along the rear stay or perhaps on the stiffening rod inside the saddlebag. Suitable bottles in bottle cages can carry water, soft drink or spare stove fuel. Additional water and the stove and similar items can be carried in the rear pockets of the rear panniers. The largest single item is likely to be your sleeping-bag, for which the saddlebag may be the best place. The tent and flysheet might be packed in a rear pannier, provided nothing else will get wet when they are removed.

One of the difficulties with cheaper tents is that the pole sections tend to be too long for convenient accommodation in the average cycle bag. If there is no other solution, make a long bag for the poles, with a secure fastener and loops for straps. The bag may then be strapped on top of the carrier or saddlebag without risk of loss on the road.

Arrange things so that items you may require during a break on your ride, or those needed first in camp, are easily reached. Spare clothes, bedding and similar items can be packed low down or packed together in one or more bags which need not be frequently opened. Remember to allow space for food which you may buy before reaching camp. Front pannier space is useful for this and for cooking-pans.

If you stop for sightseeing or shopping, always lock the machine securely to a fence or lamp-post, with a cable lock through both wheels and around the fixed object. Small or valuable items such as camera, travel documents, sunglasses, binoculars and so on should never be left on the bike. These are best carried in the bar bag, which is usually fitted with a shoulder sling. The whole bag can be removed simply and can be carried with you, even if you are leaving the bike for only a few minutes. Another thing which may perhaps be packed in this bag is a light pullover to slip on when you stop for a breather.

One final word on packing for cycle camping. Do check at frequent intervals that all straps and hooks are secure and that nothing is working loose.

On the road

The most important thing to remember is that you have a cycle which is loaded with additional weight in various places. When first starting off just take your time to adjust to the feel of it. Do not try any sudden manoeuvres until you are used to the new situation. There may be some slight shaking on the handlebars if the front load is rather heavy, but this will soon cease to be a problem.

Remember above all that you have much more rolling load to bring to a halt with your brakes. On the level this should cause little difficulty, but when running downhill you must take things very steadily. Never let the bike run away with you. Take control of the speed early on a descent by gentle application of the brakes. In fact, brakes should be applied gently at all times. Remember that the front brake is the most effective, as the weight is thrown forward when braking, increasing the grip of the front wheel. The back brake should be used to assist, and to steady the speed when running downhill. Too continuous and fierce brake application when travelling fast on a long downhill stretch can heat up the wheel rims and may overheat the tyres. So by gentle repeated application of both brakes, control the speed. When conditions are wet, it is advisable to apply the brakes sooner to dry off the rims.

The loaded bike will be more liable to spill when hitting pot-holes or bumps. Keep a good look-out ahead and take action accordingly. One very likely danger is a sharp bend on a hill with loose sand or gravel on the side. Try to cross such patches in a straight line.

Once you have got used to the feel of the loaded bike, you should practise the art of keeping a steady pedalling speed or cadence, aiming for a pedalling rate of around seventy to the minute, which means keeping the gear on the low side. Do not start off too fast, but allow your muscles to settle down. Then you will find you can keep going for a reasonable distance throughout the day. If you find your rate dropping, change to a lower gear. If a downhill stretch comes, and you find you cannot keep pressure on the pedals, do not coast, but change to a higher gear and keep pedalling. On a steep hill when your rate drops, get into your lowest gear and still keep the feet turning.

If you are not used to derailleur gears, the technique of changing will have to be mastered, but it is not difficult.

Remember that the pedals must continue to turn during the actual change, but pressure must be eased as the chain moves from one sprocket to the next. It follows that you cannot change effectively when climbing, so you must select your gear for the hill in good time, before speed drops. One of the best ways of judging when you have changed correctly is by listening. You will soon get to know the sound of the drive mechanism in different positions. Finally, always make a habit of changing down before you reach a junction or before stopping. You will then be in a low gear ready for starting.

So much for the actual riding. During the journey you will find you need to replenish lost energy and fluids, and this means carrying suitable energy-giving foods such as glucose sweets or chocolate in a handy place in the bar bag, together with drink (non-fizzy) in bottles held in cages on the down-tube of the frame. Plan your riding so that you travel about twenty miles, then stop for a short break. In this way you will be able to maintain a steady rate of pedalling without making the whole journey a marathon run.

Taking the bike on trains and ferries

Whilst on the subject of travelling, it is worth mentioning the arrangements whereby cycles can be taken on certain trains free of charge. This enables you to reach an area far from home and then enjoy riding for the maximum amount of time when you have got there. It is well to check beforehand that the route you wish to take on the train presents no problems. Certain routes are operated by high-speed trains which have no accommodation for bikes. Other routes are restricted to non-rush-hour times only. Apart from that, we have always found the railway staff very helpful. Have a length of strong cord handy to lash the machine to a convenient ring or other fixture in the luggage van to prevent it from falling over, but the bags can stay on – except, of course, your bar bag.

Sit near the van, and as soon as you reach your destination, if it is an intermediate stop, get out and leave the carriage door open until you are able to get the bike unloaded. Otherwise the train may leave with your bike still on board. There is usually some way off the platform and out of the station other than via stairs, even if it means walking across the tracks along the way made for luggage trollies.

If you go abroad by car ferry, you may be faced with a rather long ramp approaching the loading quay into the boat. The arrangements are, of course, planned for cars and lorries, but usually we have found the crew and loading personnel very friendly and helpful. Often bikes are allowed on and off first. The thing to do here, again, is to have a length of rope handy, and immediately you are on board, lean the bike carefully against the side of the car deck and loop the rope around the bike frame and tie securely to one of the many rings or other fixtures you are sure to find. When you ride off on the other side, watch for slippery, wet, oily metal ramps, and go carefully. If going to the Continent, remember to ride on the right. Watch for signs indicating cycle paths, which may be obligatory. If travelling abroad, having lamp brackets placed centrally on the front and rear carriers will avoid having to change lamps over to the other side.

Camp routine

Of course the technique of camping is basically the same whether you are backpacking or cycle camping. There is just the problem of what to do with the bike when you arrive.

The first trick is to have handy a length of strong line and two strong tent pegs. Attach the line at its centre to the seat pillar, and peg the ends down to the ground, one on each side. Then the bike will stand alone while you select the spot and pitch your tent. Then you can lift off all the bags and proceed to install and equip your temporary home for the night.

Depending on where you are, you may prefer to have the bike where you can see it from your tent door or to place it to one side so as not to spoil the view. Wherever you put it, peg it with the line, and pass your cable lock through both wheels and around and through the frame. Of course, if there is a convenient post or fence, lock it to that, provided you do not break down the fence. Take off the front battery lamp, as you will need it in the tent, and place a plastic bag or some other cover over the saddle, making sure it is secure against the wind. Before retiring to your sleeping-bag for the night, it may be as well to move the bike closer to the door of the tent for security, tether it again and lock it.

It is very pleasant to get up and on the road early in summer, which means an early night beforehand. In the morning, after breakfast, if you can air your sleeping-bag before packing, you can spend a few minutes checking over the bike, adjusting brakes if necessary, pumping tyres and so on. Then pack the bags, and down comes the tent. The bags can be lifted into position and secured, and the water-bottles filled. Then up come the pegs, the guyline is stowed and you are ready for the road again.

Tandems

Many couples use tandems for touring, and this seems an ideal way of travelling. However, the main problem is that two people's clothing and camp kit are being carried on one machine. Similar situations arise when a family is travelling on solo or tandem bikes with a child on a child's seat, as it will limit the possibilities for fitting panniers. In these situations it may be worth considering the use of a bike trailer, of which there are several on the market. Most of these are intended for shopping and round-town use. Their wheels are too small and the wheel bearing is inadequate for lengthy runs with loads along possibly rough roads. However, a trailer with cycle wheels running on pneumatic tyres is a definite possibility. The main danger would seem to be overloading. Bike handling will need to be practised, and security of the load must be studied. By security we mean both safety and freedom from theft.

10 Other Ways of Travelling

We have already looked in some detail at travelling on foot and by bicycle while camping. Advice for those travelling on foot includes some for those who go by public transport for most of the way.

We now consider some other vehicles which could be used to help you use your lightweight kit to full advantage.

Car camping

The picture which comes into most people's minds when thinking of car camping is a large frame tent with all the accompanying paraphernalia of tables, chairs and kitchen equipment. The effort involved tends to limit its use to the annual holiday, which always seems to us to be a terrible waste. The lightweight camper with a car can go off at any time of the year, at a moment's notice, and be pitched and enjoying a meal within half an hour of arriving at his destination.

With the car, there is a definite advantage in developing your own standard way of stowing everything so that it is all readily available when needed. There are obvious benefits in being able to carry everything a short distance from the car without dropping bundles and bags all over the site, and without getting it all soaking wet. For example, the car may be left on hard standing while the tent is pitched in a more suitable spot where the ground is not cut up by wheel ruts. At the same time, there is no bother from exhaust fumes blowing into the tent or any risk of cars damaging small tents after dark.

Camping light with a car gives a degree of freedom not known to people using heavier equipment, but at the same time it is possible to carry some of those extra items which are impossible for the walker or cyclist to take. The most obvious of these is a toilet tent and a chemical toilet, the possession of which is necessary when using many small campsites and is regrettably becoming an essential requirement for attendance at many club-organized rallies. Such a piece of equipment does widen the possibilities of camping when touring.

If the temptation to carry too much gear is resisted, touring over long distances by car becomes a pleasure as pitching and striking camp with lightweight equipment is so much easier. An extension of the activity into winter brings with it the realization that, with the right gear, sleeping in a small tent can be so much warmer and more comfortable than with a larger one. Additional luxuries such as pressure or gas lamps are easily carried, and these will be very welcome during the longer dark evenings. Even so, it should rarely be necessary to use a roof rack, and this in turn will help your petrol consumption.

Motor-cycle camping

In many ways, motor-cycle camping can be seen to combine the best of both worlds – that of the backpacker and that of the car camper. The equipment used for camping will be small and lightweight, but the ability to travel far and fast for very low cost gives a bonus over the car-driver. On the one hand there are those who tour in a leisurely way along minor roads and through scenic country, camping as they go, whilst at the other extreme are the long-distance tourers who travel fast with just a tent and the minimum of camping equipment, often eating in cafés.

It must be said here that all motor cyclists suffer from the fact that often commercial campsites automatically ban them without any consideration for the individuals concerned. The image of a noisy, ill-behaved group of riders wearing 'way-out' clothing is unfortunately prevalent, and it is very unfair to the perfectly ordinary, well-conducted people who happen to travel on motor cycles. Leather outer clothing, worn as an essential means of protection in the event of a spill, has no bearing on the behaviour of the individual. We hope that by quiet persistence, backed by membership of a responsible camping club, this prejudice against motorcycles among site-owners will be overcome.

The matter of clothing for the motorcyclist on tour requires understanding of the conditions involved. In addition to the leather clothing already mentioned, good stout boots are essential for protection of the feet, ankles and lower legs. However, leather clothing is very expensive and does not give much protection against driving rain. When you are riding into the wind, you can be subjected to water hitting you at speeds of up to a hundred miles an hour. Add to that the chilling effect of the wind, and you could be in real trouble. Coated nylon protective clothing which is suitable for other activities often proves unsatisfactory in these conditions, eventually leaking at the seams. The most satisfactory clothing for motor cycling is still waxed cotton, specially designed for the purpose. Even so, it has its disadvantages. It requires reproofing regularly and picks up a lot of dirt on its slightly tacky surface. A tent of the transverse ridge type, or one with an extended flysheet, is recommended for motor-cycle camping. There will be a rather large bulk of riding clothing to be stowed safely at night, which may also be very wet, so it is essential to keep it clear of any bedding.

A selection of tools and spares should be carried, including spare sparking plugs, contact points and light bulbs, and perhaps a spare clutch cable which can be taped alongside the one already fitted. If using tubeless tyres, an aerosol tyre-inflator will get you to somewhere where a more permanent repair can be made.

The motor-cycle camper is faced with the problem that the best place for carrying a load is low down and just forward of the centre-point between the wheels, which is where the engine is located!

Top boxes and box panniers, or alternatively soft panniers, are available for carrying equipment on a motor cycle. The top box is mounted on the rear carrier, where it is too high to be heavily loaded without adversely affecting stability. Many are too small to hold bulky items such as sleeping-bags. Box panniers may cause difficulties as they cannot conform to hard objects, while soft panniers often have inadequate weather protection.

An additional means of carrying gear is the tank-top bag which fits on top of the petrol tank, in front of the rider. It provides an ideal place for stowing those varied items you may need on the journey, rather like an enlarged version of the cyclist's bar bag. Unlike the bar bag, however, the tank bag is usually too big to take off and carry on a shoulder sling. It can, nevertheless, incorporate a handy map-case on its top.

A windshield and leg-shields can provide further stowage if they have small fittings or containers attached for easily accessible items. The pillion seat may be used to strap on a stuff-sack or tent bag, always provided that you are not carrying a passenger. If you are, you have the additional problem of stowing another person's kit, but again, modern lightweight equipment makes this much easier. Also, do make a habit of checking fixings at every stop because of the vibration when travelling at normal motor-cycle speeds.

One additional way of carrying some of your gear is in a rucksack. This need not cause any discomfort or loss of balance provided that it is not too heavy, and it should be close-fitting without external frame.

At the time of writing, legislation is being introduced to allow the use of a trailer behind a solo motor cycle. This must be used solely for luggage, and not for the carriage of passengers, and will bring the United Kingdom into line with other European countries, where such trailers are already permitted.

For those who do not fancy a more powerful machine, there is a lot of enjoyment to be obtained from riding one of the lightweight 'step-through' machines. Quiet and economical, some are capable of speeds averaging around 40 m.p.h. quite comfortably. With careful packing and selection of kit, the top box and a pair of throw-over panniers secured to the rear carrier or pillion seat will carry all that is needed.

Camping with a moped

We are never too sure whether a moped is a cycle or a motor

bike. This difficulty becomes more apparent when one studies the fare scales for travelling by cross-Channel ferry! Some charge them as motor cycles, some as bicycles and some as scooters. However, be that as it may, a moped provides a very handy way of travelling around the country, especially when you have found that, although the spirit may be willing, the legs or other parts of one's anatomy are no longer quite so favourably disposed to riding a pedal cycle! There are some very efficient machines on the market with normal wheels and step-through design, and these are preferable to the small wheeled models. Some machines have front carriers with baskets, intended for shopping. These are ideal for carrying some of your camping kit, balanced by panniers on the rear carrier. Large cycle panniers can usually be fitted quite well, with space still available on top of the carrier. One point to watch for is that some models of moped have the fuel tank under the rear carrier, making it difficult to get at the filler cap with kit on board. The mopeds we use have the tank incorporated into the frame behind the steering column, so there is no problem. Protection from the weather can be obtained by fitting a windscreen and leg-shields. These will add to the wind resistance, but they are probably worth considering for winter riding and can also provide support for a small pouch for odds and ends, or for holding a map.

Finding somewhere to dispose of the helmet can be a problem when shopping or sightseeing. If a top box is attached to the rear carrier, a shoulder bag can be carried in it. When removed, the helmet can be stowed in its place and locked safely away until needed again.

Normal good-quality waterproof clothing such as that used for walking or sailing can be worn. Jacket-and-trouser combinations are fine provided that adequate protection is given to the lower back. Gloves can be supplemented with waterproof over-gloves, and stout shoes or short rubber boots will give protection to the feet and ankles. It is surprising how cold the wind can be even on a warm day, once you are on the road, so have pullovers and similar garments available to put on if necessary.

One interesting problem of logistics arises with the use of

a moped for touring. The machine uses two-stroke mix, which is two-star petrol with added oil. In the United Kingdom today, very few garages seem to supply this already mixed. The only alternative is to mix it in the tank, and you may find it necessary to carry a supply of the correct oil. There is no fuel gauge on the machine, so it is essential to have a fairly accurate knowledge of the fuel consumption in terms of miles per tank-full, allowing for the reserve supply. Then, by keeping an eye on the mileage covered, you can judge when you are likely to need topping up. Since most filling stations sell petrol in quantities of not less than half a gallon, and the main tank is about that capacity, it all becomes quite an exercise. Apart from carrying a small plastic container holding sufficient oil for one refill for each bike, we have found it possible to carry a spare half-tank-full of petroil mix in a screw-top metal fuel bottle, obtainable from camping retailers. One or more of these can be held in clips or cycle bottle cages in convenient places on the machine and will provide the necessary reserve for emergencies. With our machines, we can travel fifty miles with another ten miles reserve before having to refuel. The average speed we can achieve is about twenty miles an hour in hilly country with camping kit.

If you are travelling on the Continent, the refuelling business is simpler as mopeds are more common, and the filling stations generally have two-stroke mix 'on tap'. One last little practical tip relates to parking the machines. The folding stands are very likely to sink into soft ground, so carry a small piece of flat board to place under the legs to prevent this.

Camping afloat

With rivers, canals, lakes and seashore, there is plenty of scope for camping and using kayaks, Canadian canoes, dinghies or small half-decked boats, either power or sail. Unless you are already competent in handling the type of craft you intend to use, it is best to go with an experienced companion or join a club. Safety afloat must be of prime concern.

The main consideration as regards your choice of kit and

its transportation must be damp. Synthetic sleeping-bags are preferable, and everything must be packed so that it can withstand complete immersion. Stout waterproof bags with secure fastenings, and plastic containers with screw-on or clip-on covers are recommended and should be of convenient sizes for stowing and for carrying ashore. Heavy items should be packed near the centre line of the craft, and everything must be secured against movement, especially in the event of a capsize. The cockpit of a kayak or the crew space in a dinghy must be kept clear of obstructions. When stowing kit in the ends of a kayak below the deck, leave cords attached to the necks of the bags to make it easy to pull them out.

Ski touring

The possibility of combining lightweight camping with cross-country skiing has been mentioned in Chapter 7. Travelling cross-country on skis, off the beaten track, has been likened to backpacking in the snow, and this analogy is dangerous. Before attempting it, a backpacker must have experience of winter walking and camping in the snow. After that, it is essential to learn and become reasonably proficient in the techniques of cross-country (XC) or Nordic skiing. This is not something to be learned from books, and it is not true to say, 'If you can walk, you can cross-country ski.'

Our advice is, if you are reasonably fit, join one of the courses available in XC skiing, where you can borrow the necessary equipment and get good instruction in the techniques. If you find you are getting on all right, then consider buying your own gear, but do take expert advice on this.

Ski-touring can be a very rewarding experience, but never underestimate the effects of the winter environment, and never over-estimate your own ability. Finally, never consider going alone.

Touring on horseback

The opportunities for this as an extension of lightweight camping may be rather limited in this country. It is unlikely that you will be able to purchase suitable panniers, and you will probably have to make your own. However, for anyone who has a horse and really likes the idea of combining riding and camping it would be a challenge; do not let the fact that no one else seems to do it put you off!

11 Going With the Family

Do not assume that lightweight camping is impractical with small children or babies. Travelling with a car presents few problems, but even without mechanized transport back-packing or cycle camping can be very enjoyable with a young family. Obviously it is essential that you yourselves become practised at the art before considering taking the children, especially if they are very small.

Equipment

Make no mistake about it, a small baby's requirements, especially in the shape of disposable nappies, take up a great deal of room. Both you and your partner will need rucksacks with a larger-than-average capacity, as of course it will be you who has to carry all the baby's kit. This consideration apart, your tent will have to be large enough to accommodate baby as well as yourselves, and be roomy enough to sit in and deal with his daily routine. If you are starting off with more than one child, you may find it more useful to carry two small lightweight tents so that each parent sleeps with one child. As they grow older, the children can share one tent, and the parents the other.

We believe that the best type for family use is the transverse ridge. With its two entrances, it gives plenty of storage space outside the sleeping area and allows one side to be used for access while the other side is kept as the 'kitchen', thus making a contribution to safety. There are some family-sized dome tents available, which, due to their spacious interiors, are ideal. Some of these also have double entrances, which is even better.

Sleeping-equipment for a very small baby can at first

appear to be a problem. A very tiny one can sleep in a carry-cot but if your tent is rather small, this may well take up too much room, so you will have to think of other 'beds' to try. Probably the easiest to use is a 'baby-nest', obtainable from most baby-care shops and departments. This can be laid on a small piece of closed cell foam, and extra cellular blankets can be used on top if necessary. Baby-nests, unfortunately, are suitable only for the very young, so if your child is too large to use one, try making your own, using ready-quilted fabric. If you sew a zip either side, you can unzip the nest, wrap baby in plenty of warm things and close the zips so that he cannot crawl out.

Another idea is to use a one-piece sleeping-suit, with a thick one-piece pram suit over the top. Baby can then be wrapped in a light cellular blanket, and if he crawls out, he should then still be warm enough.

Children's sleeping-bags are available, some of which are made in a mummy style with a hood – just like mum's or dad's. Some are quite expensive and may not be worthwhile unless there is likely to be another child to whom it can be passed on. Do not buy a special junior bag for an older child, but get a full-size bag and tie a piece of tape around the bag below the feet once the child is in bed, to prevent him slipping down to the bottom.

Make sure that the child has good waterproofs and good footwear. Sturdy shoes are fine if the going is reasonably easy, but if the ground you will be walking over is at all rough, boots will be needed. In the last ten years, manufacturers have realized the importance of children's outdoor clothing and footwear, and it is now reasonably easy to buy specialist items in children's sizes. All children should be kitted out with warm hats and gloves. This is particularly important when they are being 'pushed' or carried. If a toddler has a tendency to kick off his shoes when in the pushchair, try pulling on an old pair of socks over the top. A child who is at the crawling stage will need protective clothing to keep him clean and dry, and a one-piece waterproof suit is ideal for this purpose.

If you are backpacking with a young child, remember that *you* will have to decide when to take off clothing for him and when to put it on, so that he does not become overheated or chilled. Waterproof jackets are much easier to put on than the pullover type of cagoule, and are easier to ventilate. Remember too that small children cannot stand up to cold as much as you can; they can also be full of energy one minute and exhausted the next.

Transport for children

One of the best items of nursery equipment to emerge in the last few years has been the 'buggy'-type pushchair. It is possible to buy a 'pram-buggy', consisting of a carry-cot which sits on a specially made folding frame. This can be used once the 'pram' is outgrown as the base for a lie-back pushchair seat. Once the baby is over six months old, you should be able to manage with the pushchair alone. You might also consider carrying a baby in a 'Papoose' seat on your back, and carrying your equipment in a shopping trolley. These will, of course, be useful to you only if you are backpacking.

Cycle campers have more of a problem. Many years ago it was quite common to see family cyclists on the road with miniature sidecars attached to the cycles. Unfortunately it no longer seems possible to buy them, although it is possible to obtain a suitable chassis on which to build one. Some are fixed to the cycle at more than one point, whilst others are simply a 'trailer' which can be fixed to the side of the cycle. A small sidecar can carry not only the baby but quite a bit of luggage as well.

From around the age of two years, a child may be carried on a proper seat on the rear of the cycle. In these circumstances, a luggage trailer will be found to be particularly useful for carrying the camping kit. However, from about the age of five, a child is too big to carry in this manner, yet is not old enough to cycle independently on the road. Specialist cycle-dealers will be able to advise on the purchase of a tandem with a child back. There are also special trailers which can be coupled behind a cycle or tandem for a child of such age to ride. These are often much sought-after by cycling families. Look in the advertising pages of cycling magazines, or advertise your wants in the 'small ads' page. It is also possible to buy an adult tricycle complete with a double child seat behind the saddle, and a luggage tray over the axle. You may consider it worthwhile to fit a child with a cyclist's crash helmet. There are mixed views on these, but a child on the back of a cycle is very vulnerable, and if he falls off, he could suffer severe damage to the head. It is really sensible to consider such a helmet if you plan to ride with your child on the back.

Whatever method of transport you use, do use a safety harness for a baby, as you would in your ordinary pram at home. Once baby gets to the crawling and toddling stage, you can attach a length of guyline to the harness and allow him freedom to move around in camp by pegging the line to the ground so that he is away from the stove and anything else which might harm him.

Carrying their own kit

Once children get to the age of about three, if you are a backpacking family you will normally have to start them walking. Obviously you will have to cut down your daily distances, but if you plan things carefully, this need be no hardship. Give your child a small 'Diddypack' and let him carry his personal clothing and favourite small cuddly toy. He should also carry one or two light items of the family food, such as packet soups etc. We feel it is very important for children to learn to carry their share of the kit. As he gets older, the child will be able to carry his own sleeping-bag, and perhaps a storybook in addition to his clothes. Later still, you will need to get a rucksack into which he can pack all his own kit, remembering that he should not carry more than one quarter of his body weight. It must fit properly, and it is advisable to choose one with some adjustability whilst he is still growing. The external frame and separate pack is the best type to choose at this stage.

Food

So long as you make the food interesting, children will be quite happy. We never had any problems with our two. If you are planning to use dehydrated food, try it out at home first, to make sure the child can eat it. A small baby, if breast-fed, presents no problems, but if you have to deal with bottles, that is a different story. A plastic box, with a lid, large enough to contain two bottles, should be taken, and sterilizing tablets are easy to use. A plastic jug for mixing feeds in and a small thermos flask to keep hot water will be useful. Children need plenty of water to drink, and it is a good idea to let them carry their own personal supply. They should be taught not to have long draughts but to drink little and often.

As soon as you feel they are old enough, get them to take a practical interest in preparing the food. Even simple tasks such as making a fruit drink from powder and water make a child feel he is doing something important, and it is a good start to learning how to look after himself. We taught our two children to cook simple meals for themselves at a very early age, under proper supervision, of course, and by the time they reached the age of eleven, they were very competent at preparing their own food.

Many people consider that the 'Trangia'-type methylated spirit cooker is ideal for children to use. We, however, have our reservations, as it is very difficult to control the flames, and if accidentally overfilled it can constitute a real hazard. This being the case, of the types of stove currently available, the easiest to use are probably simple gas stoves with resealable cartridges. Whichever stove is used, the safety precautions outlined in Chapter 4 must be followed.

Helping in camp

Whether you are walking, 'static' or cycling, do give children some time to play each day. You will have had to cut down on your own distances covered, but remember children tire easily and need to rest. Do not allow them to become so tired that they have no time to enjoy themselves. Part of the fun should be to help setting up camp. Let a small child hold the tent pegs and pass them to you as required. An older child will very quickly learn how the tent should be pitched and will soon be asking for his own! Let him be responsible for laying out his own bedding and keeping his clothes tidy. All these little things will help him to become a good camper.

Canoe camping with children

If you have older children, you may like to consider taking them camping in a canoe or small boat. Provided that you yourselves are experienced at handling the craft, there is no reason why children should not enjoy this way of camping to the full. Obviously you will see to it that they are properly equipped with the correct size of life-jacket, and you will have given them the opportunity to get used to travelling in such craft before committing them to a long journey with camping involved. Make sure that you have sufficient dry clothing for them in the event of a 'ducking', and they will be fine. Teach them as soon as possible to take their share in the handling of the craft, and before long you will find the whole family dedicated converts to canoe-camping – or small boat camping, as the case may be.

Camping techniques with small children are much the same, whatever the mode of travel. From our experiences, we know that it is worthwhile taking children lightweight camping from a very young age. When we started, equipment was nowhere near as light or as sophisticated as it is today. We had no car but went by bus and then walked to a campsite. On the first occasion it poured with rain for most of the time we were away, yet, when it came to packing up, the reaction of our eldest daughter was, 'Daddy, do we *have* to go home?' They were well and truly 'hooked'.

12 Looking at the Weather

The lightweight camper, for a number of reasons, should be able to interpret and anticipate weather changes. For anyone contemplating walking or camping in the hills, such ability can mean the difference between an enjoyable day out and a disaster.

British weather is known to be unpredictable. Nevertheless, there are definite signs which can help the camper to make a reasonably accurate forecast. If you do not carry a radio there are other means of finding out what is in store for the day.

Many of the well-known 'weather jingles' will give a reasonable assessment of the weather to come.

Fine before seven, rain before eleven.

Red sky in the morning,
Shepherd's warning.
Red sky at night,
Shepherd's delight.

When the dew is on the grass,
Rain will never come to pass.
When grass is dry at morning light,
Look for rain before the night.

When you see a mackerel sky,
Not long wet, but not long dry.

Ring round the moon?
Rain will come soon.

Come the wind before the rain,
Be ready to make sail again

Come the rain before the wind,
Then your sheets and halyards mind.

(And your guylines!)

Wind directions

A closer look at the sky, and a study of the wind direction, will give you a more accurate forecast. Get into the habit of observing the weather every day, so that you can anticipate what is in store. Air, which is warmed or cooled by coming into contact with the earth's surface, brings our weather to us. Cold air *sinks* and sheds moisture; warm air *rises* and carries the moisture with it.

The direction from which the wind is coming will determine to some extent the weather it brings, but unfortunately this alone cannot tell us what the weather will be. Other factors, such as hills, mountains and coastal areas will have a direct bearing on the weather. For example, as the moisture-laden air from the sea reaches mountain areas, it has to rise. As it does so, it cools rapidly, forming clouds which eventually shed their moisture as rain, mostly on the windward side of the hills. The sheltered side will remain drier and warmer. On the coast, particularly in summer there will be cooling breezes off the sea. This occurs when the morning sun warms the earth, which in turn warms the air above it, causing it to rise quickly and leaving a vacuum which has to be filled. Cool air comes in off the sea to fill the space, causing the 'sea breeze'. This has the effect of altering the wind speed and the wind direction in such areas. The above factors can cause quite marked local variations in the weather, sometimes within the space of only a few miles.

Whatever the weather in the valley, you must be prepared for wind on the hills.

Watch out for changes in wind direction.

A veering wind, fair weather.
A backing wind, foul weather.

A veering wind is one which changes in a clockwise direction. This happens as the 'front' bringing the rain passes by. The wind 'backs', or changes in an anti-clockwise direction, ahead of the fronts which bring the rain.

Temperatures

Temperatures are an aspect of weather that must not be forgotten. Extremes of temperature must always be taken into account. If you listen to a weather forecast, the expected true air temperatures for the day are given. The air temperature will fall by 3°C for every 1,000 feet in height. Therefore the temperature at sea level could be 15°C (59°F) which would be a comfortable temperature for walking. However, climb to 1,000 feet and you will find the air temperature to be 12°C or 54°F. Up yet another 1,000 to reach 2,000 feet and the air temperature will drop to 9°C (48°F). This in itself can be decidedly chilly. Not only do you have to contend with these drops in temperature: the true air temperature is the shade temperature taken in *still air*. The higher you climb, the stronger the wind, and this has an additional cooling effect on the body. The combined cooling effect of air temperature and wind speed is known as 'wind chill'. So, with a 'fresh breeze' blowing (around 20 m.p.h.) at 2,000 feet, as in the example above, the equivalent temperature will become 0°C. In other words: freezing-point.

Clouds

Clouds are formed of water vapour and can tell you a great deal about the weather to come.

Cumulus clouds can be likened to a pile of cotton wool with a flat base. The small-sized ones which drift slowly across the sky often promise fine weather. The bigger ones, on the other hand, foretell sudden heavy showers and fair periods. Cumulo-nimbus clouds are bigger, much darker, and often develop into huge, towering clouds which may flatten out at the top into an 'anvil' shape. These are the thunder clouds, bringing heavy rain or hail, lightning and strong, gusty winds.

Cirrus clouds are very high clouds, composed of ice crystals rather than water droplets. They are the very 'wispy' clouds, resembling feathers, and are often present during spells of fine weather. When these clouds first appear approaching from the south-west, they are often an early warning forecast of rain to come.

Cirro-cumulus clouds are sometimes referred to as a 'mackerel sky'. They indicate that the fine weather will shortly change to unsettled, rainy weather – but it will not last long.

Cirro-stratus cloud is a thin, *white*, veil-like cloud. It is this 'veil' which gives rise to the 'ring round the moon', so watch out for rain.

Stratus clouds look rather like fog off the ground. They are very low clouds, producing drizzle and hill fog. Low stratus cloud forming overnight into early morning mist *in the valleys* means a fine day. Mist *on the hilltops* signifies a deterioration in the weather.

Alto-stratus clouds are like a *grey* veil, not so high in the sky as cirro-stratus clouds. The sun or moon will shine through them to look like a watery disc, and is a warning of wet weather to come.

Nature's forecasters

What else can you look at to help you forecast the weather? Look at nature itself. Animals and birds react very quickly to changes in the weather, and they seem to be able to tell what changes are in the offing. Sheep will always feed on the windward side of a hill, so if you see them moving round to the other side, you can be certain of a change in the weather. Cows are more troubled by stinging insects just before rain, so if you see them flicking their tails hard against their sides, rain is on the way. Rooks feeding near their rookeries means wet and windy weather. Gulls inland often mean rough weather on the coast, and swallows flying high in the sky mean fine weather. Swallows dipping very low mean rain in the offing. Often, before a storm, the birds will become uncannily quiet.

Trees in exposed areas lean away from the prevailing wind, so you will be able to tell at a glance from which direction the wind normally blows.

Local variations and advice

Local weather patterns can change very rapidly, so it is essential that you are able to obtain reliable local advice. If you have a radio, there are regular weather reports broadcast by local radio stations. The wavelengths are usually to be found in local newspapers, together with the times of transmission. You can also obtain up-to-date information from the local police or mountain rescue posts, as well as trying the local outdoor shop. Someone locally is bound to be able to advise you on the weather. Do, please, listen to what they have to say. If they advise you to keep off the hills, do so.

If you plan properly beforehand, you can find out much information to help you when you arrive. For instance, on all Ordnance Survey *Routemaster* maps, information is printed which can be copied down and taken with you. It lists all the local radio stations in the area, together with their wavelengths. Telephone numbers are also listed for detailed weather forecasts for local areas. The Meteorological Office also publishes a very useful booklet detailing weather advice.

13 Health, Hygiene and Emergencies

In this chapter we are dealing with subjects which, regrettably, are all too often ignored or 'skimmed over'. There are, however, some problems of which you should be aware, which specifically relate to living out of doors.

The element of risk is a fundamental theme running through all outdoor activities, so be prepared to help yourself if your luck runs out whilst you are out in the country, and do learn a few simple and basic ideas of first aid and how to cope with emergencies.

In any situation involving injury, the immediate priorities, before anything else, are to restart and maintain the patient's breathing, to control any bleeding and to deal correctly with any loss of consciousness. After that, what you do will depend on your knowledge as a first-aider, but the urgent need is to prevent any further risk to the patient. You may never find yourself in such a situation, but remember that even a small graze or scratch, or a minor burn caused by touching a hot pan, can spoil your own enjoyment.

If you wear the right clothing and eat properly, do not over-exert yourself and get into dry clothes after you have had a soaking, you are likely to have no problems of illness unless you are very unlucky. Minor upsets may occur, and you ought to know how to deal with them.

The elements

Sun

One of the problems which sometimes occurs is the effect of too much sun.

In very hot weather, make sure the body is kept well ventilated by wearing sufficient loose clothing. Do not walk or cycle with your shoulders bared to the sun, even if you have used some protective cream. A cotton scarf should be worn to protect the back of the neck, and a sun-hat helps to shade the eyes. A loose-fitting, long-sleeved, cotton cheesecloth shirt will be more comfortable than a T-shirt with short sleeves. It can be worn loose over the top of the waistband of a pair of cotton trousers or shorts.

Your body will lose its fluid much more quickly in hot weather, and it will be necessary to replace this fluid. It used to be thought that salt needed replacing as well, but it is now recognized that too much salt can be harmful. You should aim to drink little and often, rather than taking great draughts now and again. Do not drink quantities of very cold water, and do not drink from streams. Drink extra fluids before setting out on your travels, and when you stop again at night. When you stop for a rest or a meal break, have a drink, even if only a small one. Remember to drink *slowly* in hot weather.

Those with sensitive skins should always be prepared for sun. Take a large tube of protective cream, preferably with an ultra-violet inhibiting factor. Such preparations are expensive, but if you do possess very sensitive skin your doctor may be able to prescribe them. Frequent application to exposed skin is necessary, not forgetting the backs of the hands. Sun-rash, caused by too much ultra-violet light, can be uncomfortable. If you are unfortunate enough to suffer from this, simple calamine lotion will relieve the irritation.

Remember that, particularly in the summer months, the sun's rays will penetrate even through a cloudy sky. If you are up in the hills or on the water, the risk of sunburn is greater. Sunburn itself affects the sweat glands, preventing their proper function. As a result, further complications can arise. Apart from wearing loose covering clothing, try to stay in the shade as much as possible. If you can take a 'dip' in the sea or in a stream, this will help the body to cool off, but remember afterwards to re-apply your protective cream.

If you do become burnt, treat the burn by gently pouring cold water over the affected area. If the burning is serious, or if a child becomes burned, it is essential to get medical help.

Sometimes too much heat causes tiredness and giddiness.

The remedy is to rest for a period, in the shade, and to drink more fluids. A drink with a fairly high glucose content may help overcome any nausea.

'Prickly heat', which is caused by profuse sweating and can be most uncomfortable consists of a rash of minute blisters and can be relieved by bathing with a weak solution of bicarbonate of soda in water.

Heat exhaustion (due to lack of sufficient water intake) and heat stroke (caused by the failure of the heat regulating system of the body) are not very common in the United Kingdom. Early symptoms of the former include thirst, tiredness and giddiness, a rapid pulse and a high body temperature. The immediate remedy is to try to replace as much body fluid as possible by giving lots to drink. If the sufferer has a very high temperature, with hot, dry skin and no sign of sweating, he is more likely to be suffering from heat stroke. He may also be aggressive and irrational in the early stages. The body should be sponged down with water or covered with wet towels. Vigorous fanning may help the cooling process. In both cases, it is essential to get medical help.

During hot weather, it helps to reduce your intake of protein, but do not reduce your *food* intake too much. It is better to increase the carbohydrates a little.

If you suffer from the effects of glare from strong sun, wear good quality sunglasses or a good eye-shade: cheap ones can be harmful to the eyes. It is better to give young children an eye-shade, and small babies will be better with a proper sun-bonnet, tied on so that it cannot be pulled off.

Wind

The effect of strong winds can be quite severe at any time of the year. If you are high on the hills, or even on the downs, strong winds can cause windburn. The face should be protected with a specially formulated cream, and lip salve or lipstick should be applied to the mouth so that the lips do not become cracked and sore. Hands and ears should be kept covered.

Cold

It is far easier to insulate against loss of heat to keep warm than it is to keep cool in hot weather. The 'layering' principles described in Chapter 5 should be adhered to. If you have never encountered really cold conditions outdoors, you may not expect the difficulties presented by handling cold metal objects such as cooking-pans and stoves during lighting up, so be prepared. Clumsiness when handling such things in the cold can lead to accidents.

Wet weather

Wet weather is a nuisance, although when the weather is warm, a shower can be very refreshing. With suitable waterproof clothing you should be able to stay dry and comfortable. An accidental soaking, however, should be dealt with quickly to avoid chilling. Dry yourself off really thoroughly as soon as you can get into your tent. Change into dry clothes and have a hot drink.

Wind plus cold plus wet

The effects of all these three can lead to exposure. And make no mistake about it, you do *not* have to go into the hills to get such conditions. Never be afraid to pull out in such a situation if the need arises and the opportunity is there. If however you do have problems and have to deal with them in the hills, you should know what to do. In a case of exposure there are a number of signs to look out for, but not all may be present.

Unexpected and uncharacteristic behaviour, often accompanied by complaints of tiredness and cold may be noticed. The person may become lethargic and not understand directions or respond to questioning. He may have problems with vision, slurred speech or outbursts of unexpected energy, and may violently resist assistance or use bad language. The victim may suffer from cramp and stumble about. If any of these signs occur, it is vital to stop and act promptly. It is essential to prevent further heat loss from the body by insulating it, and to use every possible means of maintaining and improving the heat balance of the victim. If possible, get his wet clothes off and dry him. Do not rub the limbs, but put him into a sleeping-bag with a fit companion beside him to give extra body warmth. Do not apply any artificial heat. Get some insulation under him, and if it is not possible to erect a tent, put him into a survival bag. If a tent can be erected, get the rest of the party inside to provide warmth, but make sure there is good ventilation. If the party is small, one person should stay with the casualty whilst the other goes for help. Always ensure that this person carries a written message with full details of what has happened and where; he may arrive at a farm or village too exhausted to explain properly.

Whilst help is being fetched, the patient should be given glucose, condensed milk or sugar and a warm drink as soon as possible. Never give alcohol. After such treatment it is possible that he may recover sufficiently to believe himself quite fit. It is most important, however, that he remains where he is until a rescue party arrives with a stretcher. If you cannot fetch help, you will need to signal for it. The international mountain distress signal consists of six blasts on a whistle or six flashes from a torch, followed by a minute's pause, then repeated. Keep it up, and, if you are heard or seen, you will eventually receive an answering signal of three blasts or flashes followed by a pause of one minute, then repeated.

It may seem strange to you that we have dealt in such detail with health hazards which are the result of weather conditions. As a lightweight camper, however, you will certainly be subject to all kinds of weather, and you might as well know what can happen! At least if there are any signs of the above problems occurring, you will be prepared.

Internal upsets

Perhaps the most common problem for the lightweight camper is some kind of minor internal upset. This may be caused by a much-reduced fluid intake, particularly in the case of backpackers who have to carry the bulk of their supply, or a change in the water. Often the result is a certain amount of constipation, and this has to be dealt with or you will find yourself becoming increasingly uncomfortable. Increase your fluid intake and try to include some fruit juice – this can be obtained in powdered form so is easy to carry. The old Boy Scout idea of prunes is a good one. Try chewing them as you walk if you do not want to soak them and cook them, but don't ignore other dried fruits such as dates, raisins, sultanas and apricots. If you are having to use a lot of dehydrated foods, try to avoid it turning into so much 'stodge'. Add extra dried fruit to a curry, and drink several cups of tea or coffee with your meals. If necessary, take a mild laxative to relieve your problem.

Indigestion is something else that can occur with a radical change in diet. It helps to have some antacid tablets in your first-aid kit – of which more later – but try to carry the brand you know suits you personally. Psychologically that will help. Pains in the chest due to indigestion can be quite exhausting when you are carrying a pack, and it is sensible to rest for a while to let your tablets take effect.

If some food violently upsets you, and you become really nauseous, the only answer is to stay put for the day, resting in your tent and drinking as much as possible at frequent intervals. If you are not near a convenient water supply, you will have to move, but only go as far as necessary to get fresh water and set up camp again.

Hygiene and sanitation

Just because you are out camping, it does not mean that you can neglect personal cleanliness. Even if water is in short supply, there are ways of keeping clean. To neglect to do so is unpleasant for your companions, and if you should have an accident, it can create problems of infection in the wound. Use some of the cleansing tissues which can be obtained packed in sachets or small plastic boxes. These are impregnated with a spirit-based fluid which will not harm the skin and will dry quickly.

The teeth should not be neglected, even though you will have to use some of your precious water supply to keep them clean. Dentures can be a problem, especially where there is no running water. Try making a small nylon mesh bag with a drawstring closure, in which you can immerse your dentures in a stream without risk of loss.

Whilst on the subject of water, be sure to use sterilizing tablets in all 'doubtful' supplies. Not all water that comes out of a tap comes from a treated source, and you cannot automatically assume it to be safe.

It is the duty of all lightweight campers to make proper provision for sanitation. Many farm sites only have provision for the disposal of the contents of chemical toilets, which of course is of no help to the lightweight camper. Try asking the farmer if he has an outside toilet you can use, or if you may dig a small latrine hole in a discreet position. If the farmer objects to your digging a hole, he may be prepared to lend you an old bucket for the purpose.

If you are camping 'wild', a latrine hole should be sited away from your pitch and *well away* from water supplies. For digging the hole, it is convenient to carry a small metal trowel, of the type sold for children's garden tools, which are very cheap to buy. Do not dig the hole too deep – a few inches is all you need. The bacteria which act upon the excreta to disintegrate it are present only in the topsoil. It is essential to use proper toilet paper, which will disintegrate.

Rubbish

Rubbish must never be allowed to become litter! There is absolutely no reason for any camper to generate large amounts. If he carries all his provisions from home and is camping 'away from it all' where there are no disposal facilities, rubbish must be packed up and taken away until it can properly be disposed of. Wash and flatten any tins, and pack plastic and foil very small. Pierced-type gas cartridges should have the hole enlarged with a tent-peg so that they can be washed out to remove any traces of gas left in them. Paper can sometimes be burned – but do this only where there is no risk to the surroundings, clearing the ground and removing turf before you light the fire. Make sure it is completely out and there are no traces of it left before replacing the turf. Personally, we prefer to pack *all* our rubbish and take it away with us. Perhaps the only exception is food waste, which, if scattered discreetly, will quickly be disposed of by animals.

Minor accidents

As in the home, minor accidents are almost bound to occur, but you will not have all the facilities of the medicine cabinet to deal with them. You will have to carry some kind of first-aid kit and, more important, know what is in it and how to use it. Your best course is to find a class run by your local British Red Cross Society, St John Ambulance Brigade or other first-aid agency. There is usually a small fee payable, and an examination at the end of the course, but you will at least have some idea of what to do when things go wrong, and you might also be able to help someone else with your knowledge.

Cuts, stings, insect bites and splinters are all problems that you could meet when camping.

Carry some kind of antiseptic wipes for cleaning cuts and grazes. Do not carry creams as they do not clean the wound. Adhesive plaster dressings are a 'must' – probably the most useful is the waterproof strip dressing which can be cut to size. A small pair of folding scissors will deal with the problem. Very small individual plasters are useful for cuts on fingers etc.

Stings can be dealt with by applying sting-relief cream or spray. The latter, in a small aerosol pack, is very effective. Remember to take some kind of repellent to keep away the mosquitoes and other flying horrors. This can be obtained as 'wipes' packed in individual sachets, and again it is very effective.

Carry a needle and a book of matches. Splinters can be removed by using a needle sterilized in a match flame, and blisters can also be dealt with in this way. Tweezers are useful, but not essential.

Burns and scalds can be nasty at any time, but if you are out of doors, you have to be extra careful that no dirt contaminates the affected area.

Minor burns and scalds can be treated by plunging the hand or limb in cold water. This will cool the skin and reduce the pain. Be generous with the cold water; keep the affected part in the stream or bucket, or continue pouring fresh water over it until the pain is reduced to a comfortable level. A large burned or scalded area will have to be treated this way, then covered with a clean wet towel or wet cotton clothing which must be kept wet while the casualty is taken to the nearest hospital for treatment. If you are not near any hospital, go to the nearest habitation and ask them to get help. This should not be regarded as a 'minor' accident. Burns and scalds cause a sudden major loss of body fluid, causing shock. The patient should be given warm, sweet drinks and should be kept warm, but do not overheat him in your attempts. If it is possible to keep him lying still whilst fetching help, do so.

First-aid kit

We suggest that, for individual use, you make up a kit to your own preferences. This can be packed in a small plastic container or wallet. For example, you may prefer soluble pain-killers to ordinary non-soluble ones that sometimes seem to be as big as a rock to swallow when you are not feeling well.

If you buy a ready-made kit, get it from a reputable supplier, check the contents carefully and do not hesitate to replace unsuitable or unwanted items with those of your own choosing.

The following items are suggested as being suitable for a basic individual kit:

1 waterproof strip dressing, 6cm x 15cm
6 individual 'Band-Aid' or similar adhesive dressings
1 'Melolin' non-adherent dressing, 5cm x 5cm
2 antiseptic wipes (sachets)
1 sterilized medium plain lint dressing
1 small roll zinc oxide plaster, 1.25cm wide
1 book matches
1 needle
2-4 pain-killers, foil wrapped
2-4 antacid tablets, foil wrapped
1 small pack 'Moleskin'
Folding scissors
1 sachet insect-repellent (wipes)
1 tube sting-relief

You should also consider taking the following:
1 crêpe bandage, 7.5 cm wide
Sun protection cream
Lip salve
Calamine

1 large 'Melolin' dressing, 10cm x 10cm
Glucose tablets

Other emergencies

Fire

Perhaps the most feared hazard of all, the effect of fire in a tent can be tragic. Every lightweight camper should be aware of the dangers, and all precautions must be taken with stoves, lamps, candles, cigarettes and so on, but what if the worst does happen? A small fire may be quickly smothered, but the unfortunate fact is that, in a tent, this can very quickly become a large one. It is better to get out FAST, then collapse the tent poles to smother the flames. This is the only thing to do, as trying to get sufficient water to put it out is usually too slow. A stove or lamp which cannot be controlled must be taken by the base and thrown clear of the tent. Shout to warn others who may be in the way. For reasons of safety, tents should not be pitched too close together.

After a long day's travelling, you may be very tired and find it relaxing to lie in your tent reading a book. Never fall asleep with a stove, lamp or candle still burning, or whilst smoking. This is when such accidents happen. If fire occurs and you cannot get out of the tent by the normal exit, slash the rear end or side with your knife in order to get out. Shout 'Fire' at the top of your voice so that others can be warned of the danger and possibly come to your aid.

Gas

If you are using gas appliances, beware of leaks due, for example, to faulty or missing washers. Gas is heavier than air and can collect in the 'tray' of your groundsheet. When you are sleeping, therefore, you could be breathing in fatal gas. Apart from this, too much build-up of gas could cause an explosion. If you suspect any leakage, extinguish all naked lights, stoves and cigarettes. Remove the faulty appliance and container well away from the tent, which should be opened up and aired thoroughly. Do not attempt to use the appliance until the gas has been allowed to escape and the container is empty. Before re-connecting to a fresh gas container, examine everything carefully and correct the original fault.

Any stoves, including liquid-fuelled types, use up oxygen from the air whilst burning. They also produce carbon-monoxide gas in varying amounts, dependent on the condition of the stove. The dangers of running your car engine inside a closed garage are well known. The same situation can arise inside a closed tent. Leaked gas or fumes from your stove, added to a lack of oxygen, may cause headaches, dizziness and nausea. These effects may be aggravated by high altitude. If any person has been overcome by gas, apply artificial respiration immediately and air the tent completely.

Artificial respiration is always taught on first-aid courses, and to pass the examination you must be able to demonstrate that you can do it satisfactorily. You can believe us when we say 'once learned, never forgotten', as you will know yourself if you ever have to do it 'for real'.

Tent collapse

It occasionally happens that tents may collapse whilst their occupants are sleeping inside. The most common causes are strong winds or sudden snowfalls which occur unexpectedly. When snow lands on a frost-covered flysheet and the weight builds up, this may cause the poles to collapse or the flysheet to tear. For this reason, when you retire at night, always know where your clothes can be found, by feeling. If the worst happens, pull on your clothes, and get your sleeping-bag into your rucksack to keep it dry. Pack spare clothing etc in the same way, then get out and sort out the tent. Anything that will not get damaged by getting wet can stay outside. If the inner tent is made from proofed materials and is undamaged, it may be possible to use it on its own. Broken poles may be repaired by temporarily 'splinting' with a stick or long tent peg. If you cannot do either of these, you may be able to make a bivouac from your flysheet.

Flooding

If you have to evacuate due to flooding, dress as quickly as possible, put 'hard' articles in your rucksack and put it on, drop the tent and carry it with everything else in the groundsheet tray to a safer pitch on higher ground. If you cannot find a pitch, at least move higher up before packing and leaving the area.

Storms, fog and mist

The occurrence of storms is not uncommon in the hills, but the chances of your tent being struck by lightning are virtually nil. If you are out walking when a storm blows up, do not shelter under trees or, particularly in high country, under rocks or in caves. If you have to 'sit it out', try to sit on a dry rucksack, with your hands clasped round your knees, on an open slope, thus lessening the risk of your being struck by lightning. Get down off the hills if you possibly can, but if you are encamped, it is better to stay in your tent. If mist or fog comes down or you become benighted, pitch your tent and stay until the weather clears. Never try to get down off the hills by following a stream.

This chapter is intended, amongst other things, to let you know that illness and emergencies *can* happen, not that they *will*. At least we have tried to tell you what to do should such things occur when you are out camping. We hope very much that they do not.

14 Who Can Help You? Whom Can You Help?

Lightweight campers, by their very nature, are often those who wish to camp away from it all, and often away from other folk, too. Some are naturally 'loners', whilst others may be slightly more gregarious, wishing to camp in a small group. Few will wish to camp in a large group except perhaps for some special event. However, it is worth considering joining one of the clubs which has an interest in lightweight camping. There are a number of benefits on offer, even to the 'loner', not least of which is that a number offer some kind of insurance cover. However, we think the most important reason for joining such a club is that by so doing you demonstrate your support for your activity not only to other like-minded enthusiasts but to those in authority.

Camping legislation

Over the past years there has been a lot of comment in the camping Press about possible changes in the legislation regarding tent camping. In this country, the right to camp in a tent, subject to the landowner's consent, has been covered by the Public Health Act of 1936. This allows a landowner to permit an unlimited number of tents on his land for up to a total of twenty-eight days in a calendar year, subject to any specific local restrictions. This is still the situation at the time of writing. Typical local variations might apply to such places as National Parks and Areas of Outstanding Natural Beauty. A number of responsible clubs and other organizations hold 'Exemption Certificates' which enable their members to claim certain relaxations under the Act, but in general, individuals camping in tents may do so provided they have the permission of the owner or occupier of the land.

Since 1971, studies have been made of ways and means to deal with the increasing congestion on roads, public health problems and impact on the environment caused in peak holiday periods by the rapid growth in popularity of touring caravanning and tent camping. Proposals were put forward for controlling all tent camping and caravanning, based on the rather absurd view that all types of modern camping are essentially the same. After considerable discussion and constructive counter-proposals by camping organizations, it now seems likely that, although the same controls will be introduced for tent camping in general as for caravanning, a distinction will be made in respect of people using very small tents. This recognizes the undoubted fact that their impact on the environment, visually, physically and from a public health point of view, is negligible. Clearly it is important that all those who camp in this way do so in a responsible manner, in order to preserve the freedom to enjoy the outdoors. The final decisions as regards legislation on these matters have yet to be implemented, but some changes are inevitable to preserve the countryside so that we and others can enjoy it.

The 'exemption certificates' granted to organizations and clubs are issued by the appropriate government department after receipt of proof of their responsible attitude and ability to exercise an effective measure of voluntary control over their members. The certificate allows the club concerned to hold its own rallies or meets, and lays down certain conditions. Basically, proper arrangements must be made at the meets for such things as water supply, sanitation, refuse disposal, fire precautions and so on. Individual clubs vary greatly, some arranging very large rallies whilst others may be responsible for very small 'meets' with perhaps only six or seven people taking part. Some will hold area meets for most of the year, with perhaps a national gathering of members once or twice a year. Most clubs are run by voluntary officers elected from among the members, although some of the larger ones have a full-time office staff. The organization of meets and rallies is, however, almost always carried out by the voluntary officers.

What clubs are there?

The Camping and Caravanning Club

This Club, formerly known as the Camping Club, covers all types of camping but two of its specialist sections warrant consideration here.

The first of these is the Association of Lightweight Campers, recognized as the Lightweight Section of the Club, it welcomes all lightweight campers irrespective of the type of transport they use. The Association, whose officers act in a voluntary capacity and are elected annually, encourages the development of lightweight camping and equipment, and members' own comments are always welcome. Club members who belong to the Association all receive the quarterly *Bulletin*, a magazine which carries reports on equipment used by members as well as details of new equipment, news and views on various lightweight topics, news of members and information on local meets and other events, thus acting as the vehicle for keeping members in touch. An additional benefit of Association membership is the opportunity to purchase good equipment at very advantageous prices.

The second of the specialist sections of the Camping and Caravanning Club to concern us is the Canoe Camping Club. It encourages and promotes canoe camping and more adventurous voyages both at home and abroad, and offers training in canoeing skills, for both beginners and others wishing to improve their skills. There is a special group for those who enjoy sea canoeing. The club is very active in its efforts to provide access to waterways for canoeists, which is still somewhat restricted in some areas. The quarterly magazine *Canoe Camper* is sent to all members and contains details of events, reports, yarns, useful tips etc.

In addition to the special benefits and attractions of these two sections of the main Club, members also enjoy the normal advantages of membership of the parent body, which includes a certain amount of insurance cover.

Both the Association of Lightweight Campers and the Canoe Camping Club keep a close watch on any changes in legislation or local bye-laws which may affect the type of camping preferred by their members, especially where restrictions may be imposed. They keep the parent club informed of their views so that action may be taken if necessary, and also advise the Club on matters relating to their own specialized forms of camping.

The Backpackers Club
This is a small, independent club started in 1972 by a few enthusiasts whose aims were quite simple; namely, to provide an organized body to protect the freedom of backpackers and to ensure the continued right of access to meadow, mountain, woodland, moor and shore. It encourages the proper development of lightweight camping and the observance of the Country Code, and liaises with manufacturers on the design and development of new equipment.

This club can best be described as a club for 'unclubbables' and has a very informal organization. There are local voluntary 'co-ordinators' and a National Honorary Organizer. There are usually some activities each weekend in various parts of the country. Club members receive a useful *Farm Pitch Directory* for their exclusive use and are kept in touch with what is going on in the backpacking world through the quarterly magazine *Backpack*. A special insurance scheme is available to members who require it as an extra.

The Cyclists Touring Club
Whilst not a club exclusively for cycle campers, the CTC does have a considerable number among its members. As with the Camping Club and its subsidiary groups, virtually all the work involved in running the local groups is done by voluntary officers, although there is a full-time staff at the club's head office. The CTC keeps a close watch on legislation which may affect cyclists in general, but they are also concerned that any camping legislation will not penalize small groups and that consideration should be given to the needs of lightweight campers. The club magazine *Cycle Touring* is sent to all members bi-monthly. Membership subscriptions include third-party insurance, and the club's

legal department will assist members who are so unfortunate as to be involved in accidents while cycling. Insurance cover for cycles is also available for members through the club.

Youth Hostels Association

Although this organization is not a camping club, membership of the YHA can be very useful to the lightweight camper. Many hostels in England and Wales, but not all, will allow camping in the grounds of the hostel. Scottish hostels do not allow camping. Where camping *is* allowed, members may use the hostel facilities, which can be rather useful. If you carry a YHA membership card with you when camping, and if the weather turns really foul and you get a soaking, you have the chance of a night in the dry and of drying out your wet clothes overnight.

Like the CTC, the YHA has a number of local groups, which often arrange hostelling or camping weekends. A quarterly newspaper, *Hostelling News*, goes to all members, and special travel insurance is available.

All these clubs will have members who are interested in some aspect of lightweight camping. Most will be only too happy to offer their help and advice, based on the experience of their members, and will welcome you to their ranks. Generally speaking, it will be up to you to make the initial contact with your local group once you have become a member.

Other clubs

There are other outdoor clubs and associations which also deserve your support. Many of them have been instrumental in helping to keep our rights of way open, on land and on water, and also help with conservation work where it is required. The bulk of the work is done by the members themselves on a voluntary basis. (Some of the clubs which we have already mentioned also undertake such voluntary work.) We are of the opinion that, if you are going out to enjoy the countryside, you should also do your part in an active way to keep the countryside open. We do not want to see the situation which exists in some parts of the world where a 'quota' of backpackers or walkers is allowed into an area, and after that no more! It is up to us to see that this does not happen, and one way to prevent it is to take an active part in the work done by the voluntary clubs and associations to conserve our beautiful country.

The following clubs and societies will welcome your help: The British Canoe Union, The British Trust for Conservation Volunteers, The Long Distance Walkers Association, The Ramblers Association, The Scottish Rights of Way Society. Many of the above operate with local voluntary groups, which do a lot of work. Why not join one of them and take part yourself in preserving our heritage?

Appendix I

Addresses of Clubs and Other Organizations

(A stamped, addressed envelope should be sent with all enquiries.)

Association of Lightweight Campers,
11 Lower Grosvenor Place, London SW1W 0EY

Backpackers Club, Hon. National Organizer,
20 St Michael's Road, Tilehurst, Reading, Berks, RG3 4RP

British Canoe Union,
45 High Street, Addlestone, Weybridge, Surrey, KT15 1JV

British Trust for Conservation Volunteers,
36 St Mary's Street, Wallingford, Oxon, OX10 0EU

Camping and Caravanning Club,
11 Lower Grosvenor Place, London SW1W 0EY

Canoe Camping Club,
11 Lower Grosvenor Place, London SW1W 0EY

Cyclists Touring Club,
Cotterell House, 69 Meadrow, Godalming, Surrey, GU7 3HS

Long Distance Walkers Association,
Hon. Sec. Sue Coles,
29 Appledown Close, Alresford, Hants, SO24 9ND

Ramblers Association, 1-5 Wandsworth Road, London SW8 2LJ

Scottish Rights of Way Society,
28 Rutland Square, Edinburgh EH1 2BW

Scottish Youth Hostel Association,
7 Glebe Crescent, Stirling, Falkirk, FK8 2JA

Youth Hostels Association,
Trevelyan House, 8 St Stephen's Hill, St. Albans, Herts, AL1 2DY

Youth Hostels Association of Northern Ireland,
56 Bradbury Place, Belfast

Appendix II

Other Useful Addresses

Mail Order Suppliers
This list is not exhaustive. Other suppliers may be found by consulting the various outdoor magazines.

Adventure Equipment Ltd, 172 Easter Road, Edinburgh EH7 5XA

Biped, PO Box 8, Nelson, BB9 9RW

F.W. Evans, 79 The Cut, London SE1

Field and Trek (Equipment) Ltd, 23-25 Kings Road, Brentwood, Essex, CM14 4ER

Fjallraven, PO Box 5, Dallamires Industrial Estate, Ripon, North Yorkshire, HG4 1TW

Freewheel, 275 West End Lane, London NW6 1QS

Richmond Cycles, 36 Hill Street, Richmond, Surrey

Scout Shops Ltd, Churchill Industrial Estate, Lancing, West Sussex, BN15 8UG

Venturegear, 30 Cricklade Road, Swindon, Wilts, SN2 6AA

YHA Shops Ltd, 14 Southampton Street, London WC2E 7HY

Manufacturers and/or Importers
Note: Manufacturers do not generally supply direct to the public, although a few of those listed here will do so. They will, however, be able to put you in touch with your local stockist, should you have any difficulty in obtaining their products.

Adventurewear Ltd, 127 Old Street, Clevedon, Avon, BS21 6BW
(Waterproof clothing, fibre-pile clothing)

A-Form Ltd, Tower Lane, Warmley, Bristol, Avon, BS15 2XX
(Boots of all kinds)

Alpina, 67A North Road, Brighton, BN1 1YD
(Boots, rucksacks, sleeping-bags, cookwear, waterproofs)

Berghaus, 34 Dean Street, Newcastle upon Tyne, NE1 1PG
(Boots, rucksacks, waterproof clothing)

Bradsport Ltd, Camroyd Street, Dewsbury, West Yorks, WF13 1PG
(Waterproof and fibre-pile clothing)

Broadway Bikes, 65 Windmill Hill, Enfield, Middx
(Tricycles with child seats, 'side kick' sidecar chassis)

Camping Gaz (GB) Ltd, 126 St Leonard's Road, Windsor, Berks
(Gas stoves)

Carradice Ltd, Brook Street, Nelson, BB9 9PX
(Cycle bags)

Coleman UK Inc., Parish Wharf Estate, Harbour Road, Portishead, Bristol, BS20 9DA
(Stoves, rucksacks, canoes)

Craghoppers, Bradford Road, Birstall, Batley, W. Yorks
(Breeches, trousers and waterproof clothing)

Epigas International Ltd,
Viaduct Mill, Chestergate, Stockport,
Cheshire, SK3 0AJ

Europa Sport, Ann Street, Kendal, Cumbria, LA9 6AB
('Zamberlan' boots, range of socks and stockings)

Fleetfoot Ltd, 26 St George's Quay, Lancaster
(Brasher boots, Brasher bag and hill suit, Bogtrotter boots)

Giffard Newton and Sons Ltd, 71 Townsend Road, Chesham, Bucks, HP5 2AD
(Walking-boots)

Grangersol Ltd, Imperial Way, Watford, Herts, WD2 4JW
(Waterproofing agents. Pre-packed camping accessories and repair materials)

Granta Boats Ltd, Ramsey, Huntingdon, Cambs, PE17 1EZ
(Canoes of all kinds, including kits)

The Hampton Works (Stampings) Ltd, Twyning Road, Stirchley, Birmingham, B30 2XZ
(Alloy tent poles of all kinds. Alloy pegs and accessories)

G.T. Hawkins Ltd, Overstone Road, Northampton, NN1 3JJ
(Walking-boots and shoes)

Helly-Hansen (UK) Ltd, College Street, Kempston, Bedford
(Fibre-pile clothing, thermal underwear and waterproofs)

Henri-Lloyd Ltd, Smithfold Lane, Worsley, Manchester, M28 6AR
(Waterproof and insulated clothing)

Inter Footwear Ltd, 24-26 Towerfield Road, Shoeburyness, Essex
(Walking-boots)

Javlin International Ltd, Javlin House, 3-11 Edgedale Road, Sheffield, S7 2BQ
(Warmwear and thermal underwear. Wellington boots)

Karrimor International Ltd, 19 Avenue Parade, Accrington, Lancs, BB5 6PR
(Rucksacks, cycle luggage, sleeping-bags, clothing, boots, stoves)

Nikwax, 31 Clerkenwell Close, London, EC1
(Waterproofing compounds for boots and tents and clothing)

McNulty Seaglass, Victoria Road, South Shields, Tyne and Wear
(Canoes of all types)

Mountain Equipment Ltd, George Street, Glosop, Derbyshire, SK13 8AY
(Sleeping-bags and insulated clothing)

Mountaineering Activities Ltd, Wellington Mills, Duke Street, Manchester M3 4NF
(Clothing and walking- and mountaineering-boots)

North Cape Ltd, Cunningham Road, Springkerse Industrial Estate, Stirling, Scotland
(Insulated clothing and thermal underwear)

Northern Feather Leisure (UK) Ltd, 1 Newfield Drive, Menston, Ilkley, W. Yorks
(Sleeping-bags, tents and rucksacks)

AB Optimus Ltd, Sanders Lodge Estate, Rushden, Northants
(Stoves and lanterns)

Ottersports Ltd, Ash Street, Northampton
(Canoes)

P. & H. Fibreglass, Old Stanley Colliery, W. Hallam, Derby
(Canoes)

Phoenix Mountaineering Ltd, Coquetdale Trading Estate, Amble, Morpeth, Northumberland NE65 0PE
(Lightweight tents, sleeping-bags, insulated and waterproof clothing)

Primus-Sievert (UK) Ltd, 9-11 Gleneldon Road, London, SW16 2AU
(Stoves)

J.L. Priestly (Catering Services) Ltd, 93 High Street, Heckington, Nr Sleaford, Lincs, NG34 9QU
(Catering packs of dehydrated foods)

Raven Leisure Products Ltd, Unit 20, Long Furrow Trading Estate, East Goscote, Leicester, LE7 8XJ
(Freeze-dried foods and ration packs)

Rohan, Airton, Skipton, North Yorkshire, BD23 1AE
(Clothing)

Robert Saunders (chigwell) Ltd, Five Oaks Lane, Chigwell, Essex
(Lightweight tents)

Silva (UK) Ltd, 15 Bolney Way, Feltham, Middx, TW13 6DB
(Compasses)

Snowdon Mouldings, Llanberis, Gwynedd, N. Wales
(Mountain tents)

Sprayway Ltd, 5 Cambridge Street, Manchester M1 5GF
(Waterproof clothing)

Springlow Sales Ltd, Green Street, Oldham, Lancs, OL8 1TA
(Freeze-dried foods)

I. & M. Steiner Ltd, Reynard Mills Trading Estate, Windmill Road, Brentford, Middx, TW8 9LY
(Importers of accessories and tents)

Peter Storm Ltd, 14 High Pavement, Nottingham
(Waterproofs, sweaters and thermal underwear)

Survival Aids Ltd, Morland, Penrith, Cumbria, CA10 3AZ
(Accessories and survival equipment. Pile sleeping-bags)

Taymar Ltd, Wear Mill, King Street West, Stockport, SK3 0AJ
(Gas stoves)

T. & J. Food Supplies Ltd, 65 Beech Avenue, Beeston, Notts NG9 1QD
(Bulk food supplies – dehydrated food of all types)

Tilley International, Dunmurry, Belfast, BT17 9JA
(Stoves and lamps)

Touring Sport Ltd, 137 Gosport Road, Fareham, Hants, PO16 0QA
(Lightweight tents, sleeping-bags and accessories)

Trylon, Wollaston, Northants
(Canoes)

Ultimate Equipment Ltd, Ryburne Mill, Hanson Lane, Halifax, West Yorkshire HX1 4SE
(Lightweight tents, outdoor clothing, sleeping-bags)

Valley Canoe Products, Private Road 4, Colwick Estate, Nottingham
(Canoes)

Vango (Scotland) Ltd, Industrial Estate, Port Glasgow, PA14 5BE
(Lightweight tents, sleeping-bags, boots, waterproofs, rucksacks)

Walrus Waterproofs Ltd, Mersey Street, Bulwell, Nottingham, NG6 8JA
(Waterproof clothing)

Whitewater Sports, 22 Guildford Road, Woking, Surrey
(Canoes of various types)

Wintergear, Unit A10, Cibyn Industrial Estate, Caernarfon, Gwynedd, LL55 2BD
(Lightweight tents. Insulated clothing)

Woodland World Ltd, Shire Hill Works, Saffron Walden, Essex CB11 3AL
(Sidecar chassis and trailers)

Where to buy your maps etc

Cook Hammond & Kell Ltd, The London Map Centre, 22-4, Caxton Street, London SW1H 0QU
(Ordnance Survey Main Agents)

Thomas Nelson & Sons Ltd, 51 York Place, Edinburgh, EH1 3JD
(Ordnance Survey Agents for Scotland)

Stanfords (Edward Stanford Ltd), 12-14 Long Acre, Covent Garden, London WC2E 9LP

McCarta Ltd, The Map and Guide Shop, 122 King's Cross Road, London WC1X 9DS

Rallymaps, PO Box 11, Romsey, Hampshire

The Map Shop, 15 High Street, Upton-upon-Severn, Worcs, WR8 0HJ

Overseas Tourist Offices in London

Austrian National Tourist Office, 30 St George Street, London W1

Belgian National Tourist Office, 38 Dover Street, London W1

Danish Tourist Board, Sceptre House, 160-73 Regent Street, London W1

Finnish Tourist Board, 66 Haymarket, London SW1

French Government Tourist Office, 178 Piccadilly, London W1

German National Tourist Office, 61 Conduit Street, London W1

Italian State Tourist Board, 1 Princes Street, London W1

Luxembourg National Tourist Office, 36 Piccadilly, London W1

Netherlands National Tourist Office, 143 New Bond Street, London W1

Norwegian National Tourist Office, 20 Pall Mall, London SW1

Spanish National Tourist Office, 57-8 St James's Street, London SW1

Swedish National Tourist Office, 3 Cork Street, London W1

Swiss National Tourist Office, 1 New Coventry Street, London W1

Appendix III

Useful books and outdoor magazines

Books

Adshead, R., *Backpacking in Britain* (Oxford Illustrated Press, 1974)

Adshead, R., *Bikepacking for Beginners* (Oxford Illustrated Press, 1978)

Booth, D., *The Backpacker's Handbook* (R. Hale, 1972)

Constance, H., *Gear for Outdoors and How to Make It* (R. Hale, 1982)

Crane, N. *Cycling in Europe* (Oxford Illustrated Press, 1984)

Duncan, A. (ed.), *Walker's Britain* (Pan Books/Ordnance Survey, 1982)

Ennis, P. *Cycling – A Source Book* (Pelham Books, 1984)

Gausden, C. and Crane, N., *The CTC Route Guide* (Oxford Illustrated Press, 1980)

Hughes, T., *Adventure Cycling in Britain* (Blandford Press, 1978)

Jackson, J. and Lees, J.R., *Safety on Mountains*, (British Mountaineering Council, 1974)

Langmuir, E., *Mountain Leadership* (Scottish Sports Council)

Lumley, Peter, *Backpacking* (Teach Yourself Books, 1974)

Mabey, R., *Food for Free* (Fontana/Collins, 1972)

Marriott, M., *Start Backpacking* (Stanley Paul, 1981)

McNeish, C., *Ski the Nordic Way* (Cicerone Press, 1981)
Backpacker's Scotland (R. Hale, 1982)

Sharp, D., *Walking in the Countryside* (David & Charles, 1978)

Westacott, H.D., *The Walker's Handbook* (Penguin Books, 1978)

Wickens, D. and Pedersen, A., *Britain at your Feet* (Hamlyn, 1981)

Modern Lightweight Camping
'Know the Game' series (EP Publishing Ltd): *The Weather; Orienteering*
'Spur Books' series (Spurbooks Ltd): *Hill Trekking* (Lumley); *Weather Lore* (Brown and Hunter); *Winter Camping* (Brown and Hunter);

Magazines

Bicycle Times, 26 Commercial Buildings, Dunston, Tyne and Wear, NE11 9AA

Camping, Link House, Dingwall Avenue, Croydon, Surrey, CR9 2TA

Climber and Rambler, Ravenseft House, 302-4 St Vincent Street, Glasgow G2 5NL

Cyclist Monthly, Surrey House, 1 Throwley Way, Sutton, Surrey, SM1 4QQ

Footloose, 26 Commercial Buildings, Dunston, Tyne and Wear, NE11 9AA

Great Outdoors, Ravenseft House, 302-4 St Vincent Street, Glasgow G2 5NL

Practical Camper, 38-42, Hampton Road, Teddington, Middx. TW11 0JE

Appendix IV

Food Values	calories per ounce	Protein grammes per oz
Carbohydrates		
Apples, dried	88	0.4
Apricots, dried	86	1.5
Bananas, dried	89	1.0
Cabbage, dried	91	2.4
Carrots, dried	94	1.4
Cocoa	128	5.8
Dates	89	0.5
Figs	85	1.1
Honey	89	nil
Jam, marmalade	74	0.2
Lentils	98	6.9
Milk chocolate	152	1.6
Muesli	160	5.6
Pasta products	100	3.6
Potato, instant	100	1.2
Prunes	84	0.6
Raisins	84	0.6
Rice	98	2.1
Sultanas	71	0.5
Sugar, brown moist	120	nil
Soya flour	78	11.9
Wheat germ	108	3.6
Fats		
Butter	205	0.2
Cashew nuts	170	0.2
Corn oil	264	nil
Egg, desiccated whole	166	3.5

Lard	250	nil
Peanuts	168	7.5
Peanut Butter	173	7.3
Protein		
Bacon, fresh medium fat	120	4.0
Beans, dried (i.e. butter beans)	97	6.2
Cheese, Cheddar	110	6.7
Corned beef, canned	65	6.8
Egg, desiccated whole	166	13.5
Milk, dried skimmed	100	9.9
Muesli	160	5.6
Meat, canned luncheon	76	4.5
Peanuts	168	7.5
Salami	114	9.7
Shrimps, canned	32	6.3

Index